Indians and Anthropologists

Edited by Thomas Biolsi and Larry J. Zimmerman

Indians and

Anthropologists

Vine Deloria, Jr., and the Critique of Anthropology

The University of Arizona Press   TUCSON

The University of Arizona Press
© 1997
The Arizona Board of Regents
All Rights Reserved

♾ This book is printed on acid-free, archival-quality paper.
Manufactured in the United States of America
Second printing 1998

Library of Congress Cataloging-in-Publication Data
Indians and anthropologists: Vine Deloria, Jr., and the critique of
anthropology / edited by Thomas Biolsi and Larry J. Zimmerman.
    p.   cm.
Includes bibliographical references (p.   ) and index.
ISBN 0-8165-1606-5 (cloth: acid-free paper)
ISBN 0-8165-1607-3 (pbk.: acid-free paper)
1. Indians of North America—Study and teaching.   2. Anthropology—
Philosophy.   3. Anthropology—Research—North America.   4. Deloria,
Vine.   5. Indians of North America—Research.   6. Ethnocentricism.
I. Biolsi, Thomas, 1952– .   II. Zimmerman, Larry J., 1947– .
E76.6.I53   1997
301'.01—dc21   96-45804
CIP

British Cataloguing-in-Publication Data
A catalogue record for this book is available from the British Library.

The authors' royalties are assigned to the American Indian College Fund.

Publication of this book is made possible in part by the proceeds of a
permanent endowment created with the assistance of a challenge grant
from the National Endowment for the Humanities, a federal agency.

Contents

Contributors

Marilyn Bentz (Gros Ventre) received her M.S.W. from the Jane Addams School of Social Work at the University of Illinois in 1967, and her Ph.D. in anthropology from the University of Washington in 1984. Her research has focused on education on the Quinault Reservation. She served as director of American Indian Studies at the University of Washington and is on the faculty of the Department of Anthropology there.

Thomas Biolsi received his Ph.D. in anthropology from Columbia University. Since 1990 he has been on the faculty of the Anthropology Department at Portland State University in Oregon. He has had a long-standing interest in Western Native Americans and in Indian-white relations since his high school years in a suburb of New York. He is the author of *Organizing the Lakota: The Political Economy of the New Deal on Pine Ridge and Rosebud Reservations* (1992). He is currently completing a book on legal conflict between the Rosebud Sioux Tribe and the State of South Dakota.

Vine Deloria, Jr. (Standing Rock Sioux), was born on the Pine Ridge Reservation in South Dakota while his father, Vine Deloria, Sr., was serving as an Episcopalian clergyman there. He received his B.S. from Iowa State University, a master's degree from the Lutheran School of Theology in Chicago, and his J.D. from the University of Colorado School of Law. He has had a wide range of professional experience in Indian affairs, including service as the executive director of the National Congress of American Indians (1964–67), as a board member of the Oglala Sioux Legal Rights Foundation (1971–74), and as chair of the Collection Committee of the National Museum of the American Indian (1990–93). He founded the Institute for the Development of Indian Law in Washington in 1971 and served as counsel for the defendants in four Wounded Knee trials (1974–77). From 1978 to 1990 he was professor of law and political science at the University of Arizona, where he chaired the American Indian Studies Program (1978–81). He is presently professor of American Indian Studies and history at the University of Colorado. He is the author or editor of sixteen books, the most recent of which is *Red Earth, White Lies* (1995), as well as a long list of book chapters, scholarly and popular articles, and editorials.

Elizabeth S. Grobsmith received her M.A. and Ph.D. in anthropology from the University of Arizona. In 1975 she joined the faculty of the University of Nebraska — Lincoln, and until 1996 was associate vice chancellor for academic affairs and director of Summer Sessions there. She has been dean of the College of Letters, Arts, and Sciences at the University of Colorado since the fall of 1996. Following her first book, *Lakota of the Rosebud: A Contemporary Ethnography* (1981), her work shifted in focus toward the study of alcoholism and crime, and she has published several articles on the relationship between substance abuse and crime, as well as recidivism. Her most recent book, *Indians in Prison* (1994), dealt with the struggle for religious freedom behind prison walls and documented the historical and legal process prisoners underwent in obtaining access to religious expression.

Herbert T. Hoover received his Ph.D. in history from the University of Oklahoma in 1966. Since 1967 he has been on the faculty of the History Department at the University of South Dakota, where he served as director of the Indian Studies Program from 1985 to 1991 and has directed the Oral History Center since 1977. He has written and edited many books on South Dakota and American Indian history, including *To Be an Indian* (1995), *The Sioux and Other Native Cultures of the Dakotas: An Annotated Bibliography* (1993), *The Yankton Sioux* (1988), *Bibliography of the Sioux* (1980), and *The Sioux: A Crit-*

ical Bibliography (1979). He has also published numerous book chapters and scholarly articles on the same topics.

Cecil King (Odawa) is from Manitoulin Island, Ontario. He received his elementary education on the Reserve at Manitoulin and completed his education at residential school in Spanish, Ontario. He entered the field of education and received teaching certification through study at the University of Toronto and Carleton University in Ottawa. He received a graduate degree in Indian and northern education at the University of Saskatchewan. He founded and directed the Aboriginal Teacher Education Program at the University of Saskatchewan and went on to complete his doctoral degree in comparative education at the University of Calgary. He is presently full professor at Queens University, in the Faculty of Education, and director of the Ontario Aboriginal Teacher Education Program. He is currently finishing a book on the life and times of John Baptiste Assignock (Black Bird).

Gail Landsman is associate professor of anthropology at the University at Albany, State University of New York. She has conducted research on social movements of both Native Americans and women in the United States. She has twice participated as a seminar member in the "Indian Voices in the Academy" Program of the Newberry Library's D'Arcy McNickle Center for the History of the American Indian, which gave her the opportunity for continued reflection on relations between Indian and non-Indian scholars. She is the author of the book *Sovereignty and Symbol: Indian/White Conflict at Ganienkeh* (1988), and of articles on the politics of representing Indian history and Indian culture, images of Indians in the woman's suffrage movement, and activism for parental leave legislation.

Randall H. McGuire was born in Fort Collins, Colorado, and was raised in Oklahoma, Montana, and Texas. His interest in anthropology stems from his contact with Native Americans as a child and young adult. He received his B.A. in 1974 from the University of Texas, and his M.A. (1978) and Ph.D. (1982) from the University of Arizona. Since 1982 he has been on the Faculty of Anthropology at Binghamton University, Binghamton, New York. His research interests include the prehistory of the Southwest and nineteenth- and twentieth-century class relations in the United States. He is the author of *A Marxist Archaeology* (1992). He is currently directing archaeological fieldwork on the prehistoric Trincheras culture of northern Sonora, Mexico, and on the Great Coalfield War of 1913–14 at the site of Ludlow in southern Colorado.

Murray L. Wax (Ph.D. 1959, University of Chicago) has worked principally among the Oglala Sioux of Pine Ridge, South Dakota, and the tribal Cherokee of eastern Oklahoma. He has published widely in professional journals and has authored *Formal Education in an American Indian Community* (1964, with Rosalie H. Wax and Robert V. Dumont, Jr.) and *Indian Americans: Unity and Diversity* (1971). He is currently emeritus professor at Washington University, editor of *The Independent Scholar*, and completing a book titled *The Secret of the Marble Tablet: Dreams, Myth and Poetry.*

Peter Whiteley received his Ph.D. from the University of New Mexico. His research on the Hopi has focused on social structure, politics, and history. He is the author of *Deliberate Acts: Changing Hopi Culture through the Oraibi Split* (1988) and *Bacavi: Journey to Reed Springs* (1988). He is currently chair of the Department of Anthropology at Sarah Lawrence College and is working on a collection of American Indian literatures.

Larry J. Zimmerman received his Ph.D. from the University of Kansas. He is adjunct professor in the Department of Anthropology at the University of Iowa and research associate in the Office of the State Archaeologist of Iowa. He has served as editor of *Plains Anthropologist* and the *World Archaeological Bulletin* and associate editor of *American Antiquity*. From 1990 to 1994 he was executive secretary of the World Archaeological Congress. His publications focus on Plains archaeology, computer applications, and Native American issues.

Indians and Anthropologists

Introduction

What's Changed, What Hasn't

THOMAS BIOLSI AND LARRY J. ZIMMERMAN

In 1969 Vine Deloria, Jr., a Standing Rock Sioux Indian law student at the University of Colorado, published *Custer Died for Your Sins: An Indian Manifesto.* The book, widely read and commented upon, launched a writing and scholarly career of international renown. The most well known thesis of the book was contained in chapter 4, "Anthropologists and Other Friends." This piece was a biting and serious — if rhetorically humorous — indictment of the anthropological project as it pertains to American Indians. Deloria represented the anthropologist as an urban, overly intellectualized, insufficiently humanized academic who descends on Indian country every summer to confirm and reproduce essentially self-confirming, self-referential, and self-reproducing closed systems of arcane "pure knowledge" — systems with little, if any, empirical relationship to, or practical value for, real Indian people:

> Perhaps we should suspect the real motives of the academic community. They have the Indian field well defined and under control. Their concern is not the ultimate policy that will affect the Indian people, but merely the creation of new slogans and doctrines by which they can climb the university totem pole. Reduction of people to ciphers for purposes of observation appears to be inconsequential to the anthropologist when compared with immediate benefits he can derive, the production of further prestige, and the chance to appear as the high priest of American society, orienting and manipulating to his heart's desire. (Deloria 1970 [1969]:98–99)

Long before anyone in anthropology had heard of Michel Foucault or Pierre Bourdieu, Deloria had put his finger directly on what would later be called discursive formations, symbolic capital, and the micropolitics of the academy. Deloria asked, regarding Indian peoples, "Why should we continue to be the private zoos for anthropologists? Why should tribes have to compete with scholars for funds when the scholarly productions are so useless and irrelevant to real life?" (Deloria 1970 [1969]:99).

At the eighty-eighth annual meeting of the American Anthropological Association (AAA) in 1989, a group of scholars — mostly, but not all, anthropologists — convened in a session titled "Custer Died for Your Sins: A Twenty-Year Retrospective on Relations between Anthropologists and American Indians." The purpose of the session was to explore the question, What has transpired in, or how have we come to rethink, the relations between anthropologists and American Indians since publication of Deloria's book? Addressing that question is also the purpose of this book, which grew out of the 1989 AAA session.[1]

This was not the first meeting of anthropologists and others who felt compelled to speak because of issues raised by Deloria's book. In 1970 a symposium titled "Anthropology and the American Indian," funded by the Bureau of Indian Affairs (BIA), was held concurrently with the annual meeting of the AAA. Deloria's book had helped to crystalize the issues discussed at the symposium, as well as those behind the adoption by the AAA of its Code of Ethics in 1971 (Grobsmith, this volume; Henry 1972).

The publication of Deloria's book in 1969 can be seen as representative of a new period in relations between American Indian people and anthropologists in particular, between Indians and non-Indians in America generally, and between colonized peoples and the metropolis globally. Of course, other works also registered the tectonic shifts in these relations, including Talal Asad's *Anthropology and the Colonial Encounter* (1973), Dell Hymes's *Reinventing Anthropology* (1969), and the *Current Anthropology* issue on social responsibilities (1968). This new period in global political-economic, colonial, and race relations might fruitfully be called "late imperial." The reader should immediately take note that we mean by this term that there has been both change and continuity in the colonialism against which and within which American Indian people must live. On the one hand, none of the contributors to this book harbors any illusions of colonialism or racism being over. We intend not to be "prematurely celebratory" (McClintock 1994:294) about the end of the oppression of Indian people and their communities.

On the other hand, some things have changed significantly since Deloria first wrote about anthropology; qualitative changes are apparent in the realms of political consciousness, social movements and practices, and social structures. For example, beyond Deloria's own widespread personal and intellectual influence, there have been new forms of native consciousness critical of *colonial* relations of all kinds, as well as new forms of practice directed at altering those disempowering relations. The emergence of the American Indian Movement as well as other forms of pan-Indian activism (see Churchill and Wall 1988; Cornell 1988; Dewing 1985; Hauptman 1986; Landsman 1988; Matthiessen 1991; Means 1995; Steiner 1968) and the evolving struggle for national sovereignty based on indigenous readings of treaties (see *Akwesasne Notes* 1978; American Indian Lawyer Training Program 1988; Deloria 1974; Ortiz 1977) are obvious examples. So are the appearance and development of Native American Studies programs in universities (see Guyette and Heth 1988; Medicine 1972a), as well as new organs for native counterhegemonies within the academy (*American Indian Culture and Research Journal, American Indian Quarterly, Northeast Indian Quarterly, Wicazo Sa Review*) and major critical works by native scholars (see, for example, Churchill 1992, 1994; Jaimes 1992; Ortiz 1984; Warrior 1995; and, of course, the many works of Vine Deloria, Jr.). Widely read Indian newspapers such as *Akwesasne Notes* (Rooseveltown, New York) and *Indian Country Today* (Rapid City, South Dakota) disseminate many ideas from this critical scholarship among Indian people; *sovereignty* is indeed a household word among Indian people in 1997. The adoption of tribal and native national research ordinances, the creation of cultural centers, the development of a movement for the repatriation of native remains and sacred objects from museums and other institutions, and the furor over the celebration of the Columbian quincentennial are also well-known examples of the new terrain upon which any anthropological research on Native American issues must take place.

This new period in Indian/non-Indian relations is not only characterized by emergent Indian consciousness and action. It also includes a variety of ideological positions and actions among anthropologists and other scholars who do research "on" Indians. The adoption of the AAA Code of Ethics (*Current Anthropology* 1971) and the promulgation of an ethical code for research in native communities by the National Endowment for the Humanities in 1990 (National Endowment for the Humanities n.d.), along with the creation of the AAA Reburial Commission (1989), have effected change, as has the enactment by Congress of the Native American Graves Protection and Repatriation Act (NAGPRA). Of course, the scholarly role in decolonization is no more monolithic than the Indian role is. "Culture wars" rage within anthropology just as they do in the wider academy. The range of scholarly positions effectively runs the gamut from radical self-critique (Clemmer 1972 [1969]; Talbot 1979; see also the chapters in this volume) through defense of the scientific position of the anthropological tradition (Clifton 1990a,b). But no scholarship pertaining to American Indians remains untouched by what we are calling the late imperial situation; an anticolonial critique and an anticolonial practice influence all research now carried out, and even if a scholar intends to ignore the critique, he or she cannot ignore the changed laws, changed ethical rules, and changed patterns of access to research sources and funding. How much things have changed is indicated by a comparison of Margaret Mead's research methodology among the Omahas with contemporary institutional review boards' protection procedures for research on human subjects. Mead purposely deceived her Omaha consultants as part of her data-collection procedures in 1930 (Mead 1969 [1932]:16). Such a procedure, let alone the attitude behind it, would be unthinkable in the 1990s if for no other reason than the existence of institutional review boards (see Grobsmith, this volume).

Yet we recognize that the history of Indian/non-Indian relations is still in the making in America. And we recognize that what seems at first glance to be a *post*colonial emergence may really be colonial "business as usual, only *more so*" (Terry Eagleton quoted in Mishra and Hodge 1994:277). Certainly systems of domination — colonialism and racism, among them — have remarkable abilities to appease and contain resistance and to appear (at least to some) as not oppressive; and all emancipatory openings face the ongoing threat of cooptation. Some things have remained very much the same — indeed, colonial — despite cosmetic changes (see Deloria, this volume). But we would be foolish to ignore what has changed in fundamental ways, and what those changes mean both for Indian people and for anthropologists. With these complexities in mind, we hope our readers will allow us the term "late imperial" as a useful shorthand for a situation changed in important ways, the potentialities of which have yet to be worked out.

One of the fundamental changes that marks the late imperial situation is an increasing awareness, both on the part of Native Americans and on the part of anthropologists, of the *social process* of *producing* knowledges about Indians in America — particularly, for our purposes, scholarly knowledges. Most "informants" and "anthros" no longer believe that what passes for scholarly knowledge is ever universal, value-neutral, or unconnected to professional, class, and other interests (although there are always "holdouts").[2] Scholarly knowledges about Indians come from modes of knowledge production by which Indian cultures, Indian languages, and Indian objects and bodies have been subjected to scholarly appropriation and (re)presentation. One of the concerns of this book is to make clear how these modes of knowledge production are organized, how they change, what hegemonies they draw on and reproduce, and how they can be made more just and humane.

Alienation (and Repatriation)

The alienation of cultural property and its repatriation to Indian peoples has emerged as one of the most important themes in the analysis of knowledge production in the context of late imperialism in Indian/non-Indian relations. As Dell Hymes has pointed out (1991), Marx's concept of alienation applies — metaphorically, if not technically — to the experience of Indian peoples in the scholarly modes of knowledge production. Alienation for Marx involved the process by which the product of labor became an external thing, existing independently of the producer and even confronting the producer as a hostile force.

With little modification, this definition fits the case of the material culture and human remains collected from Indian peoples in the Americas. Turner (1986:1), for example, by appealing to a universal humanity whose interests anthropology claims to represent, seeks to cut any organic ties native peoples may claim with their pasts as embodied in materials: "I explicitly assume that no living culture, religion, interest group, or biological population has any moral or legal right to the exclusive use or regulation of ancient humans skeletons since all humans are members of the same species, and ancient skeletons are the remnants of unduplicatable evolutionary events which all living and future peoples have the right to know about and understand." By this logic, anthropologists, not Native Americans, become the curators—in fact, owners—of heritage. Native Americans often ask what good archaeological study does or even if findings are "true" (Zimmerman 1992:48). Some worry that studies could harm them spiritually and physically (Rhodd 1990:374). Many also understand that Native American acceptance of archaeologically constructed pasts can threaten cultural identity (Zimmerman 1990:416). Thus Indian people are forced to confront material elements of their own community as an alien, hostile force.

Alienation—in the sense in which the young Marx spoke of alienation under capitalism (see Ollman 1971)—also appears in the socially distancing research stance of traditional anthropology, which Marilyn Bentz argues can "violate the friendship and the spirit of the human relationship that binds the anthropologist and his or her research subject" (see chapter 7 and also Deloria, this volume). Anthropological research, Bentz points out, is only possible on the basis of *friendship*, and the Indian friends of anthropologists can be "betrayed" by such seemingly innocuous devices as life histories, kinship studies, and reflexive accounts—even if "informed consent" is obtained. Gail Landsman also notes the ethical problem of converting information derived from informal, fieldwork settings into permanent texts disseminated for public scrutiny; Indian people have been historically powerless to control or even influence this process of alienation.

Alienation is also clearly visible in the alien representations of Native Americans anthropologists produce and circulate. In chapter 10, Peter Whiteley identifies a "metropolitan aesthetic gaze" trained on Hopi people. Anthropology has been involved in this gaze as one among many appropriators or representers of Hopi culture—along with pot hunters, racist impersonators, and New Agers—who radically decontextualize and reinterpret things Hopi according to non-Hopi "registers of significance," registers insulated from the "material realities" of real Hopi life. The problem specifically with respect to anthropology concerns the "graduate school rationale of constructing 'problems' *in vacuo* to pursue in 'the field.'" The result is anthropology's collusion in the "contemporary intellectual reproduction of colonial oppression."

"How did it happen," Murray Wax asks in chapter 3, "that anthropologists came to think of themselves as having the mandate not only to study but to speak for Indian peoples?" The simple answer is that Indians were "available" for representation (Medicine 1972b:25), which is to say, they had been made safe and suitable for ethnography, with all the complex and brutal history that implies. A more involved answer outlined by Wax addresses the relative powerlessness of Indian people — historically, at least — to represent themselves: "Without literacy, politico-military power, or the competencies for dealing with governmental bureaucrats, they would have especially been exploited, so that anthropologists could feel morally obligated and entitled to represent them to authorities and the larger world." In this context an "alliance" existed between Indian people and the anthropologists who studied them, but Wax argues that this alliance was inherently imbalanced, contradictory, and doomed to recurrent crisis. The interests and fate of individual anthropologists and Indian people diverged, with anthropologists benefiting from the continued "underdog" status of Indian people,[3] and Indian people losing control by allowing others to represent them.

The crisis in the "alliance" became apparent with Deloria's 1969 attack on anthros, but other Native American scholars have also articulated grave concerns about the source and nature of scholarly representations of Native Americans (McNickle 1972; Medicine 1972b; Ortiz 1972; Churchill 1992). The crisis is also clear in Landsman's description in chapter 9 of the rift between Iroquoian scholars and Iroquois traditionalists. Contemporary Iroquois traditionalists not only are practically capable of representing Iroquois society but insist on it. The crisis in the "alliance" also comes through clearly in Cecil King's chapter, in which he enunciates a point of view widespread in native communities in North America: "We have been observed, noted, taped, and videoed. Our behaviors have been recorded in every possible way known to Western science, and I suppose we could learn to live with this if we had not become imprisoned in your words. The language that you use to explain us traps us in linguistic cages because we must explain our ways through your hypothetical constructs and theoretical frameworks. . . . We must segment, fragment, fracture, and pigeonhole that which we hold sacred." King clearly sees that the process of representation is rooted in the institutional framework of knowledge production: "We want to be given the time, money, luxury, and security of academic credibility to define our own constructs from within our own languages and our own words." Regarding the continued role of outsiders in representing native peoples, King asks, "When will you become instrumental to our ambitions, our categories of importance?" At minimum, representations constructed by outsiders should be subject to control by native peoples: "We want to say who comes to our world, what they should see, hear, and take away. Most important, we want to appraise, critique, and censure what they feel they have a right to say." Anthropologists may well consider such suggestions dangerous infringements upon academic freedom, but it is clear that such demands have become more vocal and more persuasive since Deloria's book; they will not go away, and scholars will increasingly need to deal with them directly, whether they choose to or not.

Social Constructivism

A second linked point to emerge from these chapters is the heuristic value of a constructivist and skeptical stance by anthropologists on anthropology itself. More specifically, anthropological research and writing on American Indians is best seen not as scholarship based on an epistemologically privileged Truth or Science standing above social life, but as a *discourse* that is a social "partial truth" — partial in the sense of incomplete and interested (Clifford 1986). Anthropological representations are, after all, no less cultural (in the sense of socially constructing a worldview) than any other mode of thinking (see Biolsi, this volume); whether they are more right or more wrong, mostly true or mostly false, science or obscurantism, or somewhere in between these extremes, they are socially constructed, socially transmitted, and socially enforced templates for interpretation and practice. Verification and replication do not magically make any set of ideas thereby less social, situated, or political. Recognizing this does not mean that we take all representations to be equally good. As Landsman points out, it can mean, rather, the (enriching) realization that the content of anthropological representations comes not from contemplative observation but from positioned stances in ongoing social struggles, such as colonialism and postcolonialism (see also Randall H. McGuire's chapter).

Both Gail Landsman and Larry Zimmerman show how our profession has stubbornly sought to force its discourse on Indian peoples as a *science* in contrast to their (prescientific) *culture*, their false consciousness. Of course, until recently, anthropology was in a position — in terms of power and authority — to do that. But Native Americans interpreted this stance, especially on the part of the archaeological subdiscipline, as no more than "scientific colonialism." The voting public has largely agreed, as the flurry of reburial acts passed by state legislatures and by NAGPRA have made clear. McGuire reveals how the discourse involving the concept of the "vanishing race" has made it easy for archaeologists to believe that they — and not contemporary Indian people — are the inheritors, and the appropriate protectors and interpreters, of the Indian past. Thomas Biolsi argues that the cultural "integrationist" conceptual apparatus of the 1930s had the unanticipated consequence of causing one anthropologist to write off most Oglala Lakotas as people unworthy of his attention.

Can We Get Along?
We should begin any attempt to answer this question with a clear recognition that anthropologists as members of an academic discipline, and Indian people as members of reservation (and other kinds of native) communities, are positioned with respect to each other in a larger scheme of political and cultural economy. Indians and anthropologists do not confront each other "in the field" as representatives of "two worlds," however "obvious" that may seem at first glance, and notwithstanding the difference in vantage points. Rather, they are ultimately parts of the same world, the same larger social formation. Of course, there are "cultural" differences between anthropologists and Indian people, and the discipline and native communities do have profoundly divergent "local knowledges." Their standpoints, their positions, within the social formation differ vastly. But this difference is not a historical accident or an occurrence unconnected to the totality; difference itself is underwritten and produced by a larger social situation. The same history and social forces that made anthropology possible and presently undergird its reproduction as an academic profession in universities also shaped the terrain for contemporary native communities and presently reproduce the material and cultural conditions of their survival (for a clear statement of this position, see Gupta and Ferguson 1992;

on the systematic production of local difference on a global scale, see Harvey 1989; Wolf 1982).

At the time that Vine Deloria was asking why Indian people should continue to be studied by anthropologists, Dell Hymes was asking if it would be necessary to invent anthropology if it did not already exist (Hymes 1969). The answer to Hymes's question is, of course, both yes and no.

Recognizing the *positionality*, as Lila Abu-Lughod (1991) calls it, of anthropologists and Indians in the larger social formation inevitably raises the issue of colonialism and anthropology's linkages to colonialism. Obviously, this question cannot be answered satisfactorily in one brief introduction or even in a single book. As Joan Vincent points out, there is a complex and "many layered relationship between anthropology and colonialism" (Vincent 1991:47; see Vincent 1990 for details on the layers), but this must not stop us from serious consideration of "the role of ethnographers on the moving edge of capitalist expansion and of the function of ethnographic writing in a larger scheme of things" (Vincent 1991:47). In the end, whether anthropologists and Indians can get along or not will depend on the critical self-consciousness of anthropology regarding its position in capitalism and colonialism — the larger scheme of things.

What are some of the layers of the relationship between anthropology and the colonization of American Indians? First of all, there is the matter of enablement. Colonialism historically made Indians available, as Medicine puts it, for anthropology, just as surely as colonialism made Indian lands available for homesteaders, railroads, mining companies, and Eastern and European investors in the development of the American West (see White 1992 for a summary of Western development). Anthropologists followed the army and the BIA to study Indian cultures (see Bieder 1986; Hinsley 1981; Vincent 1990), just as missionaries followed to save Indian souls. This historical relationship has not ended: the continued economic and political oppression of Indian communities still makes Indians (more or less) available for anthropological research. Anthropologists as individuals — or, most of them — have not been directly involved in the colonial disempowerment of Indian people, but their choice of Indians as subjects of study has been directly enabled by it. To some extent, this relationship is undergoing change as Indian communities have come to question and even fund and control research.

Another layer of the relationship concerns the situations in which anthropologists have directly served in the colonial apparatus (for good or bad) or otherwise been part of the construction of colonial discourses (wittingly or unwittingly) (see Bieder 1986; Hinsley 1981; Vincent 1990). The resonance of Lewis Henry Morgan's evolutionary paradigm with the late-nineteenth-century project to "civilize" the Indians may not make anthropology guilty of colonialism directly, but it is a political linkage at a deep level that needs to be taken seriously and explored. There has always been an "administrative version of anthropological thought" in the colonialism of the West (Hoxie 1992:973). Nineteenth-century anthropological evolutionism was part of a deeper "capitalism triumphant" (Wolf 1969) intellectual climate that helped to determine and to justify policies toward native peoples.[4] Consider Alice Fletcher, the BIA agent who supervised the allotment of the Omaha, and James Mooney, whose study of the Ghost Dance was funded by the Bureau of American Ethnology, an institution intended to provide practical information for the colonial regulation of Indian people. Mooney's excellent and sympathetic study notwithstanding, his superiors and sponsors put him in the field to figure out how to avoid further unrest among the colonized. A "reader-response" analysis of the reception of Mooney's text by his superiors and administrators would be more than a little interesting (see Hinsley 1981).

Finally, and most deeply, there is the matter with which we began this section — the relative positioning of anthropology and Native Americans in the larger political and cultural economy. The history by which Indian people were made primitive Others, conceptually and materially, subject to economic exploitation, political colonization, and scientific scrutiny — in a word, their *disempowerment* — is the same history by which generally elite white intellectuals became authorized to study the primitive as professional anthropologists in the academy, in a word, their *privilege*. Anthropology as a discipline and anthropologists as individuals have been — understandably and predictably — slow to recognize this inescapably political linkage between themselves and disempowered peoples. Indian people have not been so slow, even before they were catalyzed by Deloria's book. As Abu-Lughod (1991:148) puts it:

We need to ask questions about the historical processes by which it came to pass that people like ourselves could be engaged in anthropological studies of people like these, about the current world situation that enables us to engage in this sort of work in this particular place, and about who has preceded us and is even now there with us (tourists, travelers, missionaries, [Agency for International Development] consultants, Peace Corps workers). We need to ask what this "will to knowledge" about the Other is connected to in the world.

Anthropology is a quintessentially Western project. It now seems likely, to answer Hymes's question, that anthropology, or something very much like it, would have been invented if it did not exist. Anthropology does not provide crucial practical knowledge in the way physics, chemistry, engineering, and business administration do (after all, sponsors from the colonial apparatus often found anthropological reports practically useless [Kuper 1985]); but it does address deep questions Westerners ask about themselves and their encounter with peoples they have colonized and liquidated. In other words, anthropology is not a *universal* "science of man [sic!]." It is a set of questions asked and answered by an "interested party" in a global and highly unequal encounter, the ultimate results of which are yet to be fully worked out. Anthropology is the academic discipline that makes sense of the Others the West has both created and encountered in its global expansion since 1500 (see Biolsi, this volume; Diamond 1974). Anthropology does not work monolithically. There are deep divisions in the field about what the Other is and how to study him or her (compare, for example, Geertz 1973 and Wolf 1982, or Clifford and Marcus 1986 and Fox 1991). Scholars also debate how anthropology is implicated in colonialism and what theoretical and practical stance anthropologists should take regarding colonialism. We should note, however, that there is a well-developed, critical approach to these questions apparent in the anthropological tradition, and we would take issue with Deloria's contention in this volume that anthropology is not able to offer "any sane critique of modern civilization." Within American Indian studies, for example, Eleanor Leacock and Joseph Jorgensen stand out as prolific and influential scholars whose work has used Native American materials in a sustained critique of capitalism. Many anthropologists have followed in their paths.

The point, however, is that anthropology originates in the unique moral dilemmas and political struggles of the West, not in "man's will to knowledge." The discourses by which anthropology operates therefore make sense to Western intellectuals, but there is no reason to believe they make any sense at all to native peoples. Anthropology does not ask questions native peoples necessarily ask or need answers to. Anyone who has taught an anthropology course with Native American students in the room, or who has tried to explain a "pure research" problem to native informants, knows this. This fact of different vantage points is behind the most critical situation pointed out by Vine Deloria in his 1969 critique and reiterated in his chapter in this volume: Anthropology as a disciplinary enterprise does not so much harm Indian people (although there are enough individual cases of direct or indirect harm) as conduct studies on issues completely and utterly irrelevant to Indian welfare. Even when anthropologists and other intellectuals consciously choose to engage in research critical of colonization and colonial power relations, they do not have the same interests as native peoples; they do not bring the same questions to the research setting. Ironically, some of the most critical and radical thought in anthropology makes Indian people most uncomfortable. How would most Indian people, for example, feel about Eric Wolf's (1982:171) insistence that the Ojibwas constituted not a native nation with deep historical roots but a postcontact, historically emergent phenomenon? How would most Indian people feel about Morton Fried's (1975) insistence that tribes as political entities did not appear until Europeans arrived? Given the ongoing political, legal, and ideological struggles over sovereignty, couching Indian history in such a way is understandably threatening to Indian people. We can get an idea of what a native scholar might have to say about this kind of historicism by examining Ward Churchill's biting commentaries on Sam Gill's *Mother Earth* and on James Clifton's *The Invented Indian* (Churchill 1992).

Can we get along? To begin with, we as anthropologists need to be critically self-aware of our positionality. Some of the chapters here begin to do this. They hopefully anticipate a new kind of anthropological writing about American Indians in which these kinds of issues are addressed—writing that tells us as much about the place of study of Indians in American society as it tells us about Indians. Works like those of Robert Bieder (1986), Robert Berkhofer (1979), Douglas Cole (1985), Brian Dippie (1982), Harvey Feit (1991), Curtis Hinsley (1981, 1989), Gerald Sider (1993), George Stocking (1992), Joan Vincent (1990), and Eric Wolf (1969) also obviously move in the right direction. But more needs to be done to answer in a serious and sustained scholarly way the kinds of questions Abu-Lughod poses with regard to the study of American Indians. Not every anthropologist needs to do this, but somebody has to do it. Is it possible to write a description of the encounter between an anthropologist (perhaps, oneself) and an Indian community which positions that encounter within "a larger political-historical context" (Abu-Lughod 1991:141)? Such a description would have to show the historical, political-economic, social, and cultural forces responsible for both the Indians and the anthropologist being there at a particular time, in particular ways, with specific power relations, and with particular beliefs about, and interests with respect to, each other.

Here we see a limit to the utility of some versions of the postmodern critique of what anthropologists do. We think anthropology has a *history*; we think that what we do is not merely replace one arbitrary "narrative" (Bruner 1986) with another in an endless play of texts, or fill one "gap" (Clifford 1986) only to create another in an infinite word game with arbitrary, closed rules. Anthropology has a history because its theory has a social context (LaCapra 1983; Vincent 1991), because its theory confronts experience (Thompson 1978:7–9). We think different thoughts today than we did thirty years ago, not only because of internal discourse-driven dynamics, but also because scholars from different kinds of backgrounds with different loyalties and accountabilities entered the field, because our "natives" stopped being so compliant with our representations, and because our students — some of them from the "primitive" societies we study — stopped buying our representations. And surely it makes a difference if, because of those experiences, we now think of colonialism and racism *as concepts* in our teaching, research, and writing. In this sense, we do know more, or understand more critically and insightfully, the political-economic context in which we work and live and in which our subjects work and live — because our experience demanded that we know this, or at least confront it.

As important as such critical theory is, critical analysis of the global cultural and political economies would *still* be quintessentially a Western — not an Indian — project. We can well imagine that such an account would be organized around concepts like capitalism, mode of production, world system, class and class consciousness, hegemony, labor power, surplus extraction, technologies of power, epistemes, discursive formations, symbolic capital, and so on. These are not concepts of much interest or use to Indian communities. It is easy enough to imagine most Indian people insisting that they need not Marx or Foucault, or any technical scholarly concepts, to understand exactly what has happened to them since 1492 and how anthropology as a discipline has been implicated, even if not directly involved.

What will ultimately be required for us to get along is not new theories, paradigms, discourses, or texts (no matter how critical they might be), nor new sensitivities and ethical stances on the part of anthropologists (no matter how progressive they might be), but change in the social relations of scholarly production within the academy. Deloria, in effect, calls for this change in the final chapter in this book. It is, of course, much more difficult than changing theories or ethics — because it involves power and the (re)distribution of power. When one considers the sociology of hiring, publication, promotion, and funding in anthropology, one quickly realizes that research on American Indians will continue to reflect the agendas of the "establishment" rather than those of Indian people. The anthropological career largely involves the professional accumulation of symbolic capital through peer-reviewed publication and of (micro-)political power through institutional and disciplinary networks and seniority. The anthropologist thus necessarily has, as Wax puts it, a "hit-and-run" relationship with the native community he or she studies. This situation essentially guarantees that scholarly work will orient itself around intellectual issues in the elite, hegemonic, national intellectual culture, not around indigenous issues. To change the content of what anthropologists do we will have to develop new criteria of promotion and tenure, for example, in which outreach and service to American Indian constituencies count as much as, if not more than, traditional scholarship. Some positions in the field (especially joint appointments with American Indian Studies programs) appear to have these components in the job description or appointment letter, although like a working woman, the anthropologist so hired ends up being expected to do "double duty" — to perform both as a traditional department-based colleague and as an outreach or service person. We will also have to create professional opportunities for anthropologists in tribal government, tribal colleges, and other contexts in which accountability for scholarly work ties the scholar directly to indigenous concerns in indigenous communities. Anthropological expertise deployed on behalf of tribes in court cases and federal recognition procedures are a start, although few anthropologists presently root their careers in this kind of work. In short, native communities will have to seize anthropology for their own uses. Whether or not these kinds of opportunities will expand to make a concrete difference in the content of what anthropologists do — making the work more responsive and accountable to native communities — remains an open question.

We need to be careful about celebrating the end of colonial relations between Indians and anthropologists; put bluntly, the *structural* relationship remains in many ways a colonial one. Imagine, for example, all the courses on "Indians of North America" taught by non-Indian anthropologists in American colleges and universities, and imagine how many courses are taught by Native Americans or faculty members otherwise accountable to native communities. Are anthropologists automatically most "qualified" by virtue of their credentials to represent Indian people and native communities in college classrooms? What would we say if representatives of local native communities challenged our monopoly on, or even our right to teach, these courses? This is not at all unlikely given the present concern of Native Americans with alienation of native spirituality by non-Indians (see Churchill 1994).

Whether or not we can get along may ultimately have less to do with the will to change or politics within anthropology, and more to do with crisis and opportunity. It is not unimaginable that in the crisis of public confidence in, and funding for, public higher education apparent at this writing, novel experiments in the organization of teaching and research may be possible, experiments that would allow us to open up what we teach and what we write to Indian people.

Nevertheless, things may not change. If so, it is likely that anthropologists will be less and less welcome in Indian communities and that the field as a whole will be less and less relevant to contemporary Indian concerns. We may well end up getting along only because anthropology is no longer practiced in Indian communities and anthropology is no more a concern to Indian communities one way or the other than is medieval Chinese philosophy. Obviously, the contributors to this book desire that such an eventuality not come to pass.

Notes
1. JoAllyn Archambault, Raymond D. Fogelson, Loretta Fowler, Dell Hymes, Raymond DeMallie, and William Sturtevant presented papers at the conference session but did not contribute chapters to this book. Dell Hymes published his session paper in the

Journal of Linguistic Anthropology (Hymes 1991). Randall H. McGuire and Peter Whiteley did not participate in the original conference session but have written chapters included here.

2. We recall a 1986 panel on reburial at the AAA annual meeting in Philadelphia, at which a native spokesperson chastised the profession for its failure to come to terms with native concerns. One of our colleagues, a well-known anthropologist in Native American Studies, rose in the audience and responded that he did *science* and that he, as a scientist, would not be intimidated from doing his science.

3. At the AAA panel in 1989, Vine Deloria made the point that at one time Indian people were seen by anthropologists as essentially *primitive*; now they are often seen as essentially *oppressed*: a successful or accomplished Indian professional is somehow less Indian.

4. Perhaps the point one might want to draw here is that anthropology is trapped and contained by a larger social-cultural logic just as much as Native Americans are. Morgan's scholarly program and BIA policy emerged out of the same social context and the same deeper episteme of Western progress. As Richard G. Fox points out, anthropologists "neither own nor control the means of scholarly production" (Fox 1992:9). Global historical forces have "made us" (p. 13) just as much as they have determined the situation of Indian people.

References

Abu-Lughod, Lila. 1991. "Writing against Culture. " In Richard G. Fox, ed., *Recapturing Anthropology: Working in the Present*, pp. 115–35. Santa Fe, N.Mex.: School of American Studies Research Press.

Akwesasne Notes, ed. 1978. *Basic Call to Consciousness*. Summertown, Tenn.: Book Publishing.

American Indian Lawyer Training Program. 1988. *Indian Tribes as Sovereign Governments*. Oakland, Calif.: American Indian Lawyer Training Program.

Asad, Talal, ed. 1973. *Anthropology and the Colonial Encounter*. London: Ithaca Press.

Berkhofer, Robert F., Jr. 1979. *The White Man's Indian: Images of the American Indian from Columbus to the Present*. New York: Vintage.

Bieder, Robert. 1986. *Science Encounters the Indian, 1820–1880: The Early Years of American Ethnology*. Norman: University of Oklahoma Press.

Bruner, Edward M. 1986. "Ethnography as Narrative." In Edward M. Bruner and Victor W. Turner, eds., *The Anthropology of Experience*, pp. 139–55. Urbana: University of Illinois Press.

Churchill, Ward. 1992. *Fantasies of the Master Race: Literature, Cinema and the Colonization of American Indians*, ed. M. Annette Jaimes. Monroe, Maine: Common Courage Press.

———. 1994. *Indians Are Us? Culture and Genocide in Native North America*. Monroe, Maine: Common Courage Press.

Churchill, Ward, and Jim Vander Wall. 1988. *Agents of Repression: The FBI's Secret*

Wars against the Black Panther Party and the American Indian Movement. Boston: South End Press.

Clemmer, Richard O. 1972 [1969]. "Truth, Duty, and the Revitalization of Anthropologists: A New Perspective on Cultural Change and Resistance." In Dell Hymes, ed., *Reinventing Anthropology*, pp. 213–47. New York: Vintage.

Clifford, James A. 1986. "Introduction: Partial Truths." In James A. Clifford and George E. Marcus, eds., *Writing Culture: The Poetics and Politics of Ethnography*, pp. 1–26. Berkeley: University of California Press.

Clifford, James A., and George E. Marcus, eds. 1986. *Writing Culture: The Poetics and Politics of Ethnography.* Berkeley: University of California Press.

Clifton, James A. 1990a. "Introduction: Memoir, Exegesis." In James A. Clifton, ed., *The Invented Indian: Cultural Fictions and Government Policies*, pp. 1–28. New Brunswick, N.J.: Transaction Publishers.

———. 1990b. "The Indian Story: A Cultural Fiction." In James A. Clifton, ed., *The Invented Indian: Cultural Fictions and Government Policies*, pp. 29–48. New Brunswick, N.J.: Transaction Publishers.

Cole, Douglas. 1985. *Captured Heritage: The Scramble for Northwest Coast Artifacts.* Seattle: University of Washington Press.

Cornell, Stephen. 1988. *Return of the Native: American Indian Political Resurgence.* New York: Oxford University Press.

Current Anthropology. 1968. Symposium on social responsibilities. *Current Anthropology* 9(5):391–435.

———. 1971. Symposium entitled "Toward an Ethics for Anthropologists." *Current Anthropology* 12(3):312–56.

Deloria, Vine, Jr. 1970 [1969]. *Custer Died for Your Sins: An Indian Manifesto.* New York: Avon.

———. 1974. *Behind the Trail of Broken Treaties: An Indian Declaration of Independence.* Austin: University of Texas Press.

Dewing, Rolland. 1985. *Wounded Knee: The Meaning and Significance of the Second Incident.* New York: Irvington Publishers.

Diamond, Stanley. 1974. *In Search of the Primitive: A Critique of Civilization.* New Brunswick, N.J.: Transaction Books.

Dippie, Brian W. 1982. *The Vanishing American: White Attitudes and U.S. Indian Policy.* Middletown, Conn.: Wesleyan University Press.

Feit, Harvey. 1991. "The Construction of Algonquian Hunting Territories: Private Property as Moral Lesson, Policy Advocacy, and Ethnographic Error." In George W. Stocking, Jr., ed., *Colonial Situations: Essays on the Contextualization of Ethnographic Knowledge.* Madison: University of Wisconsin Press.

Fox, Richard G. 1991. "Introduction: Working in the Present." In Richard G. Fox, ed., *Recapturing Anthropology: Working in the Present*, pp. 1–16. Santa Fe, N.Mex.: School of American Studies Research Press.

Fried, Morton H. 1975. *The Notion of Tribe.* Menlo Park, Calif.: Cummings.

Geertz, Clifford. 1973. *The Interpretation of Cultures.* New York: Basic Books.

Gupta, Akhil, and James Ferguson. 1992. "Beyond 'Culture': Space, Identity, and the Politics of Difference." *Cultural Anthropology* 7(1):6–23.

Guyette, Susan, and Charlotte Heth. 1988. *Issues for the Future of American Indian Studies: A Needs Assessment and Program Guide.* Los Angeles: American Indian Studies Center, University of California.

Harvey, David. 1989. *The Condition of Postmodernity.* Cambridge, Mass.: Basil Blackwell.

Hauptman, Laurence M. 1986. *The Iroquois Struggle for Survival: World War II to Red Power.* Syracuse, N.Y.: Syracuse University Press.

Henry, Jeannette, ed. 1972. *The American Indian Reader: Anthropology.* San Francisco: Indian Historian Press.

Hinsley, Curtis M., Jr. 1981. *Savages and Scientists: The Smithsonian Institution and the Development of American Anthropology, 1846–1910.* Washington, D.C.: Smithsonian Institution Press.

———. 1989. "Zunis and Brahmins: Cultural Ambivalence in the Gilded Age." In George W. Stocking, Jr., ed., *Romantic Motives: Essays on Anthropological Sensibility*, pp. 169–207. Madison: University of Wisconsin Press.

Hoxie, Frederick E. 1992. "Exploring a Cultural Borderland: Native American Journeys of Discovery in the Early Twentieth Century." *Journal of American History*, December, pp. 969–95.

Hymes, Dell. 1991. "Custer and Linguistic Anthropology." *Journal of Linguistic Anthropology* 1(1):5–11.

Hymes, Dell, ed. 1969. *Reinventing Anthropology.* New York: Pantheon.

Jaimes, M. Annette, ed. 1992. *The State of Native America: Genocide, Colonization, and Resistance.* Boston: South End Press.

Kuper, Adam. 1985. *Anthropology and Anthropologists: The Modern British School*, rev. ed. New York: Routledge.

LaCapra, Dominick. 1983. *Rethinking Intellectual History: Texts, Contexts, Language.* Ithaca, N.Y.: Cornell University Press.

Landsman, Gail. 1988. *Sovereignty and Symbol: Indian/White Conflict at Ganienkeh.* Albuquerque: University of New Mexico Press.

Matthiessen, Peter. 1991. *In the Spirit of Crazy Horse.* New York: Viking.

McClintock, Ann. 1994. "The Angel of Progress: Pitfalls of the Term 'Post-Colonialism.'" In Patrick Williams and Laura Chrisman, eds., *Colonial Discourse and Post-Colonial Theory*, pp. 291–304. New York: Columbia University Press.

McNickle, D'Arcy. 1972. "American Indians Who Never Were." In Jeannette Henry, ed., *The American Indian Reader: Anthropology*, pp. 29–36. San Francisco: Indian Historian Press.

Mead, Margaret. 1969 [1932]. *The Changing Culture of an Indian Tribe.* New York: AMS Press.

Means, Russell. 1995. *Where White Men Fear to Tread: The Autobiography of Russell Means.* New York: St. Martin's.

Medicine, Bea. 1972a. "The Anthropologist and American Indian Studies." In Jeannette Henry, ed., *The American Indian Reader: Anthropology*, pp. 13–20. San Francisco: Indian Historian Press.

————. 1972b. "The Anthropologist as the Indian's Image Maker." In Jeannette Henry, ed., *The American Indian Reader: Anthropology*, pp. 23–28. San Francisco: Indian Historian Press.

Mishra, Vijay, and Bob Hodge. 1994. "What Is Post(-)colonialism?" In Patrick Williams and Laura Chrisman, eds., *Colonial Discourse and Post Colonial Theory*, pp. 276–90. New York: Columbia University Press.

National Endowment for the Humanities. N.d. *Ethics Code for Scholars Working in American Indian Communities.* Washington, D.C.: National Endowment for the Humanities.

Ollman, Bertell. 1971. *Alienation.* Cambridge: Cambridge University Press.

Ortiz, Alfonso. 1972. "An Indian Anthropologist's Perspective on Anthropology." In Jeannette Henry, ed., *The American Indian Reader: Anthropology*, pp. 6–12. San Francisco: Indian Historian Press.

Ortiz, Roxanne Dunbar. 1977. *The Great Sioux Nation: Sitting in Judgment on America.* Cincinnati, Ohio: General Board of Global Ministries.

————. 1984. *Indians of the Americas: Human Rights and Self- Determination.* New York: Praeger.

Rhodd, B. 1990. "Reburial in South Dakota: Two Perspectives." In Anthony Klesert and Alan Downer, eds., *Preservation on the Reservation: Native Americans, Native American Lands, and Archaeology*, pp. 369–75. Window Rock, Ariz.: Navajo National Archaeology Department.

Sider, Gerald M. 1993. *Lumbee Indian Histories: Race, Ethnicity, and Indian Identity in the Southern United States.* New York: Cambridge University Press.

Steiner, Stan. 1968. *The New Indians.* New York: Dell.

Stocking, George W., Jr. 1992. *The Ethnographer's Magic and Other Essays in the History of Anthropology.* Madison: University of Wisconsin Press.

Talbot, Steve. 1979. "The Meaning of Wounded Knee, 1973: Indian Self-Government and the Role of Anthropology." In Gerrit Huizer and Bruce Mannheim, eds., *The Politics of Anthropology: From Colonialism and Sexism toward a View from Below*, pp. 227–58. The Hague: Mouton.

Thompson, E. P. 1978. *The Poverty of Theory and Other Essays.* New York: Monthly Review Press.

Turner, Christy. 1986. "What Is Lost with Skeletal Reburial?" *Quarterly Review of Archaeology* 7(1):1.

Vincent, Joan. 1990. *Anthropology and Politics: Visions, Traditions, and Trends.* Tucson: University of Arizona Press.

————. 1991. "Engaging Historicism." In Richard G. Fox, ed., *Recapturing Anthropology: Working in the Present*, pp. 45–58. Santa Fe, N.Mex.: School of American Studies Research Press.

Warrior, Robert Allen. 1995. *Tribal Secrets: Recovering American Indian Intellectual Traditions.* Minneapolis: University of Minnesota Press.

White, Richard. 1992. *It's Your Misfortune and None of My Own*. Norman: University of Oklahoma Press.

Wolf, Eric R. 1969. "American Anthropology and American Society." In Dell Hymes, ed., *Reinventing Anthropology*, pp. 251–63. New York: Pantheon.

———. 1982. *Europe and the People without History*. Berkeley: University of California Press.

Zimmerman, Larry J. 1992. "Archaeology, Reburial, and the Tactics of a Discipline's Self-Delusion." *American Indian Culture and Research Journal* 16(2):37–56.

Part One

Deloria Writes Back

These three chapters explore the critique of anthropology by Vine Deloria in his earlier works. In chapter 1, historian Herbert T. Hoover places Deloria in context—as an influential author, polemicist, and activist, as a member of an old and accomplished Indian family, and as an American Indian intellectual who worked his way into prominence from a marginalized position.

Elizabeth S. Grobsmith describes in chapter 2 the reception of *Custer Died for Your Sins* when she was a graduate student in anthropology, and how she struggled to learn from the book's message. In many ways, this chapter is a dialogue with Deloria (which Deloria continues in the Conclusion). Grobsmith explains how the concerns originally raised by Deloria have affected not only anthropologists but also tribal members, tribal governments, and academic professional and institutional bodies concerned with ethics. While Grobsmith is obviously indebted to Deloria, and believes anthropology is too, she also clearly sees a need for tempering his critique and for developing a more nuanced assessment of the field's relations with Indian communities.

Murray L. Wax draws out Deloria's critique in chapter 3 and posits that one of the main issues in contemporary Indian affairs is the matter of representation—how Indians will be represented and by whom. Because of the marginalized political-economic position of Indian communities in the United States, popular perceptions of Indian people as an admirable and oppressed minority are potential resources. But this stereotype, as all stereotypes, has its decided costs, and its strategic pursuit by Indian spokespeople is a matter of walking a thin line. Thus, it is not surprising that Indian intellectual leaders focus on the issue of representation, and that Deloria has taken on those non-Indians who would represent Indians, with or without Indian consent: anthropologists. Wax explores both how anthropology came to claim the authority to represent Indians and why that authority has become problematic. He also emphasizes Deloria's insistence that only a researcher whose interests are tied to those of the community being studied will be able to produce work that is useful, work that is desired by the community, and work that is not colonial in nature.

1

Vine Deloria, Jr., in American Historiography

HERBERT T. HOOVER

Vine Deloria, Jr., is an author of obvious importance to historiography. In approximately two decades he wrote or edited at least ten books and as many articles that belong in every substantial bibliography related to Native American Studies. *Custer Died for Your Sins* and several others provide insights into all intercultural relationships of national society in the past and serve as preparation for adjustments to an increasingly multiethnic society in the future. Deloria qualifies as a fixture in the history of historical writing about the United States because his works have lasting application.

An inquiry about their principal contribution to contemporary society evoked some interesting responses among other authors in Sioux country, where Deloria spent the early years of his life. Steve Emery, the attorney general for and member of the Cheyenne River Sioux Tribe, said: "I can think of no other Native American author in the twentieth century who has contributed so greatly to trans-cultural communication by the clarification of Native American history." Frank Pommersheim, a specialist in the legal experience of Indian people at the University of South Dakota School of Law, called him "the leading Sioux intellectual" of his generation. Frederick Manfred, premier novelist in the region, portrayed him as "a critic of social problems" and not a historian at all. Said Manfred, Deloria "exaggerates the facts," using them to argue "rationally, like a lawyer." The strength of his contributions comes not from the quality of the history he wrote but through the verve of his rhetoric: "sardonic, eloquent, clear, outraged."

Norma Wilson, professor of Native American literature at the University of South Dakota, emphasized how Deloria employs the art of argument, presenting new interpretations of past events through the use of irony. Robert Stahl, professor of anthropology at Northern State University in Aberdeen, South Dakota, and specialist in tribal cultural affairs, thought Deloria's writing might best be remembered for its emphasis on a "third position" between those of whites and Indians. Deloria has stood foremost among recent tribal spokespeople who strive for the amelioration of misunderstandings by the merger of antagonistic legal systems into one acceptable to all members of national society. Together these and half a dozen other respondents supplied an image of a critic whose primary purpose is to demand public recognition for Indians, with rights more firmly rooted in history than those of other ethnic minorities; to encourage tenacity in the revival of political, economic, and cultural self-determination among the tribes; and to establish a relationship based on mutual respect between Native Americans and other citizens.

The most useful statement regarding motivation came from Leonard Bruguier, director of the Institute of Indian Studies at the University of South Dakota and member of the Yankton Sioux Tribe: "Vine, Jr." became "a principal leader in the fight for rights of Indians in the United States" because he "carried on the leadership qualities of his father, grandfather, and great grandfather." In other words, his success stems not only from his formal education and academic position but also from an extraordinary family heritage.

To overlook his heritage is to ignore both the motivation and the context of his works. Vine Deloria, Jr., has contributed as a polemicist from a "third position," as Professor Stahl indicated, using personal experience and data mainly from Sioux country in an effort to encourage the survival of tribalism across the United States and to defend Native American rights against infringement by members of non-Indian society. His distinguished performance bespeaks personal achievement, to be sure, but the role he serves comes as a bequest from his ancestors. Four generations used a special forum availed them by historical circumstance to resist the loss of Native American identity and intercede on behalf of tribes in their relationships with mainstream society.

The names Delorier and Des Laurias first appeared in the annals of upper Missouri River fur traders employed in the network of Pierre Chouteau, Jr., and

Company from St. Louis as one among many without particular distinction. The name Francis Deloria surfaced in federal records as one of prominence, however, shortly after the establishment of the Yankton Sioux Agency in 1859 at a place later named Greenwood.

Within two years more than two thousand people accepted confinement to reservation life along the valley and on the Missouri Hills nearby. This group comprised seven bands represented by as many men called chief by non-Indians; they had become leaders in civil affairs and diplomacy through traditional means. Agency leaders organized an additional band, because the 1858 treaty of land cession contained an unusual provision to support tribal members of mixed extraction, and "made" Francis Deloria its first chief. As the son of a French fur trader and a Yankton mother, he became an ideal liaison for the tribe's eighth band and looked after the rights of its mixed-blood members to special consideration under the terms of the treaty signed by Yankton leaders at Washington, D.C., in 1858. The same was true of Philip J. Deloria, who in 1877 succeeded his father in the role of chief for the mixed-blood band until he became an Episcopal priest.

At that point, "PJ" reluctantly relinquished the office of band chief (to Peter Grant) and accepted appointment as the first person of Indian heritage ever to take over mission affairs for a Christian denomination on an entire reservation in Sioux country. The performance of P. J. Deloria as a mediator between tribal and non-Indian societies continued as before, in the context of mission affairs. His children brought similar distinction to the family name, emphasizing cultural preservation as much as tribal accommodation under twentieth-century conditions. Ella Cara Deloria made her mark with ethnological studies. Vine Deloria, Sr., followed in his father's footsteps as an Episcopal priest. Vine Deloria, Jr., Vine Senior's eldest son, carried on the family tradition. Although at first attracted to the Episcopal ministry, the younger Vine Deloria earned a degree in law, gained financial support from academia, and gave popular expression to ideas supported by each generation of his forebears back to his great grandfather Francis.

Vine Deloria, Jr., flourished as a polemicist, despite an obvious disadvantage as an ethnic minority spokesman late in the 1960s. He represented one of four minority groups in national society struggling for civil and social rights who attracted attention according to force of numbers and political influence. African Americans made the greatest gain, Hispanic Americans were next in line for benefits, and Native Americans and Asian Americans may have tied for third place in gaining recognition for their distress.

Guarded public concern about the plights of Indian tribal members coupled with Vine Deloria's credentials in theology and law outside the ivory tower may have been responsible for limitations on the vehicles of publication available to him as he reinterpreted the history of Indian-white relations. His name first appeared in bylines on pulpy pages in *Mademoiselle* and *Playboy* magazines. Soon after the editors of Macmillan Company published *Custer Died for Your Sins* (1969) — one suspects with motives similar to those of editors for Holt, Rinehart, and Winston Company when they released Dee Brown's *Bury My Heart at Wounded Knee* (1970). The editors had thoughts of book sales more than belief in Deloria's polemics or Brown's slanted version of American history. At the time, men and women of means who did not want to bear the onus of opposition to social justice for people less fortunate than themselves felt obligated to purchase both volumes. *Bury My Heart at Wounded Knee* went onto the coffee tables of many Americans among whom, according to one survey conducted by the publisher's marketing representatives, only one in five read much beyond the introduction and even fewer digested its contents from cover to cover. Doubtless, the editors of Macmillan had similar profit motives in mind, and achieved like results when they released *Custer Died for Your Sins.*

The author's subsequent climb through various vehicles of publication toward acceptance from academic colleagues was slow and tortuous. Grosset and Dunlap, which released *God Is Red* (1973), was as commercial in its design as was Macmillan, and so were Doubleday Company and Harper and Row. Not until 1983 did the younger Vine Deloria enjoy equitable reviews from most other academicians following a release from the University of Texas Press. He did not reach the pinnacle of academic privilege with a publication until the University of Oklahoma Press issued a title under his name in 1985.

Historiographers should consider this observation with tongue in cheek, to be sure, yet with admiration for a popular author outside academia looking in. Some time passed before Deloria found his niche in the ivory tower — in the Department of Political Science at the University of Arizona.

Accomplishments outside academia were instrumental in his acceptance; "I suppose my prominence in . . . fields" of interest outside the ivory tower, he recently observed, "made it possible for me to get a tenured position at Arizona." Deloria became executive director of the National Congress of American Indians, found a place in the National Office for Rights of the Indigent, and gained membership on the Board of Inquiry on Hunger and Malnutrition in the United States. The younger Vine Deloria's name also appeared on the roll of awardees from Indian Council Fire, founded in 1923 to recognize no more than one Native American each year for achievement. This brief list gave recognition to his performance and put him in sterling company — with his father and aunt Ella, Lakota Congressman Benjamin Reifel, Charles Eastman, George Frazier, Louis Bruce, and Alfonso Ortiz, to name a few.

His personal background, gradual climb to academic acceptance, and many instances of administrative or honorific recognition built an image, but these factors alone could not explain the importance of the person in historiography. Deloria's obvious role has been that of the most influential polemicist writing on behalf of Native Americans since the late 1960s, and he compares favorably with two distinguished predecessors. Former *encomendero* Bartolome de las Casas was the first. He appeased his conscience and protected his soul against eternal damnation with inflated statistics and dramatic charges against fellow Hispanic colonials. However questionable his data may have been, he garnered attention, went on to serve as the Protector of Indians for King Charles I, and became so important to sixteenth-century Indian-white relations that his *Historia de las Indias* remained in print four centuries later (Casas 1965). Helen Hunt Jackson called federal employees into account during the last quarter of the nineteenth century and also had a profound, abiding effect. Except for Las Casas and Jackson, Vine Deloria, Jr., probably exceeded all others with similar motives on behalf of Native Americans. Deloria used social upheavals in the late 1960s and early 1970s as his forum, and the impact of his work survived the conservative 1980s.

He gained influence in part because of the position of credibility inherited from his forebears, as indicated earlier, to express the outrage felt by so many Indians who had no other vehicle of expression. Precisely a century after Ulysses Grant declared the installation of his acculturative Peace Policy, Delo-

ria maligned its impacts on tribal members across the country with a revision-
ist interpretation of the history of Indian-white relations in *Custer Died for Your
Sins*. Similar indignation came through in some of his other early titles: "This
Country Was a Lot Better Off When the Indians Were Running It"; "The
United States Has No Jurisdiction in Sioux Territory"; "The War between the
Redskins and the Feds"; "Bureau of Indian Affairs: My Brother's Keeper";
"White Society Is Breaking Down around Us."

His analysis included resentful comments about the philosophy undergird-
ing white cultural imperialism. *God Is Red* read like a spiritual corollary to the
Monroe Doctrine. The *Metaphysics of Modern Existence* (1979) called into
question non-Indian worldviews of modern life as they appeared in print and
recommended the reassessment of reality about moral and religious propriety.

Inevitably, he championed the ability of Indians to bring improvement.
With concomitant themes, he stated in *We Talk, You Listen: New Tribes, New
Turf* (1970) that Native Americans were better able to cope with modern conditions than were other groups, and used as evidence the enduring nature of
tribal ways.

Demands for abiding sovereignty and increased legal jurisdiction among
groups of Indians ran throughout many of his publications. One evaluation of
the history of federal-Indian relations, entitled *Behind the Trail of Broken
Treaties: An Indian Declaration of Independence* (1985 [1974]), advocated
greater legal freedom for reservation Indians as residents of enclaves within the
United States. Justification was implicit in *The Indian Affair*, an assessment of
relationships with federal agencies, churches, and educational institutions. A
Better Day for Indians provided an outline of concerns about contemporary
tribal members. Implicit in all the publications was Vine Deloria's diatribe
against the federal government—featured in *The Red Man in the New World
Drama* (Deloria, ed., 1971) and *Of Utmost Good Faith* (1971). Even an older,
professional Vine Deloria, Jr., did not change his underlying theme but chose
a softer presentation under the label of *The Plains Indians of the Twentieth
Century*. The skill of an editor with a flair for style came through. He took a dis-
jointed set of papers that reflected varying degrees of literacy and conceptualization and brought to an academic readership the call for support he had presented to lay readers all along.

The works of Deloria represent a voice of outrage on behalf of Native Americans about what has happened for centuries, and they upbraid non-Indians at the front lines of contact for their roles in cultural imperialism. They take federal leaders to task for their violations of Indians' rights, while they explain a superior and abiding quality in tribal existence and proclaim the intention of Native American leaders to return to center stage in the management of tribal affairs with tools of philosophy, education, and law.

Not all general readers who purchased the books with subtitles *An Indian Manifesto* or *An Indian Declaration of Independence* have digested the thoughtful analyses that subsequently appeared. Historiographers must assign to Vine Deloria, Jr., a place in the annals of history, however, as an outspoken critic of mainstream society who aroused an American conscience as it surfaced late in the 1960s and remained in evidence through the 1970s and 1980s.

Ongoing processes of change endorse his posture. Evidence of Vine Deloria's efforts are manifested in many forms across Indian country. The revival of native spiritual traditions and their incorporation into indigenous curricula is clear in the evolution of tribally controlled colleges since 1968. The self-determination movement has called for an emphasis on tribal objectives unencumbered by outsiders. And continuous litigation over questions of "disestablishment" or "tribal sovereignty on ceded land" makes crystal clear the claim to a new position of sovereignty. Although Professor Charles F. Wilkinson treats federal officials far more favorably than has Vine Deloria, Jr., the central theme in his publication entitled *American Indians, Time, and the Law* (1987) is not markedly different from a central theme in Deloria's works. A judicial battle over jurisdiction will continue as long as federal judges are content to rule roughly equally on both sides in their decisions and attorneys remain eager to earn handsome fees for litigation.

I intend no disrespect by the assertion that Vine Deloria, Jr., cannot fit into American historiography as a historian, as Frederick Manfred suggested, but has made another kind of contribution. His training was in theology and law; his methods are those of an attorney. It seems appropriate to say he never has produced a scholarly history on any subject but has written successfully about the histories of many developments pertaining to Indian-white relations of the past in an effort to alter the opinions of non-Indians and cut a better deal for tribal members across the country.

Beyond that, the products of his efforts have philosophical meaning in public perceptions of historical developments throughout the Western Hemisphere — from the subjection of Guaranis by Spaniards in Paraguay to the exploitation of Miskitu Indians by the British under the guise of a protectorate in Belize. His publications have contemporary application for religious and federal workers in the noncontiguous empire of the United States. Most important, editors, publishers, and readers have elevated him to a position of leadership among Native American critics about the future of the continental United States. Many lessons exist in his publications for an aggregate society that contains elements from all cultures around the world and that soon will comprise more people of color than of Anglo-American heritage.

References

Brown, Dee. 1970. *Bury My Heart at Wounded Knee: An Indian History of the American West*. New York: Holt, Rinehart, and Winston.

Casas, Bartolome de las. 1965. *Historia de las Indias*, 3 vols. Mexico City: Fondo de Cultural Economica.

Deloria, Vine, Jr. 1969. *Custer Died for Your Sins: An Indian Manifesto*. New York: Macmillan.

———. 1970. *We Talk, You Listen: New Tribes, New Turf*. New York: Macmillan.

———. 1971. *Of Utmost Good Faith*. San Francisco: Straight Arrow Books.

———. 1973. *God Is Red: A Native View of Religion*. New York: Grosset and Dunlap.

———. 1979. *The Metaphysics of Modern Existence*. San Francisco: Harper and Row.

———. 1985 [1974]. *Behind the Trail of Broken Treaties: An Indian Declaration of Independence*. Austin: University of Texas Press.

Deloria, Vine, Jr., ed. 1971. *The Red Man in the New World Drama: A Politico-Legal Study with a Pageantry of American Indian History*, by Jennings C. Wise. New York: Macmillan.

Wilkinson, Charles F. 1987. *American Indian, Time, and the Law: Native Societies in a Modern Constitutional Democracy*. New Haven: Yale University Press.

2

Growing up on Deloria
The Impact of His Work on
a New Generation of Anthropologists

ELIZABETH S. GROBSMITH

I was a new graduate student at the University of Arizona twenty-five years ago when Vine Deloria's book *Custer Died for Your Sins* was published. I had come to Arizona because I was interested in Native Americans and applied anthropology (it was acceptable to state this plainly back then; now such statements are regarded as simple, not astute, and certainly not politically correct). I sought training that would enable me to apply my newfound knowledge, although I had amorphous and undefined goals at that time. Many Indian students were enrolled in anthropology classes at Arizona, this period in our discipline's history preceding the time when Native Americans developed ambivalent or adversarial perspectives on the field of anthropology. These students, unlike those who, in limited numbers, take our classes today, seemed to consider the discipline crucial to their education. Their philosophical principles as applied scientists were implicit. Consequently, my first impressions concerning the relationship between anthropologists and American Indians were that they worked hand-in-hand to bring significant changes in the standard of living, educational opportunities, and economic conditions of American Indian communities.

In 1970, with a new master's degree in hand, I attended a symposium on anthropology and the American Indian at the annual meeting of the American Anthropological Association in San Diego, California, where a debate took place between anthropologists and American Indians over the utility of anthropology. Observing Margaret Mead hold forth on the value of salvage ethnography confirmed my commitment to applied research and to the task ethnographers cherish — preserving, for the world's permanent historical record, the substance of American Indian culture. Some Indian students argued that anthropologists were exploiters and thieves of culture, stealing and revealing secrets to bring them academic fame and fortune. Deloria's famous image of the well-meaning, naive, and undirected straggly-haired graduate student heading for the "rez" draped with cameras and tape recorders, clutching pad and pencil, became everyone's stereotype. The burden was now on the anthropologist to demonstrate that he or she was indeed useful and had some skills or knowledge that could benefit the indigenous community. The attack on anthropologists raged at that AAA session, as it did in the larger professional community. While some Indians fought diligently to keep the anthros out, others were equally adamant about the fundamental role anthropologists played in preserving their aboriginal heritage and culture. They had been raised without the benefit of learning their language and traditions, and they protested that a wealth of Native American heritage would have been lost to them were it not for recorded myth and ethnographic descriptions of religious and cultural life. Although a sad state of affairs, this threat was a reality for them. At that meeting, Mead defended the role of salvage ethnologists valiantly, delicately balancing the potential contributions with the opposing but respect-worthy perception of their being meddlesome intruders.

Custer Died for Your Sins was, among other things, an attempt to deter ethnologists from such meddling. Deloria used the rhetoric of the self-determination era, venting the frustration of Indian communities toward paternalism and government bureaucracy, and espousing the popular new activism embodied by the American Indian Movement, the National Congress of American Indians, and other political entities. Although the book's message was powerful and had a tremendous impact on those of us in graduate schools in the late 1960s and early 1970s, Deloria did not totally succeed in keeping us away; in fact, social scientists flocked to reservations to document the phenomenon of the new pan-Indianism. He did, however, impose a test on us — a new standard, which those of us who would persevere had to meet. *Custer Died for Your Sins* became our primer for how *not* to behave, conjuring up the ultimate image of the tiresome meddler we dreaded and desperately hoped to avoid. It made us defensive, in the true sense of the term: we continually had to defend and justify our existence and practice self-reflection and introspection — tasks of self-evaluation critical to good social science. We would not advocate outside control or be party to schemes of exploitation, top-down development, or paternalistic imposition; rather, we applauded the self-determination policies and attitudes of the Nixon era, and saw our role as facilitating indigenously defined agendas. After all, we "knew the system" and could enhance people's movement through it.

Those of us who chose to move forward with our plans to work professionally in American Indian communities despite Deloria's warnings blundered into them in the midst of the charged political climate of American Indian Movement (AIM) activism, in the wake of the 1973 siege at Wounded Knee by Lakota Indians on the Pine Ridge Reservation in South Dakota. AIM had fostered great antagonism toward non-Indians and deep suspicion of outsiders in general. Although local Lakotas in South Dakota knew of the Deloria family and recognized the family name with widespread respect, Deloria's works were largely unread by reservation Indians. Nevertheless, his message certainly had been carried by the moccasin telegraph: Indians were no longer to be studied as research subjects for some do-gooder's Ph.D. dissertation topic without some accountability to the Indian community; they were to hold to the self-deterministic values that encouraged development from within the community rather than accepting the impositions of outside agents. Any interference or intervention by an outsider had better be genuine, have been sought by the tribe, be approved by the local tribal authorities, and mean more than a passing summer's recreation and another meaningless article.

Years later, finished with the formal components of Ph.D. training and ready to embark on dissertation fieldwork, I had been sufficiently enculturated into the Deloria belief system that, while completing my quest for Institutional Review Board (IRB) approval at the University of Arizona to study bilingualism on the Rosebud Sioux Reservation in South Dakota, I naively wrote a letter of protest to the IRB, objecting to the federal government's use of the term "human subject" for what we more enlightened scholars termed "informants" or "consultants." "What did the term 'human subject' imply," I asked, "that these people were guinea pigs, subjects in some experiment" such as those victimized by the early Tuskegee syphilis studies? I was informed that despite my protest about terminology, the lack of Institutional Review Board approval would preclude my conducting fieldwork with "human subjects," which to me meant the end of my ethnographic research and my Ph.D. I had already obtained the approval of the Rosebud Sioux Tribal Council to conduct my study, defending it by presenting the final product as of potential interest and use to the tribe in assisting in the development of bilingual programs and funds to support its members. But, like most graduate students of this era, I lacked the understanding of institutional review of all research conducted by an institution's faculty and students. Our graduate training programs paid lip service to ethical research, but little formal training was offered in the development of ethical field methodologies or principles.

Ironically, years later, I came to serve on the University of Nebraska's IRB in Lincoln, and became its mandated representative to review research to be conducted on incarcerated subjects. The true irony of my membership stemmed from how I came to be a board member; it was again through contact on pending research that I entered into a dispute with the IRB, this time over my invitation to all Indian prisoners in Nebraska to participate in my research. The board thought the language of my invitation too complex; but I argued that any simplification of the language was patronizing to Indian prisoners. Additionally, they worried about how incarcerated individuals could give truly informed consent, a concern I shared, which we developed a plan to address. In discussion with the board's executive secretary and through presentation to me of all the board's concerns about my upcoming research project, the conversations proved to bring to the surface numerous issues of ethical research practices. Our long and fruitful exchange drew me into the ethics of research with protected groups, and I received an invitation to join the board. Four years later, I resigned my position on the board, having become fully committed to the need for institutional review of every research protocol.

Having resolved what I then perceived as "administrative details," I arrived on the Rosebud Sioux Reservation to conduct my dissertation research in the early summer of 1974, when consciousness of the AIM takeover at Wounded Knee and the deaths that had resulted had left the community fearful, vulnerable, and extremely suspicious. The political climate was inordinately tense. I had been warned that members of the American Indian Movement had supposedly set up machine guns on tripods throughout the reservation and were shooting at all out-of-state cars. The cautionary warnings did not seem unfounded: the weekend of my arrival FBI agents were swarming the reservation, a shoot-out had occurred at the local country club, and a non-Indian woman's car had been pushed over the edge of a bluff and submerged in a lake on the reservation. Tales of sexual harassment, exploitation, and assault of non-Indian women in areas of the reservation occupied by AIM abounded. I was staying at a local motel while I searched for housing, and throughout the night was frightened by beating on my door. Awakened and terrified, I tried to call the police, only to realize that the rooms had not been equipped with telephones! When I expressed my concern to the manager the following morning about my inability to contact the police, he informed me that the people at my door *had been* the police, looking for AIM members allegedly involved in the recent reservation violence. I was stunned and afraid, and thought I had better reassess whether indeed this was an appropriate time and place for me to attempt the conduct of ethnographic research, particularly when my study required that I travel throughout the reservation and interview at least eighty informants in different communities.

Was this the welcome I had come to expect? Had I anticipated that I would encounter such hostility? Actually, yes. No one had ever given me assurances that my presence would be welcomed or desired. I knew I would be regarded as an intruder, an outsider who would have to justify (repeatedly) my existence and ingratiate myself to whomever I could. Having been "raised on Deloria," I fully expected resistance to my presence. Much to my surprise and delight, I found the reaction to my presence entirely the opposite. I was welcomed and embraced; few if any local people had read Deloria's works or ever encountered an anthropologist. They were delighted that I wanted to learn about their language and culture and treated me with no prior expectations. They considered AIM members "outside agitators," and they were fearful of AIM's militancy and violent tactics, seeing these methods of solving community problems as more appropriate to the inner city. Indian friends treated me well, incorporating me as family, resulting in nearly twenty-five years of mutually rewarding friendships and exchange. I knew just how well accepted I had been when I left town for a weekend, only to return to a round of chastising by one of my informant friends for not letting anyone know that I would be away! All jokes about adoption aside, there is scarcely an anthropologist alive who has not developed strong kinlike ties while participating in reservation community life.

Still, there were also those who were deeply suspicious of my presence, who could not relate to my being there "without a job," even though I explained that research *was* my job for the time being. They certainly harassed me, adding sugar to my gas tank, stealing my tent (I stole it back), and demanding of me rides to nearby states in payment for my having taken up their time. I learned to defend myself, to know when to say "no" and how to become comfortable with the limits of my own religion and culture. One has to take a stand, ultimately, on what one *won't* give in payment for information and knowledge gained and on what one will not do, eat, or say. (I was asked to exchange sexual favors for spiritual knowledge once but managed to make a quick getaway, albeit a bit disillusioned.) I discovered that I could be myself, be accepted, and the more I didn't pretend to be something I wasn't, the greater my acceptance became. I can't say I was never duped or fooled, and sometimes the lesson was painful and disappointing. But, as all anthropologists must, one learns to sort it out.

Now, years later, I am grateful for the tough hide I have cultivated, and I have Deloria's aggressive work to thank for it. It has certainly come in handy while working with American Indian inmates in the Nebraska Department of Correctional Services. My status with this group has been and continues to be somewhat volatile, my research interests having to be delicately balanced with the institutional needs of the inmates. When years later I requested permission of Nebraska Indian inmates to conduct research on their access to religious freedom in prison, one inmate responded, "You have earned the right to eat at our table," which meant that I had paid my "dues." I had endured a substantial amount of criticism, had my safety and that of my family threatened, and had letters of protest written about my research, but I had ultimately demonstrated enough long-term commitment to earn the right to make this request.

During my many years of attending professional conferences, I have had the privilege of hearing presentations given by Vine Deloria from time to time, sharing with professional colleagues information on issues from Lummi oyster farming on the northwest coast to matters of tribal governance, jurisdiction, and sovereignty. As a fledgling anthropologist, I was quite in awe of his work and message, and took to heart, as did most of my graduate school associates, his admonitions about anthropological involvement in conflicting research agendas. Deloria's speeches emphasized self-determination, asserted tribes' rights to decide what projects were likely to benefit them, and affirmed their right to cast off those projects that had little potential for directly benefiting the community. He had an equally tremendous effect on tribal members, empowering them to reject those research projects whose outcomes stood little chance of serving tribally defined needs. Deloria and a host of sociologists and anthropologists became authors of an entire genre of social science that dealt extensively with community planning, community review of outsiders' research, principles of bottom-up (rather than top-down) grass-roots development, conflicts between priorities of funding agencies and of the local community, the uselessness of model building for its own sake, tribal autonomy, and the development of legal codes governing review of researchers' proposals. Deloria and others also addressed tribes' rights to determine who may legally have access to tribal citizens for research purposes (Deloria 1980; Moreland 1989; see also Schensul and Schensul 1978; Schensul 1980; and Wax and Cassell 1980 for an extensive discussion of philosophical issues associated with the ethics of research). Indeed, an entire area of social science research methodology has emerged around these ethical concerns. Embracing the principle of working in consultation and collaboration with and for Native Americans, I found an interesting reaction among Indian inmates when consulting them a few years ago about writing a book to document their struggle to obtain religious freedom "behind the walls" (Grobsmith 1994). Naturally, they had mixed reactions to participating in such a project. In soliciting their support, I elicited fascinating responses to my lengthy efforts to communicate about the goals of my project, my invitation to participate, and the use of written consent forms, as I discussed what effects on Indian inmates such a project would yield, what involvement they might like to have, their authority in reviewing and evaluating the final results, and how any royalties would be handled. My orientation had made me *so* cautious about this project that some Indian inmates got very frustrated with me. The

Native American Spiritual and Cultural Awareness Group (NASCA) at one of the Nebraska prisons wrote:

> You asked for the opinion of the NASCA members as to whether they would like to see this book done. The Native Americans . . . were the only ones to vote on this matter and a unanimous vote of approval for you to proceed was reached. . . . Actually, we cannot see what all the fuss has been about by some of our Brothers. . . . True, you are not Native American but what you propose does not go into our rites but only the right struggle for those rites. . . . In sum, we encourage you to proceed with your vision and we look forward to the outcome of your efforts. Little good gets done worrying about what bad might come of something done by someone else that not everybody likes. So worry more about doing a good job and less about approval before it is done. (Personal communication from Lincoln Correctional Center, April 25, 1989)

Although *Custer Died for Your Sins* established, in effect, new guidelines for anthropological research with American Indians, the federal government's Commission on Human Subjects Research (through the Code of Federal Regulations) requires that investigators obtain permission from their subjects prior to initiating any research. However, the federal guidelines can only emphasize the legality of obtaining permission (and the liabilities of the failure to do so), and do not address the greater ethical issues of the true *involvement* of subjects in proposed research. For Native American research, this issue becomes exceedingly complex because of tribal sovereignty. Tribes' legal rights empower them not only to screen and approve or disapprove research, but also to control researchers' access to community members. Tribes have the right to deny permission for investigators to conduct research in Indian communities, particularly where they see little or no benefit to be derived. Consequences of infractions may be dealt with in tribal court, and researchers may be formally penalized for violations of the tribal code. Tribal rights over their members' involvement in research may even supersede individual wishes to participate in a particular study, for an investigator may be denied permission to conduct research on tribal land even though he or she may have obtained informed consent from a prospective participant.

Deloria's work may not directly have had an effect on the refining of federal regulations governing research, but such legal questions as the right of access to research subjects (especially those on federally defined trust land) have become increasingly important in determinations about granting permission to work with Indian subjects. Furthermore, issues of informed consent, particularly with minorities or those classified by the federal government as "vulnerable" human subjects (for example, pregnant women, prisoners, and mentally disabled informants) are carefully scrutinized by review boards to maximize the protections to which citizens, especially those who historically have been at risk for exploitation, are entitled. Several years ago, for instance, a proposal came before the University of Nebraska Institutional Review Board (of which I was then a member). The investigator wished to conduct medical research with an Indian tribe, pending the receipt of tribal approval. Federal guidelines for obtaining informed consent normally require that consent be in writing, unless the researcher has grounds for requesting that this requirement be waived and oral consent be allowed instead. The investigator argued that because Native Americans are suspicious of scientists who "do experiments" on Indians in Public Health Service (Indian Health) hospitals, obtaining written informed consent was inappropriate and not in keeping with the oral traditions of the tribe. While this may have been true, the board believed that it was precisely because of exploitation of Indians that special care had to be taken to obtain written informed consent before the investigator could be permitted to proceed. If institutional review boards require written informed consent for all other investigators, would they not be remiss in permitting research to be done on American Indian subjects using a lower standard of gaining consent, the board asked. Ultimately, whose guidelines should have precedence — those of the federal government or those of the tribe? The outcome was interesting. The investigator had assumed that the tribe would not approve the research if written informed consent were required, but he had not specifically asked. The board recommended that the investigator discuss this issue with tribal council members, apprising them of the board's concern that standards for participation not be lowered for Native Americans and asking the tribe to weigh the advantages and disadvantages of written informed consent before making the ultimate decision. The tribal council decided that written informed consent would afford its members the greatest protection and help ensure full disclosure of the purposes of the study prior to anyone's individual participation.

Deloria has suggested that informed consent is irrelevant. He states: "If one is continually investigated by anthropologists or sociologists, all of whom share a common universe of discourse where fundamental questions have already been decided, informed consent is somewhat akin to firing the warning shot immediately before the fatal bullet is sent on its way" (1980:270). But consider the alternative. In the case mentioned above, the investigator was attempting to get permission to treat a skin disorder in which a high percentage of the population was allergic to certain ultraviolet rays of the sun and could therefore not go outside for much of the year. Permission was sought to invite participants into a study to test the effectiveness of an FDA-approved skin medication not currently stocked by the Indian Health Service hospital pharmacy because of its prohibitive cost, even though the ointment had already been demonstrated to be effective in similar populations. If the investigator could demonstrate the effectiveness of the drug for this particular population suffering from this skin disorder, then pressure could be brought on the health service in this delivery area to stock the drug. What if the investigator had not brought this issue forward? Must all research agendas be defined from inside the community? Would we prefer that the scientist had not presented his idea to the tribe? Although the research idea certainly did not come from within the community, the possible benefit to the tribe justified the proposed research. The tribe then had the authority to determine the best way for its members to participate. Today, both medical and social science investigators not only would defend their right to develop research agendas but also would say that, given the consequences of contact and acculturation, it is irresponsible *not* to engage in applied research.

But the question we must ask ourselves today is, Would such moral arguments have even taken place pre-Deloria? The evolution of tribal decision-making is considerable and complex, documented in several of Deloria's later works, dealing in particular with issues of jurisdiction and tribal sovereignty (Deloria and Lytle 1984). Tribal courts increasingly exercise their authority with respect to many legal issues, such as Indian child welfare and custody cases, substance abuse, juvenile delinquency, and reservation crime, and more jurisdictional conflicts will arise as tribes exert greater authority. The 1990 Supreme Court case concerning the denial of unemployment benefits to a Native American drug and alcohol counselor in Oregon terminated from his job because of his Native American Church practices provides an excellent example of jurisdictional conflict among tribal, state, and federal rights to control Indian affairs. Issues of tribal sovereignty are sure to increase in complexity as the courts face policy conflicts with state and county laws, in everything from the establishment of casinos for gambling to vehicular crime, rampant on the reservations, and other offenses committed on federal trust land by non-Indian offenders.

Deloria's view of anthropology is probably as biased as the anthropologist's perception of what is good for Indian communities. His perception that our discipline is "oriented according to the dictates of the old theory of cultural evolution which, in its most derogatory interpretation, saw dark-skinned peoples as culturally inferior to whites" (Deloria 1980:269) does not reflect nearly a century of anthropological premises nor the commitment of our discipline to assert the rights of indigenous peoples throughout the world. But then, Deloria is an attorney, not an anthropologist. And he even sympathizes with our plight when he states that although "recent research on American Indians has been primarily conducted by educators and administrators, . . . social scientists have received the negative reactions from the Indian community" (1980:268).

If one were to list all the areas of anthropology upon which Deloria's work has had a positive impact, among them would be precisely those same areas criticized in chapter 4 of *Custer Died for Your Sins*—development and economic anthropology, legal anthropology, and political anthropology. Deloria's impact on our discipline has been such that working with any ethnic or cultural group now reflects a different protocol than before. Our actions have changed, and the assumptions that underlay them have changed as well. Those of us "raised on Deloria" have had built into our knowledge of our discipline issues of ethics and morality, legality and propriety, jurisdiction and self-determination, seldom considered by pre–1950s ethnographers, their offensive and frequently unethical field techniques having been well documented. Our discipline continues to suffer internal conflict between the applied research approach and the pure research orientation. While we may agree within the discipline that contact must be made with constituents before the research is initiated, not all social scientists consult the subject group on defining the research agendas, nor is there universal agreement that the results of the research should be examined by the group prior to their release. But within anthropology, applied researchers have clearly established new research protocols, based on firm and lasting rather than casual contact with our constituencies, a commitment to advocacy and support, and an extension of their roles from culture brokers to legal consultants, expert witnesses, and lobbyists to Congress. Lest I slight a generation of applied anthropologists before me whose commitment to American Indians was and is supreme, let me add that while an evolution of ethical considerations has certainly occurred, numerous ethnologists spent their lives living such commitments: in North America alone, James Mooney, Sidney Slotkin, and more recently Omer C. Stewart, whose testimony on behalf of legal recognition of the Native American Church of North America had a more profound effect on Indian policy than any other. Few of them have publicly lashed out at Deloria for his ungrateful condemnation of their "intrusive" acts. Stewart, for instance, at the very same AAA meeting at which the confrontation between Indians and anthropologists occurred, responded in his mild, inimitable fashion:

> It is hard for me to get steamed up at Vine Deloria's picture of the anthropologist's vile role in the life of the American Indian. . . . I simply cannot identify with it myself nor do I see it in the lives of anthropologists I know. . . . Now Vine Deloria does not agree with me that there has been all this harmony in the past and he, for one, would try to see that there is no harmony in the future. Or, at least, the white man is going to pay more for it, which might keep all but the very rich anthropologists from coming on to the reservation. (Stewart 1970)

My most recent attendance at a function where Deloria was keynote speaker was typical of the experiences I had come to expect. In a conference entitled "Who Owns the Land?" held in Omaha, Nebraska, in 1989, my anthropology students and I listened attentively as Deloria, once again, told us how it was. My students, adherents to the applied orientation and to environmental responsibility, advocates for indigenous people, activists with regard to political and

economic injustice, and in many cases law degree recipients, sat in awe awaiting pearls of wisdom from the lips of Deloria. When he told us that anthropologists were the only group he had ever known who had had our "brains sucked
out of our skulls," my students shrank in horror. While I felt bad for them, I was
not surprised by his remark. I had become accustomed to the culture of Indian-
anthropologist interaction — characterized by attack and defense, inquiry and
justification. Deloria's work has indeed bred a tougher class of anthropologists,
a small but thick-skinned group who work their way through the briars of
research in a community that may initially have found them unwelcome
guests. But good anthropologists also recognize the discomfort in beginning
any field situation and are willing to withstand the ambivalence of this difficult
period. So maybe it wasn't bad that these students had their first eye-opening
experience of Deloria and his world.

Recently I experienced an event not unlike the one I witnessed at the beginning of my career at that famous AAA meeting in San Diego. Members of
the Northern Ponca Restoration Committee in Nebraska requested that I prepare an anthropological account of their history, their relationship with the Bureau of Indian Affairs and other U.S. federal agencies, and their status since
their termination, in support of their efforts to be federally restored by Congress. They stated, "We need an anthropologist to do this." I could not have
been more gratified and honored to have been asked to gather and present useful data to Congress on behalf of their quest for restoration (Grobsmith and Ritter 1992). Deloria might wonder why they came to an anthropologist and not
an attorney for the development of such testimony; but they knew — as do other
American Indian groups — that it is to the anthropological record tribes must
turn to locate information on aboriginal culture, ethnohistorical reconstruc-
tions of indigenous traditions, documentation of tribe-to-government relations,
Indian policy, and relocation and termination, not to mention contemporary
qualitative and quantitative survey data. Our expertise is based on the one attribute we possess as social scientists that Deloria has rejected most strongly —
that we are researchers. Our data may be irrelevant, extraneous, not desired, of
no relevance to tribal interests, and so on; but increasingly, our data come from
consultation with native peoples, and the result is a relationship of mutual re-
ward. In all the instances in which I have testified on behalf of Native Ameri-

can inmates in the Nebraska Department of Corrections, it has been my research on indigenous religious practices, as well as on the relationship between substance abuse and crime, that has been the basis of my being invited to serve as expert witness in the courts (Grobsmith 1989, 1991–92, 1992). We *are* a different breed of researchers — and for that, we can thank Deloria.

I have one final reflection in looking back on the effect Vine Deloria has had on anthropology. Twenty-five years ago, when I sought my first professional position in an academic environment, I found the competition tough. Many of us were trained as aspiring American Indianists, and anthropology departments had their pick of faculty with this expertise. Today, there are very few anthropologists left whose orientation within cultural anthropology is applied rather than ethnohistorical, whose geographic focus is American Indian societies, and whose outlook makes them willing to travel to the reservation, work with living community members, and research and document community concerns. The last generation of applied American Indianists has aged and too quickly draws closer to the end of its productive years in field investigation. Today many social scientists feel that reservation communities are closed, impregnable, inaccessible; and many of them are. Our generation has learned our lesson well: stay out and allow self-determination to happen — good advice on one level. But the next generation of students, far more politically conservative and complacent than we ever were, will likely not withstand or sustain challenge and will end up taking the easy route to success. They will find something else to study. We must address the consequences of this change on the discipline of American Indian anthropology as we examine the future of one of the most fundamental and important areas of American anthropology. Let us hope there are still some field researchers around willing to study these issues.

References

Deloria, Jr., Vine. 1969. *Custer Died for Your Sins: An Indian Manifesto.* New York: Macmillan.
———. 1980. "Our New Research Society: Some Warnings for Social Scientists." *Social Problems* 27(3):265–71 (special issue, "Ethical Problems of Fieldwork," edited by Joan Cassell and Murray Wax).
Deloria, Vine, Jr., and Clifford M. Lytle. 1984. *American Indians, American Justice.* Austin: University of Texas Press.

Grobsmith, Elizabeth S. 1989. "The Relationship between Substance Abuse and Crime among Native American Inmates in the Nebraska Department of Corrections." *Human Organization* 48(4):285–98.

———. 1991–92. "Inmates and Anthropologists: The Impact of Advocacy on the Expression of American Indian Culture in Prison." *High Plains Applied Anthropologist* 11/12:84–98.

———. 1992. "Applying Anthropology to American Indian Correctional Concerns." *Practicing Anthropology* 14(3): 5–8.

———. 1994. *Indians in Prison, Incarcerated Native Americans in Nebraska.* Lincoln: University of Nebraska Press.

Grobsmith, Elizabeth S., and Jennifer Dam. 1990. "The Revolving Door: Substance Abuse Treatment and Criminal Sanctions for Native American Offenders." *Journal of Substance Abuse* 2:405–25.

Grobsmith, Elizabeth S., and Beth R. Ritter. 1992. "The Ponca Tribe of Nebraska: The Process of Restoration of a Federally Terminated Tribe." *Human Organization* 51(1):1–16.

Moreland, Jerre. 1989. "Aboriginal Legal Procedures for the Enforcement of Human Research in Native American Communities." Paper presented at the National Institutes of Health/Food and Drug Administration Conference on Current Ethical Issues in the Protection of Vulnerable Human Subjects in Clinical, Behavioral, and Sociological Research, Omaha, Nebr.

Schensul, Stephen L. 1980. "Anthropological Fieldwork and Sociopolitical Change." *Social Problems* 27(3):309–19 (special issue, "Technical Problems of Fieldwork," edited by Joan Cassell and Murray Wax).

Schensul, Stephen L., and Jean J. Schensul. 1978. "Advocacy and Applied Anthropology." In George H. Weber and George McCall, eds., *Social Scientists as Advocates: Views from the Applied Disciplines*, pp. 121–65. Beverly Hills, Calif.: Sage Publications.

Stewart, Omer C. 1970. "Anthropology and the American Indian." Paper presented at the annual meeting of the American Anthropological Association, San Diego, Calif.

Wax, Murray, and Joan Cassell. 1980. "Editorial Introduction: Towards a Moral Science of Human Beings." *Social Problems* 27(3):259–64 (special issue, "Ethical Problems of Fieldwork," edited by Joan Cassell and Murray Wax).

3

Educating an Anthro
The Influence of Vine Deloria, Jr.

MURRAY L. WAX

> A warrior killed in battle could always go to the Happy Hunting Grounds.
> But where does an Indian laid low by an anthro go? To the library?
> Deloria, *Custer Died for Your Sins*

In many traditional American Indian myths, the protagonist is a being who changes shape and form: at one moment a young warrior, the next an eagle, buffalo, or raven, and finally a coyote. To the confusion of anthropologists, Vine Deloria, Jr., is that sort of shape-shifter. Just when a serious anthropologist believes that Vine has been cornered, analyzed, and refuted, he changes shape and emerges elsewhere. Sober-sided, scientific-minded anthropologists find these transformations frustrating.

We anthropologists tend to be so serious about Indians and Indian affairs that we are disconcerted by Deloria's wit and sense of comedy.[1] In the field, many of us have encountered, or painfully experienced, the wild and wonderful sense of Indian satire and ridicule, expressed nonverbally in imitative mime (as when a group of Hopis enact the behavior of a white medical team confronting a woman in the throes of labor). Deloria's jokes have an astringent quality: cutting yet healing. His prose can be both benevolent and painful, like a surgeon's scalpel, or a medicine man's injunction to fast. Because the ridicule can wound, we ache to respond; but, when we do so, we find ourselves bedazzled by the wit while ensnared by his appeal for virtue grounded in human linkages. We realize that he has seen deeply into our heads and hearts and is trying desperately to enlarge our restricted vision.

We are most comfortable with Deloria when reading his attacks on targets whom we ourselves dislike, such as those who would shield the idiocies of Custer's campaign by contending that his force was outnumbered. In fact, I first encountered Deloria's wit while reading his critique of the Custer apologia. I was living in Pine Ridge, South Dakota, surrounded by Oglalas who had been described by Gordon Macgregor as "hostilely dependent" but whom I found not to be dependent, and whose hostility was usually well grounded; so when I encountered Deloria's critique I was particularly receptive. In the best scientistic style, he began by reckoning the numbers of women, children, elders, dogs, horses, and items of baggage that would have to have been in the Valley of the Little Big Horn for the number of Indian warriors to surpass the number of Custer's forces. By this calculation, the valley was so jammed that, when Custer attacked, his forces were smothered to death!

Anthropologists are sometimes bewildered by his level of education. In my generation, they had been more accustomed to dealing with folk philosophers than with people who identified themselves as "natives" but who could match the anthropologists in erudition. Perhaps Deloria cannot match us in purely ethnographic detail (except possibly about the Sioux), but he has sufficient theological training and skill as a medicine man, priest, lawyer, and social critic to deserve the title: Doctor of Arts, Critical Theology, and Satiric Prose. True, he sometimes exhibits the idiosyncrasies of the autodidact. I read his essays and shake my head as I find him taking seriously the fantasies of an Immanuel Velikovsky (Deloria 1973:chap. 8). But, then, I discover that, unlike my academic colleagues, he has the critical genius to perceive the inadequacies of a media star such as Alvin Toffler and his notion of "future shock." He also has the especial genius to challenge immediately someone like Carlos Castaneda and his supposed accounts of a Yaqui medicine man, while numerous anthros accept that writing as if it were the product of fieldwork.[2] Understandably, anthropologists are uncomfortable when Deloria turns that perceptive intellect on their own uncritical acceptance of inflated verbiage and ethnographic fakery.

Coupled with this erudition is Deloria's intuitive understandings of the varieties of Indian peoples. Modern reservation communities can be incredibly diverse, and the social movements that thus emerge can be bewildering to the outside observer. Yet, Deloria threads his way with empathy and concern, while trying to communicate to his white audience a sense of the problems and tragedies of the Indian community and to his Indian audiences a sense of the varieties of responses that may be generated among whites: "The Indian movement today is dangerously overcommitted to antiwhite sentiments because it does not understand its own history. The reaction of whites to the movement is equally overbalanced because of a frantic desire to obliterate historical fact by contending that such events as Sand Creek and Wounded Knee were not all that bad" (Deloria 1974a:x).

Deloria's voice forms a bridge of communication across which he leads the liberal — but often foolish (Deloria 1970a:chap. 4) — white into an appreciation of the militant activist, the cautious tribal official, and the seemingly passive but discontented tribal member.

With these skills, Deloria has emerged as one of the most powerful political journalists of our time. In that capacity, he can be savagely critical of all agencies and individuals who seem to be afflicting or exploiting Indian peoples. He is often so wittily caustic that his targets accuse him of unfairness, yet his logic is such that his argument is almost impossible to refute. In many of these essays he speaks as a politician rather than as an inhabitant of the ivory tower, and to insist upon his being detached and objective would be like asking Winston Churchill, during the Battle of Britain, to have been fair to the peoples of Germany, Italy, and Japan.

The Rhetorical Bind upon the Indian Speaker

During the European colonization of North America, and the immediately subsequent years of the republic, government officials regarded Indian peoples as "nations" with which to negotiate treaties. Constitutionally, treaties are part of "the supreme law of the land"; but this does not make their workings automatic. Even though a treaty might specify an annual payment, Congress was not obliged to appropriate the funds. So, people (Native Americans) to whom monies were owed in compensation for land cessions were nonetheless totally dependent upon the whim of a legislature elected biennially by a citizenry that, until the 1920s, did not include Indians. Even today, Indians' direct political influence is marginal. When funds are allocated by the federal government, they usually are rationalized on the moral rights of a neglected and abused class of citizenry, rather than on the grounds of treaty obligation.

The status and welfare of Indian people have thus been dependent upon a legislative body responsive to special interest groups and subject to ideological fashion. As a conspicuous but powerless population, Indians have therefore been the targets of programs endorsed by Congress as being beneficial and re-formative: from the nineteenth-century educational incursions of the mission churches to the allotment program of the turn of the century, to the Indian New Deal of John Collier, to the termination and relocation programs of the post–World War II period. None of these programs was initiated by Indians; none enjoyed the consensual support of Indians. Yet each was presented as if it were the moral response to the rhetoric of the "Indian Problem." Unless the perspective of Indians is brought forcefully and eloquently into public discussion, they will continue to be subjected to programs that express the goals of others. And unless Indian peoples are willing and able to bring treaty issues into public discussion and courts of law, they will continue to be victimized.

Those who — like Deloria — would speak as Indians for Indians often find themselves ensnared in a moral dilemma. Most tribes are small, impoverished, lacking political clout. How then can they find political expression? Indian leaders often accomplish this by translating the complexities of a series of en-counters between Indians and whites into tragic dramas: the ruthless, powerful, greedy whites inflicting moral and legal wrongs upon noble creatures, living in harmony with Nature and the Deity. The present miseries of the Indian people are then sited within a set of historical tragedies. In this context, whites (at least some of them) can be shamed into acknowledging collective guilt, and thereby also into granting the legitimacy of the claims integral to the treaties drafted decades ago. If the rhetoric is successful, a club has been forged that can be used to bludgeon the government, the churches, and the benevolent founda-tions into corrective measures.

Unhappily, this rhetoric bears a price, for it portrays Indians as anchored in moments of historic confrontation with whites, and thereby prevents their es-cape from stereotype. Moreover, because the moral leverage derives from cur-rent miseries, Indians are encouraged to present themselves to the world as pas-sive and abused "noble savages," torn from the mythic wilderness of the ages of European exploration.[3] When Indians become prosperous and successful within contemporary society, they lose the moral leverage that acknowledges the justice of their claims. (In some areas of the West, a successful Native American was no longer regarded as "an Indian," and until the rise of the various movements of red power — and the legal system of affirmative action — successful people often chose not to identify themselves as Indian.) While Deloria does his share of wielding the club of moral outrage, he has also endeavored to present Indians as variegated humans rather than stereotypes, and he has been successful in eluding the trap of simplistic rhetoric.

Although his work has brought positive consequences in a larger sense, anthropologists have been disconcerted. For a long time, they believed that they had the mandate to speak for subordinated, exploited, and oppressed peoples. During the decades when most Indians were illiterate, and few were fluent in the languages of the Europeans, this mandate seemed appropriate, although we should note that from the early days of the settlement of North America there were Indians who could converse in a European language and who were literate. (Theyendanegea [Joseph Brant] journeyed to England in 1775 to present the Mohawk land grievances to the British government. Typeset in Cherokee and English, *The Cherokee Phoenix* appeared in 1828.) Nevertheless, non-Indian ethnographers felt that they had the responsibility of presenting tribal needs and desires to the larger world and that, being literate scholars and eager observers, they could draw a true and unbiased portrait. To their credit, some ethnographers filled this role conscientiously; I think especially of the legacy of Franz Boas, as exemplified in Alexander Lesser and Gene Weltfish; I think also of such amazing mavericks as Jaime de Angulo. There were others, such as Paul Radin, who were conniving in their desire to obtain and record the cultural traditions that they perceived as expiring with their bearers, but who were sustained in their quest by respect for these traditions, and indeed were forceful in their public defense of Indians as knowledgeable and responsible beings. No matter how fortified by knowledge and virtue, however, an outsider attempts at great hazard to decide the fate of other peoples, as did those early ethnographers who, via the Lake Mohonk conference, helped precipitate the movement toward general allotment of Indian lands.

Deloria most forcefully and eloquently challenged the mandate that (non-Indian) anthropologists might presume to speak for Indian peoples, and his challenge underlies his critique of anthros. The issue is who speaks for whom?

And the response must be that the voice of the political spokesperson is ideologically and epistemologically distinct from that of the anthropologist, no matter how engaged is the latter.

How did it happen that anthropologists came to think of themselves as having the mandate not only to study but to speak for Indian peoples? At the turn of the century, as anthropology was emerging as an organized university-based discipline, it took as a central mission the study of exotic nonliterate peoples. Such study had a long tradition in European thought, as exemplified by Herodotus, Snorri Sturlusson, Marco Polo, and assorted missionaries, travelers, and adventurers. While some were convinced of the superiority of their own cultures (or social caste), a significant number believed that their educational mission was in the reverse direction: Europeans might learn from the others.

Frequently, the exotic peoples had become accessible for study because they had been subjugated by a European power and were enveloped within systems of colonial administration and market economics. Without political or military power, or the competencies needed for confronting government bureaucrats, they were easy targets for manipulation. Observing those tragedies, anthropologists considered themselves morally obligated and entitled to present these peoples to the literate world. Ethnographers could feel that they were reciprocating some form of compensation to those who had been their hosts and allowed their inquiries. Moreover, their very study had demonstrated the humanity of peoples considered "savages" by colonial governments. Indeed, ethnographers sometimes thought they had demonstrated that these peoples were superior to their overlords in one or another area of moral, social, or aesthetic significance.

Over the decades, problems with this "alliance" between ethnographer and hosts have become increasingly evident. First, most ethnographers have only a hit-and-run relationship with those they claim as "their people." Here today, gone tomorrow, ethnographers dwell in their own temporal and organizational universe, where their fate is not tied to that of their onetime hosts. Thus, it becomes more likely that ethnographers will advocate measures that are morally pure but practically troublesome. And, by advocating such unrealistic measures, ethnographers may inflict more injury than provide assistance.

Second, the commitment of the alien ethnographer is rarely as stable as that

of kin or of family members (except for the few who have intermarried and set-
tled, or who have otherwise maintained long-term communal relationships).
Many ethnographers prefer to defend peoples who are underdogs — economically impoverished and exploited, militarily subjugated — and who can therefore be elevated to a morally superior status. As such peoples become stronger,
richer, or politically dominant, the anthropologist typically becomes disen-
chanted and reneges upon the alliance. Third, the authoritative stance of the
anthropologist tends to deny to the host leaders the right to speak for the people,
especially when the rational and moral anthropologist regards the host leader
as advocating a position detrimental to the larger interest of the group or to the
world as a whole, or chooses to challenge an anthropological axiom, such as the
prehistory of humans in the Americas.

Following this same model, many anthropologists of the early twentieth
century would provide an eloquent and knowledgeable defense for the natives
of the Americas. In general, Native Americans (or those identified as such)
lacked competence in written language and law; they were numerically few,
politically weak, economically disadvantaged. However, this anthropological
posture has become increasingly difficult to maintain with regard to modern
Indian communities. What Deloria called to anthropological attention was
that only those whose fate is tied to that of an Indian group have the moral right
to be their speakers.

Assuming that our stance was and is moral, we have felt the urge to defend
the anthro against Deloria's attack, and we often overlook Deloria's role as a
forceful advocate of anthropological research. He respects the abilities of anthropologists and he urges (1980) that these be put at the service of Indian communities. Thus, while Deloria's journalistic persona may be skeptical of anthros and other academics, the Indian statesman asks for scholarly assistance in
countering the ignorance of bureaucrats: "The first important fact of life in our
new research society is the recognition that most decisions affecting human beings are made by officials who are dreadfully ignorant of the actual conditions
under which people live" (Deloria 1980:265). Elsewhere (1974b:x) he has written, "Thank God somebody [historian Donald Parman] has understood that
the CCC [Civilian Conservation Corps] is far more important for this generation of Indians to understand than the number of warriors Red Cloud used at

the Wagon Box fight or what Lewis and Clark had for breakfast on the Yellowstone. The only memory that Indians in South Dakota had of good times was the days of the CCC."

Although here too, he has issued a caution: anthropologists should not presume that, because their intentions are noble, they have the privilege of intruding into an Indian community and subjecting its people to study.

> I don't believe, in view of the awakening of the nonwestern European peoples in this country, that an observational science can be a valid science if the person observing is not intimately tied in with the community that he's observing and shares some of the burdens and responsibilities for what is happening in that community. . . . It is time for Indian organizations and the American Anthropological Association to sit down and discuss what issues are relevant in the Indian community. (Deloria 1970b:97–98)

Certainly, Deloria has ridiculed anthropologists, sometimes so caustically as to elicit irate retorts. (I recall the outrage stimulated by that fourth chapter of his *Custer Died for Your Sins.*) However, behind the ridicule is a respect, a hope that anthropologists (and other social scientists) will emerge worthy of Indian trust, as becomes evident in Deloria 1974b and 1980. Clearly, his efforts have been beneficial to our discipline and to others.

A Personal Note

To convey some of my personal feelings about Deloria, I need to provide a bit of biographical background.

As a young and relatively innocent ex-seminarian, Deloria was the victim of a typical Indian trick, being offered a great title and hollow office.[4] In 1964 the affairs of the National Congress of American Indians (NCAI) were in dismal shape. Membership was low; member tribes were delinquent in dues but involved in bitter, even Byzantine, rivalries and intrigue. The previous executive director had been strong on rhetoric while lacking in organizational capacities. In short, the NCAI was a paper organization with neither budget nor staff. Seemingly naive, Deloria was offered the honor of being executive director, with great responsibilities, and a compensation contingent upon his ability to persuade tribes to join and member tribes to pay dues.

I remember encountering him in Denver at that time. The NCAI office was small, dingy, and lacking in equipment. Deloria drove me to my destination in a decrepit car with brakes so poor that I panicked each time he had to stop. With quiet but bitter humor, he recounted occasions when scientists, funded with grants, had visited in order to locate the tribes they had received monies to study. To him this seemed a crazy commentary on the Indian situation. Many tribes were so impoverished they were in danger of political, social, and cultural destruction; nevertheless, scientists were being funded to study these peoples whose address they did not even know and whose conditions they could scarcely conceive.

At the beginning of this essay, I commented on Deloria's ability to play the mythical hero: to transmute his outer shape and manifest the strengths and virtues of another being. So it was in the case of his position at NCAI. He might easily have remained in the persona of the abused, passive, noble red man; as easily, he might have become the loudmouth agitator, scoring points with the dissatisfied Indian population but dismissed by the powerful organizations. Instead, using his pen alternately as tomahawk, scalpel, and feather, he bludgeoned, dissected, humored, and ridiculed his audience. The NCAI increased in membership and power; and the larger public of whites and of national organizations came to redefine their relationship to the Native Americans.

My meeting with Deloria in Denver was but the first of several encounters and the prelude to a considerable correspondence, during which I tried to entice him into acquiring a graduate education (a Ph.D. at my university), and he tried to educate me with wit, insight, and simple fact. Since I realized that he was a decent and moral man, I could somewhat allow him to educate me, even though — as a university-type Jewish intellectual, weighted with a considerable burden of abstract ideology — I must have been a difficult case.

Of course, the irony is that, even without the Ph.D., Deloria himself has been made a distinguished member of the academy. Were he an ordinary mortal, instead of a figure with mythic gifts, he would now be in danger of being shafted with his own satiric arrows — or, worse yet, of being shot by his own people, as were the "patriot chiefs" of the last century (1970:chap. 2).

I was tempted to end this essay by quoting the story that was narrated to Deloria in 1965 by an old Tohono O'odham who explained that his people were "like the old mountains in the distance. The Spanish had come and dominated them for 300 years and then left. The Mexicans had come and ruled them for a century, but they also left. 'The Americans,' he said, 'have been here only about 80 years. They, too, will vanish, but the [Tohono O'odham] and the mountains will always be here'" (1976 [1970]:187–88). But, I realize that while this faith may continue to sustain many traditional Indians, it fails to do justice to what is happening in modern America. On the one hand, the political and legal status of Indians has been changing and evolving, as tribes (often spearheaded by a lawyer named Deloria) use the court system with ingenuity and determination. On the other hand, the cultural portrait of Indians has been transmuted, as traditional Indian themes and rituals have become the basis for an efflorescence of a new religious subculture. And for the social scientific disciplines, there is a shift in orientation from that of the detached observer, linked to exterior networks of power, to that of the committed and engaged participant, linked to the local community. Among those who should be credited for these transformations, the shape-shifting Deloria — lawyer, priest, political scientist, prophet, educator, and satirist — is the preeminent candidate.

Notes

1. For a small sample of general Indian humor, see chapter 7 of *Custer Died for Your Sins*; a distinctive wit pervades much of Deloria's writing, even when the naive reader anticipates serious prose.

2. "A substantial number of young people took up the Carlos Castaneda books as if they were the final word on Indian religion. . . . Few Indians recognized anything to do with Indian religion in the books. Where were the sacred mountains, the healing ceremonies, the tales of creation and historical migrations?" (Deloria 1973:52–53).

3. Indians also lose the capacity to examine realistically their contemporary relationship to the natural world: "We tell our audiences at Indian Awareness weeks on university campuses that Indians do not worship money. Yet our tribal councils are leasing our sacred mountains for royalties, and our tribal politicians are seeking better and higher-paying jobs. . . . Our activists chastise the white man for his destruction of nature, and admonish people to respect the Sacred Mother Earth, while they themselves are throwing empty beer cans along the road. Many of our communities look like junkyards. . . . While we are poor there is no excuse for being either destructive or dirty about the way we live" (Deloria 1978:24).

4. "In 1964, while attending the annual convention of the National Congress of American Indians, I was elected its executive director. I learned more about life in the

N.C.A.I. in three years than I had in the previous thirty. Every conceivable problem that could occur in an Indian society was suddenly thrust at me from 315 different directions" (1976 [1970]:184).

References

Deloria, Vine, Jr. 1969. *Custer Died for Your Sins: An Indian Manifesto.* New York: Macmillan.

———. 1970a. *We Talk, You Listen: New Tribes, New Turf.* New York: Macmillan.

———. 1970b. "Some Criticisms and a Number of Suggestions." In Jeannette Henry, ed., *Anthropology and the American Indian: A Symposium*, pp. 93–99. San Francisco: Indian Historian Press.

———. 1973. *God Is Red: A Native View of Religion.* New York: Grosset and Dunlap.

———. 1974a. *Behind the Trail of Broken Treaties: An Indian Declaration of Independence.* New York: Delacourte.

———. 1974b. Foreword. In Norris Hundley, ed., *The American Indian: Essays from Pacific Historical Review*, pp. vii–xi. Santa Barbara, Calif.: Clio Press.

———. 1976 [1970]. "This Country Was a Whole Lot Better off When the Indians Were Running It." In Murray L. Wax and Robert W. Buchanan, eds., *Solving "The Indian Problem": The White Man's Burdensome Business*, pp. 177–89. New York: New Viewpoints/Franklin Watts.

———. 1978. "The Indian Student amid American Inconsistencies." In Thomas Thompson, ed., *The Schooling of Native America*, pp. 9–28. Washington, D.C.: American Association of Colleges for Teacher Education.

———. 1980. "Our New Research Society: Some Warnings to Social Scientists." *Social Problems* 27(3):265–71 (special issue, "Ethical Problems of Fieldwork," edited by Joan Cassell and Murray Wax).

Part Two

Archaeology and American Indians

Randall H. McGuire examines in chapter 4 how archaeologists came to see themselves as the (only) stewards of the past and how the field has avoided "engagement with an enduring people whose interests and beliefs should have a major role in structuring [archaeological] practice." He sees this history as rooted in an American narrative that is much bigger than archaeology or anthropology: the myth of the "vanishing Indian." "Indians" were a self-referential discursive construction of the colonizers, and by definition were either already gone or were not long for the New World after the Europeans and modernity arrived. Thus any serious or reliable connection of contemporary Native Americans to the archaeological past of North America was denied, and it would be up to professional archaeologists to preserve the past. This view has been seriously challenged in the last five years, however, mostly by Native Americans and by federal law.

Larry J. Zimmerman describes in chapter 5 the range of responses on the part of archaeologists to demands by American Indians for reburial of native remains in the possession of archaeologists. He finds that archaeologists have denied the Indian demands as "merely political" (and therefore somehow not legitimate), while claiming that the data that would be lost are too important a part of the human heritage. Some professionals have attempted to enter into dialogue with Indian people, which can be useful but is also limited without serious self-reflection on the part of the profession. This self-reflection must involve analysis of the differing worldviews of archaeologists and Indian people before any workable compromises can be reached. Ultimately, Zimmerman argues, archaeology must design research agendas that serve not merely the dictates of "pure science" but also the interests of Indian people. He believes mutually beneficial partnerships are possible that will necessarily *reinvent* archaeology and have a transformative effect upon the way archaeologists "do their science."

4

Why Have Archaeologists Thought the Real Indians Were Dead and What Can We Do about It?

RANDALL H. MCGUIRE

> None of the whites could understand that they were not helping living Indians by digging up the remains of a village. . . . The general attitude [of the archaeologists] was that they were the true spiritual descendants of the Indians and that the contemporary AIM Indians were foreigners who had no right to complain about their activities.
> Deloria, *God Is Red*

In his book *God Is Red* (1973) Vine Deloria, Jr., recounted a 1971 confrontation between American Indian Movement activists and archaeologists at an archaeological dig in Minnesota. The archaeologists were clearly surprised that the activists objected to what they were doing and that Indian people thought of archaeology as a form of oppression. The archaeologists saw themselves as the preservers of a dead Indian culture, while the activists, through their protest, sought to establish that their culture and their pasts lived on. The archaeologists had been seduced by one of the defining myths that has structured white perceptions of Indian people for almost two hundred years: the myth of the vanishing American — or, as Deloria (1973:33) phrased it, the notion that "the only real Indians were dead ones." This myth alienates living Indian peoples from their pasts and persuades anthropologists, archaeologists, and historians that *they* are the inheritors of Indian pasts. Deloria confronted archaeologists with the idea that the pasts they study are the pasts of a living people. Over twenty-five years later archaeologists are just now coming to this awareness.

As a discipline archaeology has been slow to transform its practice from the study of a "vanished race" to an engagement with an enduring people whose interests and beliefs should have a major role in structuring that practice.[1] In the United States this change has begun largely owing to federal legislation that forces archaeologists into this engagement. The change has not, as many once feared, meant the end of archaeology, but most archaeologists have not yet realized how profound a transformation of the discipline it requires. Today many archaeologists are honestly striving to enter into a dialogue with Native American peoples that they hope will improve the practice of archaeology, and they have produced a number of exemplary studies. Many Native Americans are also now more hopeful about archaeology then they were in 1971. But fundamental, and perhaps irresolvable, differences still exist between the worldviews of the two communities.

Stewards of the Past

It used to be commonplace for archaeologists to present themselves as the only ones who could really know the past of Indian people (Zimmerman 1989). Often we saw ourselves as the stewards of extinct Indian cultures (Meighan 1985; Turner 1986). We sometimes assumed that Indian people did not know their past, had no interest in that past, or were unable to preserve it (Deloria 1973:31–33). Even though there has been a profound move away from these views, I suspect they are still held by a large portion of the profession.

Brian Fagan's (1985:11) widely used textbook *In the Beginning* includes a typical assertion of this type:

> Most American Indian groups came into contact with literate Western civilization only in the past three centuries. Before European contact, Indian history was not written; it consisted mostly of oral traditions handed down from generation to generation. Archaeology and archaeological sites are the only other possible sources for American Indian history. Only as archaeologists probe into their ancestry will the first chapter of American history be written.

Fagan goes on to laud archaeologists who work with Indian people. He indicates that by working with Indians we can interpret the objects we find and can bring the forgotten history of Native Americans "into the consciousness of the Indians themselves" (Fagan 1985:11).[2]

In the United States, archaeologists and anthropologists have been the authorities on Native American pasts, and this authority has given us a power over those pasts. Courts of law and government commissions call us as expert witnesses and have often given our testimony more weight than that of tribal elders. We are the ones who write about Indian pasts for the general public, who prepare teaching materials for public schools, who instruct college students; and it is, by and large, archaeologists and anthropologists who control the great museum collections of objects from that past. An eighty-plus-year legacy of historic preservation law, beginning with the Antiquities Act of 1906, reserves the archaeological record of Indian peoples for our study. We often assert this authority in the books, articles, and exhibits we prepare for the general public. We make the archaeologist the hero of the story and either split Indian peoples from their past or treat them as artifacts of that past. Rarely have our public presentations given an Indian view of the past or treated that past as part of an ongoing native cultural tradition.

Many archaeologists have taken what they perceive, rightfully, to be liberal stances regarding Indian people. They have actively worked to protect Native American sites and promote acceptance by the general public and the powers that be in the United States of the proposition that Native American pasts are a legitimate part of the American heritage, deserving of the same level of attention, protection, and understanding as the European heritage. They see their actions and concerns primarily in terms of their own intentions, debates about national heritage, and the history of archaeology. Some are honestly at a loss to understand why many Indian people do not appreciate these efforts. Most Indian people cannot escape the larger history of white-Indian interactions because that history dwells in the relations of their day-to-day lives. It lives in the regulations, bureaucracies, poverty, and discrimination that deny them the ability to determine their own lives and futures. In this larger set of relations the archaeologist's authority over Indian pasts is simply one other aspect of their lives that has been taken from their control. To understand how Native Americans see us, and to gain the awareness that Deloria tried to thrust upon us over twenty-five years ago, we need to look at our place in this larger history.

The Vanishing American

How did archaeologists become the stewards of Indian pasts? The answer to that question lies in the relationship of archaeology to the larger history of white–Native American relations in the United States. White American attitudes about Indian people have usually stemmed from a definition of the Indian as an alien and singular Other (Berkhofer 1978:xv; Trigger 1980). Defining Indian people as alien placed them outside the usual rights and privileges of white society, and lumping all Indian people in a single group denied them an identity except in relationship to whites. Whites have tried to characterize the "otherness" of Indian people in terms of an opposition between the noble savage and the ignoble savage. Two more basic ideas about Indian people, however, mediate this seemingly incompatible dichotomy. Most white observers have agreed that the Indian Other was a primitive Other, and that this Other had vanished or was vanishing.

The Image of the Indian in the New Republic

At the end of the eighteenth century the elite members of colonial America forged the new nation of the United States. They consciously built it around a new concept of nationhood grounded in Enlightenment thought. This concept legitimated the state as the government of a nation, that is, a people united by a common culture, language, territory, and history (Commager 1975). Many in Europe, arguing that the United States was too big, and too socially and environmentally diverse, to create the cultural unity and economic integration needed for a nation-state, predicted the new nation would wither and fail (Gerbi 1973).

At the same time the nature of relations between Indian people and Europeans on the East Coast changed.[3] For over 150 years most Europeans had lived in frequent, even daily, contact with Indian people. Before the Revolutionary War the military power of native confederacies, such as the Iroquois and the Cherokee, rivaled that of the colonies, and the confederacies could raise large armies to strike at the colonies. These confederacies had been key players in the conflicts between French and English, and English and Colonist. But by 1814 Indian groups posed no threat, either real or imagined, to the security of the nation and were a "problem" only on the frontiers. In the early nineteenth century the government removed, destroyed, or concentrated the East Coast tribes. For the first time in 150 years a majority of white Americans would have little, or no, firsthand contact with Indians in their lifetime. The day-to-day lives of most whites confirmed the myth of the vanishing Indian (Dippie 1982:12–18). Scholars reinforced the popular image with a litany of lost tribes and declining numbers (Emerson and Forbes 1914:23; Heckewelder 1876 [1818]:93).

Many of the founders of the new nation were urbane gentlemen of the Enlightenment. They accepted the primacy of nature along with the theory that rational men could arrive at an objective understanding of the world by uncovering the laws of nature (Leaf 1979). In Enlightenment philosophy, primitives stood in a special relationship to nature: they were noble savages, untarnished by the corrupting might of civilization, but such pure souls were unable to adapt to civilization. The evils of civilization, which the rational man could endure, could only sully the nobility of the savage. So, the noble savage had to be left to the untamed wild lands of the West; and as the advance of American civilization transformed the wilderness, the noble Indian had surely to perish (Berkhofer 1978:89; Dippie 1982:28). The Indians that survived the advance of civilization and lived in small concentrations in the East, or on the fringe of the frontier, denied the noble image. The Enlightenment gentlemen blamed the drunkenness, beggary, and savagery of these people on social decay resulting from their contact with civilization. They were fallen savages, not worthy of their heritage (Dippie 1982:25–28).

The eighteenth-century theory of environmentalism held that differences in the natural and social environment produced the diversity of the human species. Therefore, the primitive state of the Indian ensued from the environment of the New World, raising the chance that the new American republic might in the end sink to the same state (Berkhofer 1978:42–43; Gerbi 1973).

Thomas Jefferson accepted the environmental theory but tried to refute the idea that the North American environment begot a lesser flora, fauna, and people. He gathered ethnographic data and dug in an Indian burial mound, being the first to intrude upon Indian graves for the sake of scholarly inquiry. Jefferson (1964 [1785]:91–92) depicted the Indians as a noble race that had faded from the East Coast because of civilization's vices, not environmental defects. White Americans, who enjoyed the virtues of civilization, could build a great nation in this land. Jefferson, and many other enlightenment nationalists, called Native Americans the first "Americans" to give the new republic its own, distinct, national identity (Commager 1975:187).

The scholarly and political polemic of the late 1700s and early 1800s equated Indian people with the environment of North America. In 1794 Charles Willson Peale institutionalized the Indian as an object of natural history in his museum of natural history in Philadelphia (Goetzmann and Goetzmann 1986:15; Sellers 1980). Five years later the American Philosophical Society issued an appeal for data on the archaeology, flora, and fauna of the new nation. In 1812 Isaiah Thomas founded the American Antiquarian Society in Massachusetts for the study of American antiquities as well as fine and rare products of art and nature (Willey and Sabloff 1980:29).

These acts and institutions laid the groundwork for a liberal program of study to record the nation's Indian and natural heritage before they both faded away (Mitchell 1981). Henry Rowe Schoolcraft (1857) and John Heckewelder (1876 [1818]) talked to elderly Indians and read old documents to capture the waning memory culture of the Eastern tribes. Adventurers, like George Catlin (1841) and Prince Maximillian, went west to paint the primitive culture of the Plains Indian before it too disappeared (Dippie 1982:25–29; Goetzmann and Goetzmann 1986:15–35, 44–57).

The Mound-Builder Myth

Not all white Americans believed in the noble savage, and many winced at the idea of an Indian first American. The noble savage was an urbane, East Coast ideal. People living on the frontier or in rural areas, where whites were, or had recently been, locked in struggle with real Indian people, rejected it. Enlightenment ideals also faded in the third decade of the 1800s, displaced by a more xenophobic nationalism (Horsman 1967) that cast a new vision of the American people. The new nationalism preached that Americans were God's chosen race. Indian people, the ignoble savages, were not part of the nation (McLoughlin 1986:xvi). Even as the U.S. Army drove Indian people west (Every 1966; McLoughlin 1986; Satz 1975), white scholars and preachers tried to rout their ancestors from the history of the nation. They promulgated the "myth of the mound builders." The myth insisted that a civilized, white, race had built the great earthen mounds of the Midwest only to be overrun by red savages (Silverberg 1968). The whites of the United States, not Indian people, were the inheritors of the mound-builder heritage. Those who promoted the myth of the mound builders were, by and large, frontiersmen active in the removal of Indian people, who stood to profit from the economic growth of the region (Silverberg 1968).

· These conservative thinkers tried to build a national heritage for the United States in much the same way Europeans resurrected Celts, Goths, Magyars, and Anglo-Saxons to legitimate their nation-states (Hobsbawm 1983; Lowenthal 1985:337–38). One unnamed contributor to the *Literary World* noted: "We have, what no other nation on the known globe can claim: a perfect union of the past and present; the vigor of a nation just born walking over the hallowed ashes of a race whose history is too early for a record" (Anonymous 1848). A number of writers tried to pen a New World *Iliad* or *Aeneid.* Cornelius Mathews wrote *Behemoth: A Legend of the Mound-Builders* (1839) and roughly a decade later William Pidgeon authored *Traditions of De-Coo-Dah* (1852).

During, and after, the Mexican-American War, U.S. Army columns crisscrossed lands that would become the states of Arizona and New Mexico. The officers of these units described the great stone ruins of the region, and on the pages of their journals they composed a southwestern variant of the myth of the mound builders. They argued that the huge ruins had been the abodes of the Aztec race. Inspired by William Prescott's *History of the Conquest of Mexico* (1843) and the legend of an Aztec origin in the north, they gave the ruins names like Aztec and Montezuma's Castle (Brandes 1960). They speculated that the savage ancestors of the contemporary pueblo peoples had driven the Aztecs from their homeland.

This tale rent the Pueblo people from their past. The Pueblos looked civilized with solid stone homes, fields, and livestock, and the Treaty of Guadalupe-Hildalgo required that the United States respect their rights and extend them citizenship. But, Anglos coveted Pueblo fields, rangelands, and water, and they needed a rationalization to justify taking them. They used the Aztec myth to argue that Pueblo civilization was nothing more than a thin veneer taken from the Spanish (Hall 1984:118). The Pueblo people were only latter-day imitators of the lost race that had left the great ruins. This idea legitimated the taking of Pueblo assets and the denial of their civil rights (Lekson 1988).

Despite these attacks on Native American pasts, the dual image — of the noble Indian and the first American — survived and grew among East Coast artists, scholars, and intellectuals. Noble savages thrived in paintings, poems, and novels from 1830 to 1860. They showed up on the canvases of Karl Bodmer, Paul Kane, and Albert Bierstadt (Goetzmann and Goetzmann 1986:36–57, 145), in Henry Wadsworth Longfellow's poem "Hiawatha," and in the Leatherstocking Tales by James Fenimore Cooper (Mitchell 1981). Liberal scholars contested the theory of a lost mound-builder race. Schoolcraft (1857:135–36) dug at the Grave Creek Mound in Ohio to try to prove that Indian people had built the mounds (Silverberg 1968:107–8).

Both the notion of the Indian as a fallen noble savage and the mound-builder myth used the Indian past to legitimate the white nation. Throughout the nineteenth century, anthropological and archaeological debate focused on the clash of these two positions. The conservative position denied the humanity of Indian people and gave them no place in the nation. The liberal position upheld the humanity of Indian people but allowed them a place in the nation only if they gave up their Indianness. Few people saw the need to ask Indian people how they felt about their past, or the white's uses of it.

The Indian in Victorian America

By the late 1870s, the U.S. Army had herded all the tribes into small, isolated areas or forced them into the less desirable corners of the West (Hagan 1979:112–19). This confinement of the tribes to reservations eliminated Indians from the day-to-day experience of most whites in the West, as well as in the East (Dippie 1982:162). The Indian people on the reservations, contrary to earlier predictions, did not vanish as a race but lived on as "fallen noble savages." The notion of the vanishing Indian endured because liberal reformers thought that Indian people could survive as human beings only if they were lifted from their debased condition. They had to assimilate and put aside their Indianness to escape a debased life (Dippie 1982:162–64). Policy makers envisioned not a romantic death for the Indian but rather a less dramatic cultural extinction as Indians cast off their primitiveness to join the melting pot of U.S. society.

The scientific world reinforced the movement of Indian policy to assimilation with a theory of cultural evolution. Some used the theory to argue that Indian people could not be raised from their savagery because such progress took thousands of years and could not be hastened or guided. Others used it to hold out the hope that whites could teach Indian people to be like them (Dippie 1982:106). In 1879 John Wesley Powell founded the Bureau of American Ethnology (BAE) and began social research based on evolutionary ideas. His goals resembled those of Indian scholars a generation before, to record the vanishing culture of the American Indian and to advise the government on Indian policy (Berkhofer 1978:54; Dippie 1982:167–69). Powell, along with many other late-nineteenth-century ethnologists (such as McGee, Morgan, and McClintock), made their study of the Indian part of a larger study of natural history (Dippie 1982:223–28). By 1870 this view was firmly institutionalized in the BAE and in the major natural history museums — the National Museum, the Peabody Museum, the Field Museum, and the American Museum of Natural History (Willey and Sabloff 1980:41–45).

In the latter half of the 1800s archaeology became a professional career, and bit by bit people with special technical training and academic credentials took over the doing of archaeology (Willey and Sabloff 1980:34). Archaeologists began to argue that they should control Indian sites because only they had the special skills and knowledge to study them. In the United States, archaeology became an academic discipline as part of a holistic, anthropological study of the disappearing American Indian, and was housed in the museums of natural history. The new professionals did more than dig sites. They also studied language, myth, custom, and crafts. They were by and large from the East Coast, and an East Coast establishment paid for their work (Patterson 1986, 1995). They tended to take the liberal view of the Indian past and to reject lost race theories (Silverberg 1968:174–221).

Cyrus Thomas finally proved that Indian people had built the mounds and resolved the mound-builder controversy in 1894. Thomas was not the first to say that Indians built the mounds, and most of the data he used had been available for many years. By 1894, however, few people felt the need to justify the taking of Indian land or the breaking of tribal military power. Four years earlier, on December 29, 1890, the Seventh Cavalry had slaughtered over 250 men, women, and children at Wounded Knee, South Dakota, bringing the "Indian Wars" to a bloody conclusion (Hagan 1979:133). The Dawes Act of 1887 sought to break up the reservations into small parcels for individuals to farm and own. By 1934, this last great land grab had cost Indian people two-thirds of their remaining acreage (Hagan 1979:147). With the Indian nations defeated and Indian people dispossessed, the data could now carry the field in the debate over the past.

At about the same time, the Aztec theory was set aside in the Southwest. In 1876 the Supreme Court ruled in *United States v. Joseph* that Pueblo lands were not reservation lands, and therefore could be bought and sold. Anglos rushed to take Pueblo lands, using the Aztec theory to argue that the Pueblos' claim to their lands had only a superficial historical basis. The first archaeological technicians to work in the region, Adolph Bandelier (1884), Frank Cushing (1886), Jessie Fewkes (1896), and Cosmo Mindeleff (1891), rebuffed the Aztec theory of the Indian past and by the late 1890s had proved that Pueblo people built the ruins.

These and other analyses that asserted the humanity of Indian people, and their place in an American heritage, were an antidote to ideas and policies that would have meant genocide for Indian people. They did not, however, allow Indian people self-determination in their lives and cultures; they framed the pasts of Native Americans in terms of white interests, debates, and agendas. Even among liberal scholars the potential of Indian people continued to be denied. As Bruce Trigger (1980) points out, the nineteenth-century cultural evolutionists did not recognize Indian progress along the unilinear evolutionary ladder. Archaeologists classified Indian cultures at only two stages of evolution, savagery and barbarism (Patterson 1995), and argued that both the mounds in the Midwest and the stone-wall ruins in the Southwest dated to, at most, a few hundred years before European contact and conquest.

Into the Twentieth Century

During the first third of the twentieth century, both the public and the scholarly community accepted that the demise of the first American was both inevitable and imminent (Dippie 1982:273). Franz Boas wrenched U.S. anthropology away from an evolutionary theory, but like several generations of researchers before him, he and his students took to the field to record what they could of fading Indian cultures (Berkhofer 1978:61–69). In archaeology, researchers such as A. V. Kidder, Nels Nelson, and Manuel Gamio shifted the aims of archaeology away from the study of myth and evolution to the building of chronologies and the tracing of cultural boundaries (Willey and Sabloff 1980:83). Archaeology became more specialized. Interest in Indian ethnology on the part of most archaeologists declined so that only a few gained any appreciation for Native American views of the past (Trigger 1980:667). The model of diffusion and migration, which ruled in archaeology until the 1960s, allowed for little innovation by Indian people and reinforced popular ideas that the tribes had never been sedentary.

At the turn of the century many Americans feared for the survival of the natural wonders of the United States, and a nationwide conservationist movement developed to save them (Mitchell 1981). This movement linked the protection of Indian sites with the defense of nature (Dippie 1982:222–36). In 1906 the U.S. Congress passed the Antiquities Act to protect Indian sites on federal land and to allow for the establishment of national monuments to save both sites and the wonders of nature. Laws passed in the 1930s, 1960s, and 1970s carried on this precedent of defining Indian sites as archaeological resources and reserving the study of them for archaeologists (King, Hickman, and Berg 1977). The linchpin of modern U.S. environmental law, the National Environmental Policy Act of 1969, included Native American sites as environmental resources.

The first serious and widely accepted challenge to the notion of the vanishing American came from New Mexico in the 1920s (Dippie 1982:274–79). In 1922 H. O. Bursum introduced a bill in the U.S. Congress to settle the land claims of whites on Pueblo lands. The bill would have ransacked the Pueblo land base. White groups, led by the artist colony in Santa Fe, fought the bill. Edgar L. Hewitt and Charles F. Lummis used archaeology to portray the Pueblos as an ancient people and as an enduring race that would not fade away (Lekson 1988). In 1923 the bill went down in defeat.

Not all archaeologists accepted the idea that the Indian people of the Southwest would endure. Many voiced honest concern for Indian people, but in their popular presentations they still spoke of a race that would soon fade away — a race that had left its past for their study. Ann Axtell Morris, the wife of archaeologist Earl Morris, wrote one of the most popular books on southwestern archaeology of the period, *Digging in the Southwest* (1933). In it she soundly rejected the Aztec theory and clearly identified the Anasazi as the ancestors of the Pueblos. Nevertheless, she spoke of the modern Pueblo people as if they were an anachronism of the past. She wrote, "they are archaeology still alive" and their time is almost done: "Their course is about run. They are swamped on all sides, and although some friends at court are laboring to procure them freedom from molestation, the deadly absorptive White American culture is creeping into their lives, with its inevitable tendency to level and destroy whatever of the primitive it touches" (Morris 1933:74). Like Jefferson over one hundred years before, she valued the noble savage but lamented that he must perish with the onrush of white civilization.

In 1938 John Collier, then director of the BIA, announced that the Indian was no longer vanishing. In a major policy reversal the federal government moved to save the tribes with the Indian Reorganization Act of 1934, an Indian New Deal (Deloria and Lytle 1984; Taylor 1980). The tribes that reorganized along the lines set out by the act got federal aid, but traditionalists on the reservations fiercely opposed the new European governmental forms imposed by the act. They saw themselves as sovereign, independent, nations, with their own governments. For them, the act was simply a device of the federal government to usurp their sovereignty.

From Termination to Self-Determination
In the mid- to late 1940s U.S. Indian policy reverted to its old course. Relocation moved thousands of Indian people to the cities, while at the same time, termination dissolved tribal governments and distributed tribal land and assets to tribal members (Deloria and Lytle 1984; Fixico 1986). The tribes fought the new policy, but the specter of termination would haunt them until the late 1960s.

In 1946 Congress set up the Indian Claims Commission, which met until 1978, to settle all treaty-based land claims with Indian tribes (United States Indian Claims Commission 1978). The commission was established to aid the policy of termination by cleaning the slate of all government obligations to the Indian tribes (Deloria and Lytle 1984:191; Fixico 1986:28). Archaeologists and anthropologists helped the tribes by researching and testifying before the commission. Many archaeologists point with pride to the discipline's involvement in these cases as evidence of how archaeology has helped Indian people (Ford 1973). While pride may be justified, most archaeologists seem unaware that many Indian people hold much more ambiguous feelings about this testimony. For it soon became clear to Indian people that the commission gave little weight to the traditional knowledge of their culture, and that it favored the testimony of white experts. In fact, the commission functioned as part of a general strategy to destroy their existence as a people, and in the minds of these Indian people the white experts who testified were tainted by their association with the process.

The thrust of cultural anthropological research on Indians shifted in the 1930s to studies of cultural change, and then in the late 1960s to a glorification of the survival of Indian tribes and groups. These shifts had little impact on archaeology. The new archaeology's emphasis on scientific method and the discovery of universal laws of cultural change only increased the alienation of archaeologists from Indian peoples' interests in their own past (Trigger 1980:672).

Indian people won their battle against termination in the late 1960s. Since the early 1970s the official Indian policy of the United States has been self-determination — that Indian people should decide their own fate and control their own reservations. At least this is the theory. In the 1980s self-determination was often used as an excuse to cut off government aid to Indian people (Deloria and Lytle 1984). Three laws, the Indian Self-Determination Act of 1975, the Indian Child Welfare Act of 1978, and the Indian Religious Freedom Act of 1978, codify this policy. It is also embodied in recent reburial and repatriation legislation.

Archaeologists have viewed the trends of the last twenty-five years — the growing expression of Indian self-awareness and the increased control of tribal lands by Indian people — with some alarm. Most U.S. archaeologists were genuinely shocked and confused in the early 1970s when AIM activists obstructed digs and seized collections. On most reservations the tribe has taken over the permitting of archaeological excavations from the BIA, and many tribes do not allow excavation except when historic or environmental protection law requires it (see, for example, Gila River Indian Community 1982; Salt River Indian Community 1986). Some tribes also do their own contract archaeology on their reservations and have started their own tribal museums. The Zuni, Hopi, Navajo, and Makah nations, among others, have had their own archaeology programs for many years. The provisions of the Indian Religious Freedom Act for the first time give Indian people a legal protection for off-reservation burials and sacred sites. The act seems to be at odds with the provisions of historic preservation laws that treat these things only as objects of scientific inquiry (Echo Hawk 1986; Moore 1989). Throughout the 1980s many Indian people openly challenged the archaeological privileges that have been built up over the last two hundred years (Antone 1986; Hammil and Cruz 1989; Hammil and Zimmerman 1984; Hill 1977; Quick 1985; National Congress of American Indians 1986; Talbot 1984; Turner 1989).

The general public has been slow to discard the notion of the vanishing Indian. Very few Americans have regular contact with Indian people, and the vast majority derive what they do know about Indians from the media and public school education. The popular media, and many public school texts, tended until recently to stereotype Indians as a vanishing race (Hoxie 1985; Stedman 1982; Wilson 1986).

Archaeologists still reinforce this popular image in their public programs and statements, even when such a view directly contradicts what we know about prehistory. Often the myth is an unintended consequence of some other explicit moral about ecology or pothunting. Other times the archaeologist is made the hero of the story for solving the riddle created by the disappearance of the people in the past. The notion of the vanishing American affects the way archaeology is done. The image allows archaeologists to glorify their object, the Indian past, and yet detach it from the descendants of this past, living Indian people. The heros of the prehistoric tale become the archaeologists who have been able to interpret this past and not the Indian people whose lives flow from it.

A recent children's book, *The Village of Blue Stone* (Trimble 1990), does an excellent job of linking archaeology, modern Indian peoples, and the past. The book weaves a story around a prehistoric village in the Four Corners area of the Southwest, using archaeology as well as Pueblo oral history and religion. The book explicitly links the prehistoric Anasazis of the Four Corners region with their modern Pueblo ancestors. Archaeologists would do well to promote Trimble's reflection that "Anasazi culture is not dead: It continues to give meaning to the lives of modern Pueblo Indian people" (p. 52).

Archaeology and Living Native Americans

Native Americans, of course, never vanished, nor did they forget their own histories and heritages. They have always taught their children this culture — histories that ended with the archaeologists digging through the bones. For at least two centuries, two sorts of histories have existed for Native Americans. One has been a dominant history, researched in universities, taught in schools, preached from the pulpit, and published in books. This history has been dominant both because it reflects the viewpoint of the conquerors of the continent and because it overshadows all others. It resides in the institutions, such as schools, universities, and museums, that produce and control knowledge in our society. The other type of history was covert. Native elders taught it to their children in the home to resist the dominant history thrust upon them in the larger world.

Vine Deloria used words and ideas to confront white America with this covert history, at the same moment in time that AIM members physically confronted archaeologists to challenge how the dominant history was created and validated. Deloria, and many others, informed us that the pasts we had taken as our own were the heritages of living peoples — peoples who have a present and a future, as well as a past. We archaeologists did not listen well, and it took us over twenty-five years to hear the message.

I would like to say that this was a process of creeping self-awareness, but it was not. It required the passage of federal legislation to unstop our ears. The institutions of knowledge resisted the message throughout the 1970s and the 1980s. As Rick Hill (1994:185–86) comments: "In most cases, however, it has only been the force of law that has brought museums to the negotiating table. The history of the relationship between American Indians and Museum proves this to be true. Only when Native Americans arm themselves with lawyers can they obtain audiences with museum boards of trustees to discuss their concerns. The majority of museums will return items requested by American Indians only if legally required to do so." In 1989 Congress passed the National

Museum of the American Indian Act to establish a separate Native American museum within the Smithsonian Institution. This act also mandated that the Smithsonian Institution inventory all Native American and Native Hawaiian human remains and funerary items in its collections, notify native nations and communities of this inventory, and repatriate these remains and objects to the appropriate communities. The next year, Congress passed the Native American Graves Protection and Repatriation Act, which applied the same requirements to all museums receiving federal funds and broadened the mandate to include sacred objects and items of cultural patrimony. These laws in essence require that archaeologists work closely with Indian people in the future. It is no longer legally possible in the United States to engage in archaeology without involving Indian people.

Changing Attitudes and Practice in Archaeology

The 1990s have brought important transformations in both the doing of archaeology and the attitudes of U.S. archaeologists. The repatriation of human remains and sacred objects is proceeding around the country with thousands of individual remains and objects already returned to Native American nations. The largest single repatriation to date has been the Smithsonian Institution's return in 1991 of about a thousand human remains and hundreds of funerary objects from Larsen Bay in Alaska to the Kodiak Area Native Association (Bray and Killion 1994). Few, if any, archaeological excavations occur in the United States today without some consultation with Native American communities. Many, if not most, archaeologists have sincerely sought to alter the practice of the discipline in response to legislation. These efforts are manifest in the institutional makeup of archaeology and in the public discourse of the major archaeological society in the United States, the Society for American Archaeology (SAA).

The National Park Service (NPS) has taken a leading role in the interpretation and implementation of NAGPRA. In December of 1990 the Park Service held the Tribal Cultural Heritage and Historic Preservation Conference, which led in 1991 to the establishment of a national organization of Native Americans called the Keepers of the Treasures Committee. This committee represents Native American positions on issues of religion and patrimony.

Since March of 1992 the *Federal Archaeology Report* has included a regular column on issues related to NAGPRA. In 1993 the NPS issued a special volume of the *Federal Archaeology Report* (volume 6, number 2) entitled "Our Native American Partners in Preservation," and in 1995 it followed with a special volume on NAGPRA (volume 7, number 3). The national-level committee, which oversees NAGPRA, has been active since August of 1991. The Park Service published draft regulations for NAGPRA in May of 1993, but as of this writing final regulations have not been accepted.

Since the passage of NAGPRA the Society for American Archaeology has taken an activist stance in trying to improve relations between archaeologists and Native Americans. The SAA invited Vine Deloria to address its national meeting in 1992 and later published his comments in *American Antiquity* (Deloria 1992). The following year the *Bulletin of the Society for American Archaeology* initiated a regular column, "Working Together," with an essay by Walter Echo Hawk (1993), a Pawnee lawyer with the Native American Rights Fund.

Perhaps the most significant move by the society has been the framing of a new statement of ethical principles for archaeology. The SAA initiated the process in 1991 and published drafts of the principles in 1995 (Lynott and Wylie 1995). Previous statements of ethics by the society had primarily concerned the relationship of archaeologists to pothunting and the definition of what constituted a competent archaeologist. The new principles address these two questions but also consider additional issues. The statement includes six principles: (1) Stewardship; (2) Accountability; (3) Commercialization; (4) Public Education and Outreach; (5) Intellectual property; and (6) Records and Preservation. Of these six, the first two, stewardship and accountability, bear most directly on relations between archaeologists and Native American peoples.

The SAA identifies stewardship as the central principle of archaeological ethics (Lynott and Wylie 1995). Stewardship springs from a declaration that archaeological materials are a public trust that should be used to benefit all people, and from an assertion that archaeologists are the stewards of these materials. As stewards archaeologists are both the caretakers of, and the advocates for, archaeological materials. The principles recognize that various groups within the "public" may have differing interests in archaeological materials, and they charge archaeologists to address these interests. Even though the principles argue that no one person or group should have exclusive access or control of archaeological resources, they clearly give archaeologists priority as the managers and specialists who must advocate the scientific study and preservation of archaeological materials.

The principle of accountability elaborates on archaeology's responsibilities to the various publics that have interests in the archaeological record (Watkins et al. 1995). Accountability charges archaeologists to establish working relationships with various groups to the ultimate benefit of the profession and all groups involved. This principle clearly responds to the issues raised by Deloria in 1973 and the Minnesota AIM members in 1971. It is a direct response to the debates about reburial and repatriation that began in the early 1970s (Levy 1995:89). It is noteworthy that two Native Americans, Leigh Jenkins and Jo Watkins, participated in the drafting of the principle.

The path that archaeology has taken in the last five years represents a dramatic, commendable, and important change in how archaeologists relate to Native American peoples. Archaeologists are actively seeking to reunite the object of research, Native American pasts, with Native American peoples. We are, however, only just beginning to learn how to do this. Many people, having taken the first step, now realize that such a reunion requires more than just public relations or education. We have initiated a dialogue with Indian peoples that will fundamentally alter the practice of archaeology in the United States. It is important that we remain self-critical in that dialogue because the path we have embarked upon is fraught with danger and pitfalls, many of which we should be able to avoid through informed action, or praxis.

The Native American Graves Protection and Repatriation Act

NAGPRA stands at the center of the evolving dialogue between Native Americans and archaeologists. The requirements, processes, and structures that it establishes enable the dialogue, but they also limit and shape it in ways that may not prove productive. There are immense practical problems with the implementation of this dialogue through the mechanism set up in NAGPRA. The processes and structures established by the act violate notions of tribal sovereignty held by traditionalist and radical members of Native American communities. Finally, framing the dialogue in terms of these requirements, processes, and structures may gloss over profound differences of viewpoint between Native Americans and archaeologists.

Implementation of the NAGPRA requirements is an enormous task. At the present time the federal government recognizes 764 distinct tribes, Alaskan villages and corporations, and Native Hawaiian organizations. Museums must contact each group that might have an interest in their collections. In 1993, 539 institutions (museums, universities, and so on) submitted repatriation summaries to the NAGPRA committee (National Park Service 1993:19). These summaries ranged in length from one page to six volumes, and altogether took up thirty feet of shelf space. Tribal offices have been swamped by inquiries from museums, and most cannot begin to reply adequately or deal with the volume of requests coming in. Museums and other institutions have also been overwhelmed by the inventory and paperwork requirements.

NAGPRA does provide for federal grants to assist tribes and institutions in the process, but very little money has actually been appropriated. No grants were made until 1994, when 200 proposals totaling $23 million were submitted to compete for $2.3 million in grants (NPS 1994:44). In 1995 Congress appropriated $2.295 million for NAGPRA grants (NPS 1995:35).

NAGPRA treats Native American nations as entities within the federal governmental structure. This reflects an ambiguous notion of Native American sovereignty that traditionalists and radicals within Native American communities largely reject (Deloria and Lytle 1984). These people hold that Native American nations are sovereign nations, and that the United States is bound by treaty to recognize and deal with them accordingly. The elected tribal councils of most nations were established under the Indian Reorganization Act. In many cases their authority is controversial, with a large faction of the nation not recognizing them as the legitimate government of the people (Deloria and Lytle 1984). In some cases, a clear majority of people of the nation oppose the tribal council. Thus, a dialogue carried out through NAGPRA may not include large and important segments of Native American nations, and these segments may reject resolutions of controversies that come from NAGPRA. Archaeologists will find themselves thrust into complex, and long-standing, local political debates that they are ill prepared to deal with.

The optimistic tone of much of the discussions about implementing NAG-PRA may be overstated. Kurt Dongoske (1995:7), tribal archaeologist for the Hopi tribe, noted that the "warm and fuzzy" experiences of the cases presented in the SAA's "Working Together" column probably represent the exceptions, not the rule, in relations between Native Americans and archaeologists.

Francis P. McManamon (1995:2), the consulting archaeologist for the U.S. Department of the Interior and chief of archaeological assistance for the National Park Service, has stated: "Clearly, archaeologists and Native Americans share the same goals — understanding the past and preserving the remains related to it." There can be little question that Native Americans and archaeologists share the practical goal of preservation, and that this can be the linchpin for cooperation between the two groups. But, saying that they share the goal of understanding the past papers over enormous differences. As Tessie Naranjo (1995:16), a member of Santa Clara Pueblo and the NAGPRA committee, observes, "But we [Tewa People] do not share the assumptions underlying what museums do: collection preservation, documentation, and exhibition." Native Americans come to a dialogue with archaeologists from fundamentally different views of the past, of its relationship to the present and future (Zimmerman 1989), and of the nature and importance of the objects under discussion (Naranjo 1995).

The purpose of my critique is not to suggest that we should turn away from the advances that have been made in the NAGPRA process, or that we should attempt to overturn NAGPRA. The act is an essential component of a new relationship between Native Americans and archaeologists. We will, however, be making an enormous mistake if we become complacent in the bureaucratized solution that NAGPRA offers to the strife between these two groups. We have to go deeper and question the fundamental assumptions that we use to justify our discipline. One of the most basic of these is the notion that archaeologists are the stewards of the past.

Stewardship or Craft

The new SAA statement of archaeological ethics is a significant step forward for relations between Native Americans and archaeologists, but it does not go far enough. It recognizes the importance of nonarchaeological interests in the past, but it does not question why archaeologists should be privileged as the stewards of the past.

Zimmerman (1995) points out that a basic contradiction exists within the SAA's Principles of Archaeological Ethics. The principle of stewardship springs from an assertion that archaeologists are the only ones who really care about archaeological materials. Yet, the principle of accountability assumes that there are many communities with valid interests in archaeological materials. From this contradiction he goes on to ask a series of questions that the SAA statement does not address: (1) Who appointed archaeologists stewards of the past? (2) Are we self-appointed? (3) Are there valid ways of knowing the past other than archaeology? (4) Is the past really a public heritage, or do we declare it so just to justify our existence and privilege? and (5) Are archaeologists deluding themselves about a conservation ethic?

Stewards are servants, they work for somebody. Whom do archaeologists work for? The SAA principles incorporate a long-standing position in American archaeology: that the archaeological record is a public trust, and that archaeologists are stewards for that public. Who is that public, and how did it choose us to be stewards (Klesert and Powell 1993)? Several scholars have argued that archaeology is a form of middle-class[4] practice that serves the interests of that class (Kristiansen 1981; McGuire 1992a:258–60; Patterson 1986; Trigger 1989). Most archaeologists come from middle-class backgrounds, and the vast majority of people who visit archaeological parks, take our classes, subscribe to *Archaeology Magazine*, and visit archaeological museums are middle class. When archaeologists fall back on appeals to a generalized public, it is the white middle class of their origin they are thinking of. The first half of this chapter describes part of the process by which archaeologists became the stewards of the past. This was a process rife with relations of power, class, and race. As long as we refused to recognize these relations, and saw the public as the white middle class of this country, we could advance our own agenda as the public's and justify our privilege and interest in these terms. Voices, like that of Vine Deloria, and actions, such as the confrontation in Minnesota in 1971, made this position untenable and led us to think about our accountability to multiple publics. We have not, however, questioned deeply enough the old position, and thus archaeologists arrive at Zimmerman's contradiction.

Zimmerman (1995:66) suggests that we start by recognizing that a diversity of valid interests in the past exists (and has always existed); we should thus assert that "all people are stewards of the past." Archaeologists should be among these stewards, but stewardship is not our special responsibility or a justification for our interests taking priority over those of others. We may then ask what it is that we have to offer a diversity of interests. I would answer that it is archaeology's craft — the skill of using material remains to interpret past experiences and situations. This skill is the basis of the archaeologist's authority, for not everyone has mastered the craft of dealing with the past archaeologically. This is our scholarship.

The craft of archaeology may serve many different communities: a municipality, a Native American nation, an ethnic group, the academy. Different interests may involve different archaeological products, and these products may sometimes come into conflict with one another. In most cases archaeologists will involve the interests of various communities, and a single project may require multiple products. The interchange between archaeologists and client communities should not be one-way. We cannot simply accept the terms and interests of the client. A good work of craft enhances, alters, and creates new possibilities of experience, however modest. It involves a complex dialogue that changes and shapes those who participate in it.

Recognizing a multiplicity of interests in the past does not necessarily mean that all interests are valid or worthy of our support. Archaeologists must combat groups that find no value in the past other than dollars and cents and that despoil the archaeological record simply for personal gain and profit. We should oppose them because their actions destroy archaeological materials without regard to the multiplicity of other interests, and thus rob other communities of the values and rewards that they derive from the past. We should also challenge those, such as the Nazis in Europe (Arnold 1990), Stalin in Russia (Klejn 1977), or the Afrikaners in South Africa (M. Hall 1984), who would distort the past and use it as a tool of oppression.

Back to Minnesota

We better the craft of archaeology through practice. Redefining the relationship between archaeologists and Native Americans is part of this practice. The last five years have seen a substantial growth in the number of successful collaborations between archaeologists and Native Americans. There are now far too many to attempt to summarize or even list here. It is perhaps appropriate, however, to return to Minnesota, where Deloria observed AIM activists confronting archaeologists in 1971 for an exemplary tale of such collaboration.

Janet Spector (1993, 1994) initiated her studies at the Little Rapids site in south-central Minnesota in 1979 with little or no involvement of Native American peoples. Little Rapids is the location of a nineteenth-century Wahpeton Dakota village, and descendants of the people who once lived in the village still reside in Minnesota. Spector did not initially consult these people because her training and the common expectations for archaeological research at the time did not guide her to do so.

As Spector became involved in feminist anthropology she began to question what she had been taught and the standard practice of the field. As she increasingly thought about how archaeologists had treated women as subjects and colleagues, she also came to question how they had treated Native Americans. This led her to make contact with Dakota people about her research at Little Rapids.

The process of involving Native American people in the research was not easy, but it transformed the entire project. Spector encountered skepticism, and even hostility, when she first approached Dakota individuals about the project. Building trust took time and required the identification of Dakota, as opposed to archaeological, interests in the site. As Spector incorporated these interests and Dakota people in her work, they built trust and transformed the goals of the project. In the end Spector produced a report, *What This Awl Means: Feminist Archaeology at a Wahpeton Dakota Village* (1993), which is singular in the discipline. The report communicates a complex human story of the excavations, of the collaboration between archaeologists and Native Americans, and of the lives of the people who lived at Little Rapids. It speaks to multiple communities and multiple interests.

Conclusion
Archaeology is changing. This change requires that we see our discipline as a study of people, not just of things. The change challenges many of the taken-

for-granted practices of our discipline. Most simply, we can no longer practice archaeology without consulting and involving Indian people, even if the descendants of the people we study now live on the other side of the continent. We need to rethink how we train students, and we need to educate them as anthropologists who can engage in archaeology as a human endeavor and not simply as a study of material culture. In publishing and disseminating results, we must consider the sensitivities, interests, and concerns of Indian people. Finally, the change disrupts the notion that archaeology should have a sole, or even primary, goal and suggests, instead, that a diversity of archaeologies should arise from our relationships with different communities — Native American and scholarly.

The change will not be easy. It raises a host of problems we are poorly prepared to deal with. Substantial mistrust exists between many Indian communities and the archaeological community — a situation difficult to overcome. Indeed, we may never overcome it as a group, and succeed only as individual researchers. Archaeologists will find themselves involved in the politics of these communities, politics that can be a morass for any outsider. And we will have to make long-term commitments to Indian peoples part of our long-term commitments to archaeology in a region. We need not give up our scientific and scholarly interests, but we must recognize that those interests are not the only legitimate ones at stake. We have initiated a process of dialogue with Native Americans that will modify our scholarship within a diversity of interests. Through this dialogue we may yet gain the awareness that Deloria tried to thrust upon us over twenty-five years ago.

Acknowledgments

I would like to thank Larry Zimmerman and Tom Biolsi for inviting me to prepare this chapter and for their comments on it. A number of people read earlier versions and offered me valuable remarks, including Rodger Anyon, Mark Cassell, Nancy Chabot, Lynn Clark, Linda Cordell, Thomas Emerson, Matthew Johnson, Mark Leone, Tom Patterson, Parker Potter, Michael Shanks, Louanne Wurst, and Alison Wylie. Conversations with George Armelagos, Kurt Dongoske, Walter Echo Hawk, Rick Effland, Jan Hammil, Ian Hodder, Jane Hubert, Leigh Jenkins, Weldon Johnson, Charles Merbs, Maria Pearson, Glen Rice, Paul Robinson, Roderick Sprague, Ernest Turner, and Peter Ucko were instrumental in the formulation of my ideas. I especially thank Cecil Antone for the dialogue we initiated in Denver in 1985 that reawakened my awareness of Indian peoples' concerns with what we archaeologists do.

Notes

1. I first developed the historical discussions of this chapter in a paper for the World Archaeological Congress (McGuire 1989). In their present form they are summarized directly from a previous work of mine that appeared as an article in *American Anthropologist* (McGuire 1992b) and as a chapter in my book *A Marxist Archaeology* (McGuire 1992a). I include them in this chapter at the urging of the editors of the volume. Envisioning this book as a text in courses, they thought my historical discussions worth repeating for a student audience. The later part of the chapter, "Archaeology and Living Native Americans," is original to this work.

2. In a more recent editorial in *Antiquity* magazine Brian Fagan (1991) called for a dialogue with Native Americans. His proposal is in the spirit of and compatible with the suggestions made in this chapter.

3. This historical summary is taken from Dippie 1982 and Hagan 1979.

4. By "middle class," these scholars do not mean the common U.S. equation of middle class with middle income. They are talking about a structural middle class that mediates between the interests of other classes. In modern capitalism the middle class comprises the managers, administrators, professionals, and small-business owners who do not control the means of production, but who tend to have significant control over their own labor and to direct the labor of others.

References

Anonymous. 1848. "The Western Mound Builders." *Literary World* 5:134–36.

Antone, Cecil F. 1986. "Reburial: A Native American Point of View." Paper presented at the World Archaeological Congress, Southampton, England.

Arnold, Bettina. 1990. "The Past as Propaganda: Totalitarian Archaeology in Nazi Germany." *Antiquity* 64:464–78.

Bandelier, Adolph F. 1884. "Reports by A. F. Bandelier on His Investigations in New Mexico during the Years 1883–1884." In *Archaeological Institute of America, Fifth Annual Report of the Executive Committee*, pp. 88–98. Cambridge: John Wilson and Sons.

Berkhofer, Robert F., Jr. 1978. *The White Man's Indian: Images of the American Indian from Columbus to the Present.* New York: Knopf.

Brandes, Ray. 1960. "Archaeological Awareness of the Southwest as Illustrated in Literature to 1890." *Arizona and the West* 1:6–25.

Bray, Tamara L., and Thomas W. Killion, eds. 1994. *Reckoning with the Dead: The Larsen Bay Repatriation and the Smithsonian Institution.* Washington, D.C.: Smithsonian Institution Press.

Catlin, George. 1841. *North American Indians, Being Letters and Notes on Their Manners, Customs, Written during Eight Years of Travel amongst the Wildest Tribes of Indians in America.* Edinburgh, Scotland: John Grant.

Commager, Henry Steele. 1975. *Jefferson, Nationalism, and the Enlightenment.* New York: George Braziller.

Cushing, Frank Hamilton. 1886. "A Study of Pueblo Pottery as Illustrative of Zuni Cultural Growth." *Fourth Annual Report of the Bureau of American Ethnology*, pp. 467–521. Washington, D.C.: Government Printing Office.

Deloria, Vine, Jr. 1973. *God Is Red: A Native View of Religion.* New York: Delta.

———. 1992. "Indians, Archaeologists, and the Future." *American Antiquity* 57(4):595–98.

Deloria, Vine, Jr., and Clifford Lytle. 1984. *The Nations Within: The Past and Future of American Indian Sovereignty.* New York: Pantheon.

Dippie, Brian W. 1982. *The Vanishing American: White Attitudes and U.S. Indian Policy.* Middletown, Conn.: Wesleyan University Press.

Dongoske, Kurt E. 1995. Letter. *Bulletin of the Society for American Archaeology* 13(2):7.

Echo Hawk, Walter R. 1986. "Museum Rights vs. Indian Rights: Guidelines for Assessing Competing Legal Interests in Native Cultural Resources." *New York University Review of Law* 14(2):437–53.

———. 1993. "Exploring Ancient Worlds." *Bulletin of the Society for American Archaeology* 11(4):12.

Emerson, E. W., and W. E. Forbes, eds. 1914. *Journals of Ralph Waldo Emerson*, 10 vols. Boston: Houghton Mifflin.

Every, Dale Van. 1966. *Disinherited.* New York: Avon.

Fagan, Brian M. 1985. *In the Beginning: An Introduction to Archaeology*, 5th ed. Boston: Little, Brown.

———. 1991. Editorial. *Antiquity* 65:183–91.

Fewkes, Jesse W. 1896. "The Prehistoric Culture of Tusayan." *American Anthropologist* 9:151–74.

Fixico, Donald L. 1986. *Termination and Relocation: Federal Indian Policy, 1945–1960.* Albuquerque: University of New Mexico Press.

Ford, Richard I. 1973. "Archaeology Serving Humanity." In Charles Redman, ed., *Research and Theory in Current Archaeology*, pp. 83–93. New York: John Wiley.

Gerbi, Antonello. 1973. *The Dispute over the New World: The History of a Polemic, 1750–1900.* Pittsburgh: University of Pittsburgh Press.

Gila River Indian Community. 1982. Archaeological Licenses Ordinance GR–01–82.

Goetzmann, W. H., and W. N. Goetzmann. 1986. *The West of the Imagination.* New York: W. W. Norton.

Hagan, William T. 1979. *American Indians.* Chicago: University of Chicago Press.

Hall, G. Emlen.1984. *Four Leagues of Pecos.* Albuquerque: University of New Mexico Press.

Hall, Martin. 1984. "The Burden of Tribalism: The Social Context of Southern African Iron Age Archaeology." *American Antiquity* 49(3):455–67.

Hammil, Jan, and Robert Cruz. 1989. "Statement of American Indians against Desecration before the World Archaeological Congress." In Robert Layton, ed., *Conflicts in the Archaeology of Living Traditions*, pp. 46–59. London: Unwin Hyman.

Hammil, Jan, and Larry J. Zimmerman, eds. 1984. *Reburial of Human Skeletal Remains: Perspectives from Lakota Spiritual Men and Elders.* Vermillion: University of

South Dakota Archaeology Laboratory, and Indianapolis: American Indians against Desecration.

Heckewelder, John. 1876 [1818]. *History, Manners, and Customs of the Indian Nations Who Once Inhabited Pennsylvania and the Neighboring States.* Philadelphia.

Hill, Richard. 1977. "Reclaiming Cultural Artifacts." *Museum News*, May/June, pp. 43–46.

———. 1994. "Repatriation Must Heal Old Wounds." In T. L. Bray and T. W. Killion, eds., *Reckoning with the Dead: The Larsen Bay Repatriation and the Smithsonian Institution*, pp. 184–86. Washington, D.C.: Smithsonian Institution Press.

Hobsbawm, Eric. 1983. "Mass-Producing Traditions: Europe, 1870–1914." In Eric Hobsbawm and T. Ranger, eds., *The Invention of Tradition*, pp. 263–308. Cambridge: Cambridge University Press.

Horsman, Reginald. 1967. *Expansion and American Indian Policy.* Kalamazoo: Michigan State University Press.

Hoxie, Frederick E. 1985. "The Indians versus the Textbooks: Is There a Way Out?" *Perspectives* 23.

Jefferson, Thomas. 1964 [1785]. *Notes on the State of Virginia.* New York: Torchbooks.

King, Thomas, Patricia Parker Hickman, and Gary Berg. 1977. *Anthropology in Historic Preservation: Caring for Culture's Clutter.* New York: Academic Press.

Klejn, L. S. 1977. "A Panorama of Theoretical Archaeology." *Current Anthropology* 18:1–42.

Klesert, Anthony, and Shirley Powell. 1993. "A Perspective on Ethics and the Reburial Controversy." *American Antiquity* 58(2):348–54.

Kristiansen, Kristian.1981. "A Social History of Danish Archaeology." In Glyn Daniel, ed., *Towards a History of Archaeology*, pp. 20–44. London: Thames and Hudson.

Leaf, Murray J. 1979. *Man, Mind, and Science: A History of Anthropology.* New York: Columbia University Press.

Lekson, Stephen H. 1988. "The Idea of the Kiva in Anasazi Archaeology." *Kiva* 53(3):213–34.

Levy, Janet E. 1995. "Ethics Code of the American Anthropological Association and Its Relevance for SAA." In M. J. Lynott and A. Wylie, eds., *Ethics in American Archaeology: Challenges for the 1990s*, pp. 86–93. Washington, D.C.: Society for American Archaeology.

Lowenthal, David. 1985. *The Past Is a Foreign Country.* Cambridge: Cambridge University Press.

Lynott, Mark J., and Alison Wylie, eds. 1995. *Ethics in American Archaeology: Challenges for the 1990s.* Washington, D.C.: Society for American Archaeology.

Mathews, Cornelius. 1839. *Behemoth: A Legend of the Mound-Builders.* Boston: Weeks and Jordon Company.

McGuire, Randall H. 1989. "The Sanctity of the Grave: White Concepts and American Indian Burials." In Robert Layton, ed., *Conflicts in the Archaeology of Living Traditions*, pp. 167–84. London: Unwin and Hyman.

———. 1992a. *A Marxist Archaeology.* Orlando, Fla.: Academic Press.

————. 1992b. "Archaeology and the First Americans." *American Anthropologist* 94(4):816–36.

McLoughlin, William G. 1986. *Cherokee Renascence in the New Republic.* Princeton, N.J.: Princeton University Press.

McManamon, Francis P. 1995. "The Reality of Repatriation: Reaching Out to Native Americans." *Federal Archaeology* 7(5):2.

Meighan, Clement W. 1985. "Archeology and Anthropological Ethics." *Anthropology Newsletter* 26(9):20.

Mindeleff, Victor. 1891. "A Study of Pueblo Architecture." *Eighth Annual Report of the Bureau of Ethnology.* Washington, D.C.: Government Printing Office.

Mitchell, Lee Clark. 1981. *Witness to a Vanishing America.* Princeton, N.J.: Princeton University Press.

Moore, Stephen. 1989. "Federal Indian Burial Policy: Historical Anachronism or Contemporary Reality?" In Robert Layton, ed., *Conflicts in the Archaeology of Living Traditions,* pp. 59–65. London: Unwin Hyman.

Morris, Ann Axtell. 1933. *Digging in the Southwest.* Garden City, N.Y.: Doubleday.

Naranjo, Tessie.1995. "Thoughts on Two World Views." *Federal Archaeology* 7(3):16.

National Congress of American Indians. 1986. Resolution Passed by the National Congress of American Indians, P–86–57-CC, Phoenix, Ariz., October.

National Park Service. 1993. "NAGPRA News." *Federal Archaeology Report* 6(3):19–20.

————. 1994. "NAGPRA News." *Federal Archaeology* 7(2):44–45

————. 1995. "NAGPRA News." *Federal Archaeology* 7(4):35.

Patterson, Thomas C. 1986. "The Last Sixty Years: Towards a Social History of Americanist Archaeology in the United States." *American Anthropologist* 88(1):7–26.

————. 1995. *Toward a Social History of Archaeology in the United States.* Orlando, Fla.: Harcourt and Brace.

Pidgeon, William .1852. *Traditions of De-Coo-Dah.* New York: Horace Thayer.

Prescott, William H. 1843. *History of the Conquest of Mexico.* Philadelphia: J. B. Lippincott.

Quick, Polly McW. 1985. *Proceedings: Conference on Reburial Issues.* Washington, D.C.: Society for American Archaeology.

Salt River Indian Community. 1986. Antiquities Ordinance SRO–102–86.

Satz, Ronald, N. 1975. *American Indian Policy in the Jackson Era.* Lincoln: University of Nebraska Press.

Schoolcraft, Henry, R. 1857. *Information Respecting the History, Condition, and Prospects of the Indian Tribes of the United States,* 6 vols. Philadelphia.

Sellers, Charles Coleman. 1980. *Mr. Peale's Museum.* New York: W. W. Norton.

Silverberg, Robert. 1968. *Mound Builders of Ancient America.* Greenwich, Conn.: New York Graphic Society.

Spector, Janet D. 1993. *What This Awl Means: Feminist Archaeology at a Wahpeton Dakota Village.* St. Paul: Minnesota Historical Society Press.

————. 1994. "Collaboration at Inyan Ceyaka Atonwan (Village of the Rapids)." *Bulletin of the Society for American Archaeology* 12(3):8–10.

Stedman, Raymond William. 1982. *Shadows of the Indian.* Norman: University of Oklahoma Press.

Talbot, Steve. 1984. "Desecration and American Indian Religious Freedom." *Akwesasne Notes* 16(4):20–21.

Taylor, Graham D. 1980. *The New Deal and American Indian Tribalism.* Lincoln: University of Nebraska Press.

Thomas, Cyrus. 1894. "Report on the Mound Excavations of the Bureau of Ethnology." In *Bureau of American Ethnology Twelfth Annual Report,* pp. 3–730. Washington, D.C.: Government Printing Office.

Trigger, Bruce G. 1980. "Archaeology and the Image of the American Indian." *American Antiquity* 45:662–76.

———. 1989. *A History of Archaeological Thought.* Cambridge: Cambridge University Press.

Trimble, Stephen. 1990. *The Village of Blue Stone.* New York: Macmillan.

Turner, Christy G. 1986. "What Is Lost with Skeletal Reburial?" *Quarterly Review of Archaeology* 7(1):1.

Turner, Ernest. 1989. "The Souls of My Dead Brothers." In Robert Layton, ed., *Conflicts in the Archaeology of Living Traditions,* pp. 189–94. London: Unwin Hyman.

United States Indian Claims Commission. 1978. *Final Report.* Washington, D.C.: Government Printing Office.

Watkins, Joe, Lynne Goldstein, Karen Vitelli, and Leigh Jenkins. 1995. "Accountability: Responsibilities of Archaeologists to Other Interest Groups." In M. J. Lynott and A. Wylie, eds., *Ethics in American Archaeology: Challenges for the 1990s,* pp. 33–37. Washington, D.C.: Society for American Archaeology.

Willey, G. R., and J. A. Sabloff. 1980. *A History of American Archaeology.* London: Thames and Hudson.

Wilson, James. 1986. *The Original Americans: U.S. Indians.* London: Minority Rights Group.

Zimmerman, Larry J. 1989. "Human Bones as Symbols of Power: Aboriginal American Belief Systems toward Bones and 'Grave-Robbing' Archaeologists." In Robert Layton, ed., *Conflicts in the Archaeology of Living Traditions,* pp. 211–16. London: Unwin Hyman.

———. 1995. "Regaining Our Nerve: Ethics, Values, and the Transformation of Archaeology." In M. J. Lynott and A. Wylie, eds., *Ethics in American Archaeology: Challenges for the 1990s,* pp. 64–67. Washington, D.C.: Society for American Archaeology.

5

Anthropology and Responses to the Reburial Issue

LARRY J. ZIMMERMAN

Indigenous peoples first openly challenged anthropology slightly more than two decades ago, asserting intellectual property rights[1] for their cultures. In the United States, for example, Vine Deloria, Jr., launched a scathing attack on anthropology in *Custer Died for Your Sins*, challenging the validity of anthropological intent, method, and product. Responding to similar reactions by those in other cultures, anthropological involvement in activities such as Project Camelot and the Thai Affair (see Hymes 1969; Marcus and Fischer 1986: 34–35), and political activism from the Vietnam War, anthropologists began an examination of their practice that resulted in an ethics code, the American Anthropological Association's (1976) "Statement of Professional Responsibilities." The bulk of these ethical concerns focused on study of living peoples and said nothing about indigenous concerns regarding the archaeological study of their pasts.

Eventually controlling or stopping archaeological research also became part of the agenda for more militant indigenous groups. The political activism of the late 1960s and early 1970s led to the creation of the American Indian Movement. AIM sought to target archaeologists as exploiters of Indians, especially when archaeologists excavated human remains the Indians claimed to be from their ancestors. AIM tactics ranged from disrupting digs to destroying field equipment and excavation notes. In 1973, in his book *God Is Red*, Deloria directly attacked archaeologists for their excavation and treatment of human remains. Archaeologists began to address the issue, but the attention of AIM and other groups, as well as that of the nation, shifted to the uprising at Alcatraz and to events surrounding a similar takeover at Wounded Knee in South Dakota.

The issue did not surface again until the early 1980s, but events have moved rapidly since that time. Archaeologists generally responded poorly to indigenous concerns, not realizing the intensity of feelings over the matter and generally misjudging the level of support of the public for indigenous peoples' demands for ethical and proper treatment of the dead. In the United States, the enactment of Public Law 101–601, the Native American Graves Protection and Repatriation Act, brought to the fore the issue of the reburial of human remains now in public institutions. Although anthropological organizations have slowly taken steps to resolve the issue, because of what indigenous groups and legislators saw as anthropological intransigence, events have largely bypassed the profession.

My intent in this chapter is to examine the responses of the profession of anthropology to the demands of American Indians about the treatment of the dead they claim as ancestors. The issue is complex, and the feelings and statements of both Indians and anthropologists have been mixed. The media, and to some extent both groups, have presented the issue as completely bipolar. That notion is entirely inaccurate. Some Indian people support excavation and study, especially when they have a say in how it is done (see Fredin 1990 for an example). And some archaeologists support reburial (King 1986). In short, the issue is a complicated one, and though this chapter necessarily simplifies some matters, I have attempted to be evenhanded and avoid blaming anthropology for the problem.[2] Rather, I seek to understand the anthropological response, which requires some understanding of Indian views, especially when Indians point out apparent inconsistencies in anthropological behaviors.

Anthropological responses seem to have followed four patterns or stages, neither mutually exclusive nor entirely linear. The *denial* reaction challenges Indian claims, arguing that academic freedom has precedence and that the remains are the heritage of all cultures, and is marked by the efforts of professional groups to pass anti-reburial resolutions or to ignore the problem. The *dialogue* response includes numerous face-to-face meetings between scholars and Indians in an effort to seek mutual understandings and solutions. The *analysis* reaction attempts to understand the intellectual roots of the confrontation. Finally, the *compromise* approach seeks to reach agreements on local, state, and national levels while attempting to maintain control over the conduct of the study of the past. These responses derive from anthropology's substantial history of dealing with American Indian skeletal remains.

Collecting American Indian Human Remains

American anthropology has intellectual roots inextricably linked to American Indians. For amateur and professional scholars, as well as the general public, the questions of who the Indians were and where they came from were some of the most pressing academic matters from the late eighteenth century onward. Even today, American curiosity about Indians is intense (see all of Williams 1991, but especially pp. 28–60; see also McGuire 1992, this volume; Trigger 1980).

The curiosity came from several sources. Chief among them was the presence of Indians, which challenged biblical notions of how people were created and distributed across the earth, combined with ethnocentric notions about human cultural evolution and Social Darwinism. People did not know where Indians had come from. At the same time, it seemed that Indians had reached a fairly complex level of cultural development apart from the European and Asian heritages, a level not thought possible because these peoples were seen as savages. Pyramids and sophisticated arts, after all, could be achieved only by those descended from more advanced cultures.

Europeans and Americans engaged in a variety of wild speculations about the origins of Indians ranging from lost continents to voyages of exploration and colonization by everyone from Phoenicians to the lost tribes of Israel. American notions of Manifest Destiny and assumptions that the New World had no history of its own further inspired imaginations.

United States expansion needed a rationale, and that was provided by Manifest Destiny, a doctrine stating that Anglo-Saxon nations, especially the United States, were destined to dominate the entire Western Hemisphere. The native inhabitants stood in the way, and genocide was a particularly un-Christian moral concept, unless the inhabitants could be found to be less than fully human. Thus, unilinear evolutionary principles were incorporated into political and religious doctrine: Indians had to become like whites in order to be "saved." Until Indians changed, they could be exploited. They also became objects of scientific curiosity. Europeans saw the newly formed United States as a country without a history and within an environment they considered prone to decadence (why else would there have been the Revolutionary War?). To prove that the continent did have a long and impressive history, all that remained for Euro-Americans was to find archaeological evidence of the contacts with the Old World. In essence, this meant proving that the Indians were not the first inhabitants of the hemisphere.

Against this intellectual backdrop, American anthropology made its debut. The historical relation of American anthropology to American Indians is well explored by others (Bieder 1986; Hinsley 1981; Willey and Sabloff 1980; Williams 1991). Still, a specific interest in Indian skeletal remains stands out as an important aspect of that history.

Robert Bieder (1990) has provided an excellent summary of anthropological interests in American Indian human remains. He contends that the early view of the remains reflects European social interests and cultural values. Specifically, he sees the primary catalyst for collecting Indian craniums as coming from the debates between monogenists and polygenists. Monogenists believed in a single human ancestor and in the malleability of human beings. In their view environmental circumstances caused racial differences. Polygenists used skeletal remains to argue that humans had changed little over thousands of years and had instead developed from multiple sources. Using skulls, polygenists concocted schemes to determine both personality and intelligence, assigning nonwhites to inferior positions.

After the Civil War, museums became preoccupied with collecting Indian skeletal remains. Organizations such as the Army Medical Museum began to collect from both battlefields and graves under orders from the U.S. surgeon general. Museums such as the Field Museum in Chicago and the American Museum of Natural History did the same. Part of the impetus for collection came from a view that American Indian populations were disappearing. As an adjunct to skeletal collecting, the newly created Bureau of American Ethnology within the Smithsonian Institution set out to gather information on cultural practices before Indians vanished.

Public interest in Indian origins dictated the research focus for the BAE (Judd 1967). The quest for answers to the so-called mound-builder question dominated both the BAE and private academies of science, leading to the excavation of numerous mounds in order to collect both bones and funerary remains. It is from this intellectual medium that American anthropology was born; with little question, though its motives were scientific, it was a tool of colonialism.

By the 1890s, the mound-builder question had been more or less put to rest with a demonstration that Indians were indeed long-term inhabitants of the Western Hemisphere (though the amount of time remained uncertain) and that the ancestors of contemporary Indians were responsible for the earthworks and artifacts that were the focus of such controversy. At the turn of the century the interest in human remains waned, but skeletal analysis remained an important part of such interests as the eugenics movement, which desired to perfect the "Caucasian race" through selective breeding and legal prevention of "racial mixing." During the war years, little attention to human remains was apparent, but the war-dead studies during the Korean conflict sparked limited interest. During the 1960s, human remains became important in attempts to reconstruct culture histories through statistical analysis of genetic traits evident in skeletal material, reconstruction of diet, and disease patterns. Late in this period, American Indians began to assert political power, partly in pursuit of return and reburial of human remains and grave goods.

American anthropologists cannot deny their discipline's ties to American Indians, but the discipline is vastly more complex than it was at the time of its origins. Certainly anthropological research today ranges far beyond Indian issues. Discipline specialities have proliferated to the point where only small numbers of anthropologists actually ever deal with human remains (physical anthropologists and some archaeologists). Attachment of anthropology to academic institutions has brought the questions surrounding academic freedom into consideration. As anthropology matured, it became a bureaucracy that was slow to respond to change and confident in its own right to exist. Faced with challenges, bureaucracies also tend to deny that problems exist. This is exactly what many individual anthropologists and their organizations first did with the reburial issue.

Denial

Denying that a problem exists seems a common enough approach to handling serious issues; if one waits long enough, the problem may go away. In the process, a series of approaches or rationales is developed to avoid actually facing the issue. Cultural anthropologists were taken by surprise when Deloria attacked the discipline in *Custer Died for Your Sins.* One can hardly blame them for being defensive. Many anthropologists had worked closely with American Indians over the years and become attached to "their people." In point of fact, many Indian people were also attached to "their anthropologist." As well, anthropologists had often put themselves at substantial personal, financial, and political risk for Indian people in issues ranging from land claims to religious freedom. What anthropologists failed to understand was that their discipline sometimes was seen as exploitative and intrusive, often getting information "wrong,"[3] paying little attention to integration of Indian people into the whole research process except as informants. In archaeology the situation was very similar.

Over the years many archaeologists have worked with Indian people, and archaeological information has been used to Indian benefit in land-claims cases. Often, when work was done on reservations, Indians were hired as excavators or laboratory assistants. More important, archaeologists believed they were providing an important service to Indians, documenting an Indian past that Indians couldn't access through their own oral history. When AIM members began to disrupt excavations, calling archaeologists "grave-robbers" and making demands for return of remains, archaeologists became frustrated. In *God Is Red* Deloria (1973:31–33) documented a dig in Minnesota disrupted by the American Indian Movement. When Clyde Bellecourt and colleagues filled in trenches, took shovels, and burned notes, a disturbed student excavator commented, "We were trying to preserve their culture, not destroy it."

Scholarly responses to Native American demands have been mixed. Some scholars considered the reburial issue part of a broader political agenda, with militants seeking publicity for their cause (see Neiburger 1990; Stamps 1989:2), charging that reburial was of concern only to the vocal element in indigenous society, especially radical spokespeople. Some of these scholars authored "anti-reburial" resolutions to counter the radicals. They urged colleagues to pass statements condemning reburial in the hope that consciousness about the problem might be raised and that legislators or other governmental agencies might notice and give assistance to scientists "under siege." Several groups did pass such resolutions at the national and state levels, most notably the American Association of Physical Anthropologists (AAPA). Another organization's efforts to take a stand on the issue might serve as an example.

The Society for American Archaeology made one of the first attempts at drafting a resolution about repatriation of Indian museum objects and display of skeletons. At its 1968 annual meeting Deward Walker, Jr., drafted and submitted a resolution expressing the need for greater respect for American Indian wishes by American archaeologists. The resolution did not even make it to the floor of the business meeting (Sprague in Quick 1985:16–17). In an excellent commentary about the matter in *American Antiquity* Roderick Sprague (1974:1) noted, "Hopefully, the experience of the American Anthropological Association concerning the effectiveness of resolutions can serve as a lesson for the Society for American Archaeology. Resolutions, if not so insipid as to be worthless, have a unique ability to alienate a portion of the membership while lulling the remainder into complacent self-satisfaction. At the same time, resolutions create serious doubts in the minds of the public while not giving any real assurance to the subject population."

With Sprague's warnings about the effectiveness of resolutions apparently forgotten, the SAA attempted to pass an anti-reburial resolution at its 1982 annual meeting. Heavy pressure and dire warnings from Indians present at the meeting that such a resolution would exacerbate already difficult relations prevented passage, but with few Indians present the next year, the SAA Executive Committee passed such a resolution, only to rescind it a year later. The resolution indeed made matters worse, alienating Indians and a number of archaeologists who were working toward compromises. In an effort to appear more evenhanded, the SAA sponsored a plenary session on reburial at its 1986 New Orleans meeting with both Indian and anthropological presenters. The next day the SAA Executive Committee came forward with a policy that essentially restated the anti-reburial resolution from earlier years. The policy alienated Indian groups enough that some like American Indians against Desecration stopped trying to work with the SAA and moved more rapidly into the legislative arena. Resolutions are part of a political approach to the problem, but other denial responses have also appeared.

Native Americans consistently have demanded to know what good comes from the study of human remains. Anthropologists have often responded not with specific answers but with suggestions about why the questioners don't already have the answers. Some scholars have contended that the simple fact that Native Americans and others ask such questions shows that human osteologists have failed to educate both indigenous peoples and colleagues about the importance of skeletal study (Goldstein and Kintigh 1990:588–89). Many anthropologists also have expressed the opinion that neither Indians nor colleagues in anthropology know or truly appreciate what it is that human osteologists do, or the value of the information they provide. Some have even felt that their colleagues have "sold them out" (Sullivan and Overstreet 1985:53). If Indians and colleagues were "properly" educated about the study of bones, certainly they would not press for reburial.

Anthropologists have decried the anticipated loss of data (Buikstra 1981) and the destruction of global heritage (Goldstein in Wolinsky 1989:11; Ontario Council of Professional Osteologists 1987:3), and some have articulated concerns for the very survival of biological anthropology. There is apparently no disagreement among physical anthropologists, archaeologists and even some Native Americans that data will be lost with reburial. A commonly expressed analogue, often stated with politically volatile overtones, is that reburial of bones is like book burning (Brues 1987). Others, promoting compromise, have offered suggestions such as returning all material without provenience, placing the bones in "keeping places" that will allow future access, or somehow sampling small pieces of bone or keeping especially important specimens for eventual analysis with new technologies (Cybulski in Quick 1985:75).

Others have extended the data loss arguments by claiming that bones are an important heritage for indigenous peoples and all other peoples. Some have suggested that the current generation of indigenous peoples, though well intended, is perhaps denying information about the past to future generations of its own people (Anderson 1990; Brues 1987; Stamps 1989:3). Some claim that the remains and the information generated from them are a global, rather than tribal, heritage and that anthropology has an obligation to protect them for the benefit of humankind (Leone 1989).

This list of responses is certainly not complete, but it does suggest a pattern of denial that reburial demands are serious. What many anthropologists fail to understand is that Indian concern for the dead is long term and not just political. It simply is not going to go away. Such concerns go back well into the last century, as is eloquently stated in an often quoted (and elaborated!) speech by Chief Seattle, discussed by Ernie Turner (1989), an Athapaskan.

Beyond the individual problem is the tendency of bureaucracies such as anthropology to deny that a problem exists and act as if it will simply go away. Indeed, the AAA initially did not address the issue. It already had an ethics code and seemed to believe that it should stay out of the reburial issue. Only when a *New York Times* story confused the AAA with the SAA, did the AAA move to establish a commission on the problem (American Anthropological Association 1991).[4]

I do not mean to imply that individuals within anthropology who practiced denial did not actually believe what they were saying about reburial. The persistence of the problem eventually forced all but the most dogmatic into an effort to understand what the problem was. And to begin the process of understanding, some opened dialogue with Indian people about their demands.

Dialogue

Some anthropologists did not understand why the problem existed but, to their credit, did not deny that the problem was real or important. They wanted information and found ways to get it.[5] They began a series of dialogues, first among themselves and then with American Indians. Those involved from the start seemed to have been those directly confronted by Indians.

After initial disruptions of digs in the Midwest, John S. Sigstad (1971) organized a meeting of archaeologists to discuss the matter at the twenty-ninth Plains Conference in 1971. A transcript of the session entitled "American Indian Militants v. Archaeology" is instructive. Mostly a document of the denial stage, it nevertheless records that issues of ethics were raised and there was some notion that talking directly with Indians about the issue might be useful.

The first meetings to include larger groups of anthropologists and American

Indians came as the result of events in Iowa that have been well documented elsewhere (see Anderson, Finnegan, et al. 1977; Anderson, Pearson, et al. 1980, 1983). From 1983 onward, numerous meetings were held across the United States, and some have published transcripts (Hammil and Zimmerman 1984; United States Air Force 1985). Among the most important of these (and to the credit of the SAA) was a meeting held at the Newberry Library in 1985, sponsored by the SAA and the Society of Professional Archaeologists (Quick 1985). Many of these meetings were open, frank, and honest, but others, such as the 1986 SAA New Orleans Plenary, were seen by many as too staged or at least heavily managed (Zimmerman 1989b:63–64).

The process of dialogue continues and is essential. In fact, regular dialogue goes on in Iowa as part of the implementation of that state's reburial law. Archaeologists meet regularly with an Indian Advisory Board that oversees the law. From that dialogue has come an important relationship of trust which has solved most problems and has created a powerful alliance that has worked to save a number of burial sites from destruction (see Schermer 1991 for an example). The South Dakota Association of Professional Archaeologists recently completed its second on-reservation meeting about the treatment of human remains and mutual Indian and archaeologist concerns over cultural resources. Dialogue does not solve all problems, apparently, but it seems to promote some understanding. Still, communication is hardly perfect. Anthropologists have begun to reflect on the problem and have started to recognize that there is a profound difference in worldview between Indians and scientists.

Analysis

As the reburial controversy "heated up," many physical anthropologists simply reacted to Indian demands in an understandably defensive way. After all, many had invested years of their lives in the study of human skeletal remains. With some justification, they felt that an important database was being threatened and, perhaps, their livelihood as well. As time wore on and the issue proved to be more than just a brief political struggle, some anthropologists became curious about why the controversy arose and why it continued. The issue itself became a matter of intellectual investigation.

One physical anthropologist who addressed the reburial issue reflexively

was the Smithsonian Institution's Douglas Ubelaker. At the Society for American Archaeology and Society of Professional Archaeologists (SAA/SOPA) conference on reburial issues, he stated:

> We won't stop looking at this issue as physical anthropologists, but we also
> have to look at the issue as anthropologists. We have to try to fit what we
> think ought to be done with our science into the broader context of what is
> going on in terms of revitalization of American Indians in this country and
> larger issues. I think if physical anthropologists could do that, there is a
> greater chance of providing a level of sensitivity . . . that can lead to amiable
> solutions. (Quick 1985:172)

Even though Ubelaker saw reburial in a political context of revitalization of
American Indians, he concluded that physical anthropologists needed to step
outside the strictures of their own specialities and apply the tools and perspectives developed by the discipline to a vexing problem.

Some anthropologists have recognized that at least some of the conflict
stems from differing worldviews and values (Anderson in Quick 1985:54; compare Price 1991:2–3). On the surface this may seem an almost too facile anthropological thing to say. Exactly what values differ, and how are varying
worldviews expressed?

Essentially, there is an underlying contrast between Native American views
about the past and those of physical anthropologists and archaeologists (Zimmerman 1987). The former is one of a substantive, value rationality that actively seeks to reconcile the felt contradictions between ideal, "thought about"
realities — such as the mythic process of creation — and real experiential realities such as human history (Hill and Wright 1988:103, especially note 2). The
latter is a subjective, or instrumental and purposive, technical rationality that
reduces the past and all else it examines to a simple "dead" exteriority open to
all manner of investigation and manipulation (that is, *science*).

Native American expressions of the past are couched in terms of mythic, sacred space-times of creation, and these mythic understandings of the past are
intermingled with historical reckoning (Hill 1988:8; Walker 1991:104). Physical anthropologists and archaeologists have a positivist objectification that gives
them exclusive, nearly godlike power to create the past. This implicitly denies

that power to Native Americans, who are removed from the past as they make it. In a very important sense, this relationship is what the repatriation and reburial issues are all about.

Anthropologists stating that the past is gone, extinct, or lost with reburial send a strong message to Indians that Indians themselves are extinct. Acceptance of the past as anthropologists view it would actually destroy the present for Indians. If the past is the present, excavated human remains are not devoid of personality and must be respected as a living person should be. Anthropologists dealing with the remains using any other approach to the past are actually showing disrespect to the person that is the remains and to contemporary Indians. If anthropologists expect Indians to accept anthropological views of time and the past, Indians, to paraphrase Ong (1982:15), would have to die to continue living. This is what Deloria (1973:49) meant in *God Is Red* when he stated, "[t]he tragedy of America's Indians . . . is that they no longer exist, except in the pages of books."

Worldview differences other than time and past are also important, but they have not received so much attention. Uses of the law may be important. Archaeologists tend to see law in terms of dispute resolution, but American Indians also attach a notion of natural or god-given law to their view of how remains should be treated (Watson, Zimmerman, and Peterson 1989). Finally, the various reburial meeting transcripts are permeated with references to the land, but the differences in how land is viewed have not yet been analyzed.

If there is to be resolution to the reburial issue that is satisfactory to all concerned, then anthropologists and Indians must recognize the political power of what are deceptively simple concepts. Useful compromises must incorporate varying worldviews and protect them. Compromise, therefore, is not very easy.

Compromise

Some archaeologists worked out compromises with American Indians long ago. In 1967–68, Roderick Sprague and Deward Walker established a policy at the University of Idaho under which the Laboratory of Anthropology would not maintain a skeletal collection. This policy resulted from some unhappy occurrences during excavation of Nez Perce burials. With the policy in place, much to the satisfaction of the Indians, word of it spread throughout tribes of the Columbia Plateau. Sprague and Walker eventually were called upon to handle most burials in the region. The approach meets most anthropological and Indian needs and has been quietly successful (Sprague in Quick 1985: 124–26).

Sprague and Walker obviously handled the issue with sensitivity and were able to develop local and eventually regional resolution of the reburial issue. Generally, however, anthropologists have not been so successful. Because of their denial that the matter was more than a transient political problem and because of the discipline's perceived or real intransigence, American Indians had to struggle to force compromises in many states or regions. Iowa passed a law early, and although other states like South Dakota only recently passed a reburial law, the professional community there early on adopted reburial policies satisfactory to both Indians and archaeologists (Zimmerman and Gregg 1989). It would be an understatement to suggest that such compromises were reached with difficulty. Nor, when reached, did they solve all problems, as we can see from recent difficulties between the Nebraska State Historical Society and the Pawnee tribe (Peregoy 1992; Svingen 1992).

Those states with relatively large resident Indian populations were among the first to reach compromise, but many places where few Indians live, usually in the East, have had more difficulty. As of 1989, just before the passage of the National Museum of the American Indian Act, twenty-seven states had an aboriginal reburial law in place (Price 1991:122–25). Local or regional compromises seem to be most effective, but some American Indians have pushed for national solutions to the problem, which are far more difficult to achieve.

In their process of denial, organizations like the SAA, AAPA, and AAA implied in their policy statements, resolutions, and reports that local compromises would be best, and they strongly urged that no broader solutions be attempted. There is truth in the idea that local or regional solutions are necessary to handle most problems. At the same time, many Indian groups saw this approach as a ploy. For instance, they saw that in states with little Indian population, anthropologists could essentially have their own way, continuing to excavate human remains and to maintain skeletal collections. They also recognized that these solutions would have no power on federally controlled lands or projects, nor on federal museums that had large skeletal collections. Consequently, some American Indian groups such as the Native American

Rights Fund (NARF), American Indians against Desecration, and the National Congress of American Indians pushed for national legislation. Initially their target was the Smithsonian, and they successfully pushed through legislation that has already repatriated many of the remains in the National Museum of Natural History. Following that bill, they lobbied for passage of what eventually became the Native American Graves Protection and Repatriation Act.

The anthropological community lobbied hard against passage of both laws but apparently failed to realize that the public supported Indian concerns on this matter. Eventually, Democratic senator Daniel Inouye (of Hawaii), chairman of the Senate Select Committee on Indian Affairs, essentially stated that if the professional community couldn't solve the problem on its own, the compromise would be legislated. Although the SAA and other groups worked to effect compromise with NARF and NCAI, the generally accepted view is that the SAA "lost." In fact, at a meeting on implementation of NAGPRA by the National Park Service, held at the 1991 SAA annual meeting in New Orleans, a frustrated past SAA president commented: "We've been hoodwinked!" Tom King, an archaeologist who has struggled to get anthropologists to compromise, told me in a hallway conversation: "There will be a few more battles, but the war is over." Anthropology's poor response to Indian demands apparently has been costly, not only in terms of a perceived loss of power over the past, but also in terms of image with the public. It may be deserved.

Where Should Anthropology Go from Here?
Although some are apparently willing to fight a rear-guard action (Neiburger 1990) or to put a different "spin" on it (Goldstein and Kintigh 1990), anthropology must find another solution. Quite simply, anthropologists must learn to share control over the past. This means that an archaeological view cannot be seen as the only legitimate view of the past. In practice, this means working with indigenous peoples to formulate both research questions and methods. In other words, anthropologists and indigenous peoples need to find out how the archaeological use of materials from past times can be used to solve questions posed by indigenous peoples (see McDonald et al. 1991 and Pardoe 1988, 1991, for examples).

Some organizations have been working toward institutionalizing this sort of cooperation. In 1989 the World Archaeological Congress (WAC) held an intercongress in Vermillion, South Dakota, on archaeological ethics and the treatment of the dead and reached an accord on the issue (Berman and Brooks 1991; Hubert 1989). The Vermillion Accord contained six clauses, all relating to the concept of respect for the rights of the dead, those claiming to be descendants, the local community, and scientific and educational purposes. The accord insisted that agreement on the disposition of the dead be reached by respectful mutual negotiation. Some felt the accord did not go far enough or provide enough protection for indigenous rights or science. Nor did it provide formal mechanisms through which negotiations could be made (Zimmerman 1990). At the same time, the accord did accomplish recognition by all parties of the rights of others concerned in the issue. In point of fact, the accord received wide recognition and has been used as a baseline in a number of disputes in Canada, the United States, and Australia.

At the second World Archaeological Congress, in Venezuela in 1990, the indigenous members of the WAC Executive Committee proposed an ethics code for archaeologists who deal with indigenous people that was accepted by the full WAC Executive Committee and Council. This code consists of two parts — eight "Principles to abide by" and seven "Rules to adhere to." They read as follows:

Principles to abide by:
Members agree that they have obligations to indigenous peoples and that they shall abide by the following principles:

1. To acknowledge the importance of indigenous cultural heritage, including sites, places, objects, artifacts, human remains, to the survival of indigenous cultures.

2. To acknowledge the importance of protecting indigenous cultural heritage to the well-being of indigenous peoples.

3. To acknowledge the special importance of indigenous ancestral human remains, and sites containing and/or associated with such remains, to indigenous peoples.

4. To acknowledge that the important relationship between indigenous peoples and their cultural heritage exists irrespective of legal ownership.

5. To acknowledge that the indigenous cultural heritage rightfully belongs to the indigenous descendants of that heritage.

6. To acknowledge and recognize indigenous methodologies for interpreting, curating, managing and protecting indigenous cultural heritage.

7. To establish equitable partnerships and relationships between Members and indigenous peoples whose cultural heritage is being investigated.

8. To seek, whenever possible, representation of indigenous peoples in agencies funding or authorizing research to be certain their view is considered as critically important in setting research standards, questions, priorities and goals.

Rules to adhere to:
Members agree that they will adhere to the following rules prior to, during and after their investigations:

1. Prior to conducting any investigation and/or examination, Members shall with rigorous endeavor seek to define the indigenous peoples whose cultural heritage is the subject of investigation.

2. Members shall negotiate with and obtain the informed consent of representatives authorized by the indigenous peoples whose cultural heritage is the subject of investigation.

3. Members shall ensure that the authorised representatives of the indigenous peoples whose culture is being investigated are kept informed during all stages of the investigation.

4. Members shall ensure that the results of their work are presented with deference and respect to the identified indigenous peoples.

5. Members shall not interfere with and/or remove human remains of indigenous peoples without the express consent of those concerned.

6. Members shall not interfere with and/or remove artefacts or objects of special cultural significance, as defined by associated indigenous peoples, without their express consent.

7. Members shall recognise their obligation to employ and/or train indigenous peoples in proper techniques as part of their projects, and utilize indigenous peoples to monitor the projects.

Both the indigenous people who drafted the code and the archaeologists who agreed to pass it understand that it is a first step, one reason why it is called a "first" code of ethics. The WAC view is that ethics are not a static device but are subject to refinement, change, and sometimes even revocation as situations warrant and times change.

The fundamental notion behind the code is that it gives direction to archaeologists in their dealings with indigenous peoples. Ethical codes are not panaceas; they are only guidelines. What is most important in the WAC code is that this first version recognizes the importance of the indigenous voice in intellectual property rights and provides some mechanisms for interaction between archaeologists and indigenous groups on heritage issues.

The code has already been widely distributed among indigenous groups, though it has circulated less thoroughly among archaeologists. Many indigenous groups have hailed the code's spirit as have some individual archaeologists. Some archaeological groups such as the Australian Archaeological Association have already adopted the code. It has already influenced cultural heritage legislation in Manitoba and British Columbia.

The SAA also began a reconsideration of its ethical code and at its 1994 meeting in Anaheim presented the membership with several principles including one indicating that professional archaeology needs to be more attuned to the concerns of various publics. A supportive statement on accountability uses American Indians as a primary example but does not explicitly state that reburial is a major concern. The draft ethical principles have numerous contradictions, including one on stewardship that may conflict with accountability, especially on reburial. Still, the statements are at the early stages of discussion, and many of these problems may yet be resolved.

In the end, the WAC code and the proposed SAA ethical principles are furthering a process of bringing indigenous peoples into partnerships with archaeologists. The result may be an almost inevitable syncretism of archaeological and indigenous approaches that will change the way anthropologists do their science. The process will eventually "reinvent" archaeology and make it more responsive to all peoples' concerns.

The reburial issue has been costly for anthropology. It has turned colleague against colleague. It has reinforced for some indigenous people the conviction that anthropology and archaeology are simply a form of scientific colonialism. Many in the public have wondered about the apparent insensitivity of anthropologists to what they see as reasonable indigenous demands. If these costs cause anthropology to be more responsive, then wrestling with the issue will have been worth it. By doing so, anthropology will have become capable of meeting both the scientific and humanistic potential of which it is certainly capable.

Notes

1. Intellectual property rights might be defined as control of information or access to information about a people or culture.

2. Some physical anthropologists and archaeologists who read this chapter will sense that I favor reburial, and that is generally true. At the same time, I do recognize that reburial causes losses for science. I believe I have maintained a fairly consistent position over the years that anthropology must work out compromises with indigenous peoples or risk losing all access to human remains (see Zimmerman 1986, 1989a:215–16, for what I consider to be fair assessments of my position on the issues). I would be less than honest, however, if I did not admit to pointing out anthropology's failings sometimes in a rather harsh way.

3. "Wrong" here may simply mean that it did not coincide with the Indians' view of their own culture. An anthropological view is an outside or "etic" view that may or may not overlap the inside or "emic" perspective. However, incorrect information sometimes was given to the anthropologist to protect privileged information; sometimes informants didn't know answers, and sometimes information was misunderstood or incorrectly recorded.

4. The timing on the development of the AAA Commission on Reburial is intriguing. After the World Archaeological Congress Intercongress on Archaeological Ethics and the Treatment of the Dead in August 1989, a reporter at the *New York Times* called me, as organizer of that meeting, for a story about reburial (*New York Times*, August 20, 1989, p. 1). In quoting me the reporter confused the AAA with the SAA. AAA President Roy Rappaport called me to complain about my misinformation. Although plans for action may have been in the works, I believe this "bad press" finally forced AAA to move forward.

5. One way to get information was to use questionnaires to ask Indians directly about their concerns. This was tried early by Sigstad (1973) and more recently by Klesert and Holt (1985).

References

American Anthropological Association. 1976. *Professional Ethics: Statements and Procedures of the American Anthropological Association.* Washington, D.C.: American Anthropological Association.

———. 1991. "Reburial Commission Report." *Anthropology Newsletter* 32(3):1, 26–28.

Anderson, Duane C. 1990. Letter to Steve Moore, Native American Rights Fund, July 14. Files of author.

Anderson, Duane, Michael Finnegan, John Hotopp, and Alton Fisher. 1977. "The Lewis Central School Site (13PW5): A Resolution of Ideological Conflicts at an Archaic Ossuary in Western Iowa." *Plains Anthropologist* 23:183–219.

———. 1983. *The Study of Ancient Skeletal Remains in Iowa: A Symposium.* Iowa City: Office of the State Archaeologist of Iowa.

Anderson, Duane C., M. Pearson, A. Fisher, and D. Zieglowsky, eds. 1980. *Planning Seminar on Ancient Burial Grounds.* Iowa City: Office of the State Archaeologist of Iowa.

Berman, Tessa, and James Brooks. 1991. "From Global Politics to Local Policy: A Conference Report on Repatriation." *Anthropology UCLA* 18(1):12–31.

Bieder, Robert. 1986. *Science Encounters the Indian, 1820–1880: The Early Years of American Ethnology.* Norman: University of Oklahoma Press.

———. 1990. *A Brief Historical Survey of the Expropriation of American Indian Remains.* Boulder, Colo.: Native American Rights Fund.

Brues, Alice. 1987. Letter to John Echo-Hawk, Native American Rights Fund, July 13. Files of author.

Buikstra, Jane. 1981. "A Specialist in Ancient Cemetery Studies Looks at the Reburial Issue." *Early Man* 3(3):26–27.

Deloria, Vine, Jr. 1969. *Custer Died for Your Sins: An Indian Manifesto.* New York: Macmillan.

———. 1973. *God Is Red: A Native View of Religion.* New York: Delta.

Fredin, Adeline. 1990. "Colville Confederated Tribes." In A. Klesert and A. Downer, eds., *Preservation and Reservation: Native American Lands and Archaeology,* pp. 289–300. Navajo Nation Papers in Anthropology 26. Window Rock, Ariz.: Navajo Nation Archaeology Department.

Goldstein, Lynne, and Keith Kintigh. 1990. "Ethics and the Reburial Controversy." *American Antiquity* 55(3): 585–91.

Hammil, Jan, and Larry J. Zimmerman, eds. 1984. *Reburial of Human Skeletal Remains: Perspectives from Lakota Spiritual Men and Elders.* Vermillion: University of South Dakota Archaeology Laboratory, and Indianapolis: American Indians against Desecration.

Hill, Jonathan D. 1988. "Introduction: Myth and History." In Jonathan Hill, ed., *Rethinking Myth and History: Indigenous South American Perspectives on the Past,* pp. 1–17. Urbana: University of Illinois Press.

Hill, Jonathan D., and Robin Wright M. 1988. "Time, Narrative, and Ritual: Historical Interpretations from an Amazonian Society." In Jonathan Hill, ed., *Rethinking Myth and History: Indigenous South American Perspectives on the Past,* pp. 78–105. Urbana: University of Illinois Press.

Hinsley, Curtis M., Jr. 1981. *Savages and Scientists: The Smithsonian Institution and the Development of American Anthropology.* Washington, D.C.: Smithsonian Institution Press.

Hubert, Jane. 1989. "First World Archaeological Congress Inter-congress, Vermillion, South Dakota, USA." *World Archaeological Bulletin* 4:14–19.

Hymes, Dell, ed. 1969. *Reinventing Anthropology*. New York: Pantheon.

Judd, Neil M. 1967. *The Bureau of American Ethnology: A Partial History*. Norman: University of Oklahoma Press.

King, Thomas F. 1986. "Ethics for the Living." *Anthropology Newsletter* 27(2):12.

Klesert, A. L., and H. B. Holt. 1985. "Archaeologists, Native Americans, and Archaeology on Indian Land." Paper presented at the fiftieth annual meeting of the Society for American Archaeology, Denver.

Leone, Mark. 1989. "Society for American Archaeology Statement on H.R. 2668, National American Indian Museum Act, 20 July 1989." Manuscript, files of author.

Marcus, George E., and Michael Fischer. 1986. *Anthropology as Cultural Critique: An Experimental Moment in the Human Sciences*. Chicago: University of Chicago Press.

McDonald, J. Douglas, Larry J. Zimmerman, A. L. McDonald, W. Tall Bull, and Ted Rising Sun. 1991. "The Northern Cheyenne Outbreak of 1879: Using Oral History and Archaeology as Tools of Resistance." In R. H. McGuire and R. Paynter, eds., *The Archaeology of Inequality*, pp. 64–78. Oxford: Basil Blackwell.

McGuire, Randall H. 1992. "Archeology and the First Americans." *American Anthropologist* 94(4):816–36.

Neiburger, E. J. 1990. "Why Preserve Bone Artifacts?" *Indian-Artifact Magazine* 9(2):8–9, 46–47.

Ong, Walter J. 1982. *Orality and Literacy: The Technologizing of the Word*. London: Methuen.

Ontario Council of Professional Osteologists. 1987. "Ontario Heritage Review Policy: Comments and Recommendations." Manuscript, files of author.

Pardoe, Colin. 1988. *Ancient Aboriginal Burials at Cowra, NSW: A Report on the Study of Two Skeletons Spanning 7,000 Years*. Canberra: Australian Institute of Aboriginal Studies.

———. 1991. "Farewell to the Murray Black Australian Aboriginal Skeletal Collection." *World Archaeological Bulletin* 5:119–21.

Peregoy, Robert. 1992. "Nebraska's Landmark Repatriation Law: A Study of Cross-Cultural Conflict and Resolution." *American Indian Culture and Research Journal* 16(2):139–96.

Price, H. Marcus III. 1991. *Disputing the Dead*. Columbia: University of Missouri Press.

Quick, Polly McW. ed. 1985. *Proceedings: Conference on Reburial Issues, Newberry Library, June 14–15, 1985*. Washington, D.C.: Society for American Archaeology.

Schermer, Shirley J. 1991. "Archaeological Investigations and Osteological Analyses at 13SR18 and 13SR19, Northridge Subdivision, Ames, Story County, Iowa." *Office of the State Archaeologist of Iowa Research Papers* 16(2).

Sigstad, John S. 1971. "American Indian Militants vs. Archaeology." Manuscript, University of South Dakota Archives, Vermillion.

———. 1973. "Research Report on Native American Skeletal Materials." Manuscript, University of South Dakota Archives, Vermillion.

Sprague, Roderick. 1974. "American Indians and American Archaeology." *American Antiquity* 39:1–2.

Stamps, Richard B. 1989. Testimony given before the Committee on Interior and Insular Affairs of the United States House of Representatives, July 20. Files of author.

Sullivan, Norman, and David F. Overstreet. 1985. "Analysis of Human Skeletal Remains from the Fitzgibbons Site, Gallatin County, Illinois." Draft report submitted to Shawnee National Forest, purchase order no. 40–51A8–5–183.

Svingen, Orlan. 1992. "The Pawnee of Nebraska: Twice Removed." *American Indian Culture and Research Journal* 16(2):121–38.

Trigger, Bruce G. 1980. "Archaeology and the Image of the American Indian." *American Antiquity* 45:662–76.

Turner, Ernest. 1989. "The Souls of My Dead Brothers." In Robert Layton, ed., *Conflicts in the Archaeology of Living Traditions*, pp. 189–94. London: Unwin Hyman.

United States Air Force. 1985. *Conference on Reburial.* Norton Air Force Base, Calif.: United States Air Force.

Walker, Deward E., Jr. 1991. "Protection of American Indian Sacred Geography." In C. Vecsey, ed., *Handbook of American Indian Religious Freedom*, pp. 100–115. New York: Crossroad.

Watson, Norman, Larry J. Zimmerman, and P. M. Peterson. 1989. "The Present Past: An Examination of Archaeological and Native American Thinking." In D. Topping, ed., *Thinking across Cultures*, pp. 33–42. Hillsdale, N.J.: Lawrence Erlbaum.

Willey, Gordon R., and Jeremy Sabloff. 1980. *A History of American Archaeology.* San Francisco: W. H. Freeman.

Williams, Stephen. 1991. *Fantastic Archaeology: The Wild Side of North American Prehistory.* Philadelphia: University of Pennsylvania Press.

Wolinsky, Howard. 1989. "Unburying Indian Bones: Science vs. Spirituality." *American College of Physicians Observer* 9(7):1–2, 9, 11.

Zimmerman, Larry J. 1986. "On Meighan and the Ethics of Reburial." *Anthropology Newsletter* 27(2):2, 12.

———. 1987. "The Impact of the Concepts of Time and Past on the Concept of Archaeology: Some Lessons from the Reburial Issue." *Archaeological Review from Cambridge* 6(1):42–50.

———. 1989a. "Human Bones as Symbols of Power: Aboriginal American Belief Systems toward Bones and 'Grave-Robbing' Archaeologists." In Robert Layton, ed., *Conflicts in the Archaeology of Living Traditions*, pp. 211–16. London: Unwin Hyman.

———. 1989b. "Made Radical by My Own." In Robert Layton, ed., *Conflicts in the Archaeology of Living Traditions*, pp. 60–67. London: Unwin Hyman.

———. 1990. "Reflections on the Issues: Implications for the Scholarly Disciplines." *Death Studies* 14(6):629–40.

Zimmerman, Larry J., and John B. Gregg. 1989. "A History of the Reburial Issue in South Dakota." *South Dakota Archaeology* 13:89–100.

Part Three

Ethnography and Colonialism

This section examines the connections between ethnography and colonial discourses and modes of domination. In chapter 6 Cecil King (Odawa) presents a concise statement of an indigenous view of ethnography. He concentrates on the issue of representation, and the intellectual violence done to indigenous thinking by the "conceptual packages" deployed by anthropology. It is not just an intellectual matter, however, because the anthropological representations have a lot to do with the stereotypes of Indians that circulate in the wider society.

Marilyn Bentz (Gros Ventre) argues in chapter 7 that compliance with formal ethics is not sufficient to protect the interests of informants. Her particular concerns are the reporting of life histories (even with "informed consent"), "reflexive" accounts, and descriptions of family history. All of these methods, while formally consistent with the letter of current ethical standards, may inadvertently harm informants. She calls for a more direct recognition of the reliance of the anthropologist upon the *friendship* of Indian people, for self-awareness training before entering the field (on the order of the training given to social work graduate students), and for a more substantive professional ethics.

Thomas Biolsi focuses attention in chapter 8 on a young ethnographer who worked on the Pine Ridge Reservation in the 1930s. Biolsi analyzes how the ethnographer, Haviland Scudder Mekeel, chose the "object" he did for anthropological study, and how that choice of object influenced what Mekeel saw on Pine Ridge. Biolsi argues that Mekeel approached his studies of the Oglala

Lakota through a romanticist and primitivist vision of Indian people, which caused him to "write off" most Oglala people and to misconstrue important parts of reservation political and economic life.

Gail Landsman analyzes in chapter 9 a dispute between Iroquois traditionalists and professional Iroquoianist scholars over the role of the Six Nations as a model for the U.S. Constitution. The dispute focused on a draft of a curriculum resource guide designed for use in New York State public schools. The guide, prepared by Iroquois people, argued that consideration of the Iroquois political system had indeed been an influence on the drafting of the U.S. Constitution. Iroquoianist scholars — anthropologists prominent among them — strongly criticized the work as unprofessional and untrue. While Landsman identifies the logic of the politics of Iroquois-anthropology relations, she perhaps draws her most critical conclusions regarding the sociology of anthropology itself.

Peter Whiteley examines in chapter 10 a range of appropriations of Hopi culture — Hopi ritual and religion through material culture — by non-Hopi, mostly white, Americans. These non-Hopis are positioned by a global political economy to be able to *collect* things Hopi, and are motivated by a global cultural economy to *desire* things Hopi. While most readers will be troubled by the descriptions of the "Smokis" (pot and art collectors) and the New Age Hopiphiles, more troubling still is Whiteley's insistence that there is a "family resemblance" between anthropology and the aforementioned modes of appropriation. Whiteley does, however, suggest some possibilities for making anthropology a discipline pursued in the interests of Hopi people.

6

Here Come the Anthros

CECIL KING

N'dahwemahdik giye n'weehkahnisidok g'dahnamikohnim meenwa dush g'meegetchiwinim geeweekomiyek monpee nongo weenashamigabwitohnigok djigeegidotamah manda enjimowndjidihying. -N'geekahwe bigossehnimah dush Wo kinah gego netawtot, weebi-weedji-yawyung, weemeezhiyung nihb-wakahwin meenwa dash nah gihnihgehn-nah n'dahkidowinan djiminokahgo-hwing, mee gahzhi bigossehndahmah . . . My sisters and my brothers I greet you and also I thank you for inviting me to speak to the topic at hand. As I was preparing my thoughts, I begged the Maker of all things to be among us, to give us some wisdom and also maybe to make my words be as a medicine for us all — those were my thoughts.

We, as Indian people, have welcomed strangers into our midst. We have welcomed all who came with intellectual curiosity or in the guise of the informed student. We have honored those whom we have seen grow in their knowledge and understanding of our ways. But unfortunately, many times we have been betrayed. Our honored guests have shown themselves to be no more than peeping toms, rank opportunists, interested in furthering their own careers by trading in our sacred traditions. Many of our people have felt anger at the way our communities have been cheated, held up to ridicule, and our customs sensationalized. Singer Floyd Westerman (Dakota), for example, expressed this anger in his 1969 recording of "Here Come the Anthros."

We have been observed, noted, taped, and videoed. Our behaviors have been recorded in every possible way known to Western science, and I suppose we could learn to live with this if we had not become imprisoned in the anthropologists' words. The language that anthropologists use to explain us traps us in linguistic cages because we must explain our ways through alien hypothetical constructs and theoretical frameworks. Our *ezhibemahdizowin* must be described as material culture, economics, politics, or religion. We must segment, fragment, fracture, and pigeonhole that which we hold sacred. The pipe, *d'opwahganinan*, becomes a sacred artifact, a religious symbol, a political instrument, a mnemonic device, an icon.

We have to describe our essence, *d'ochichaugwunan*, to fit academic conceptual packages, and we have become prisoners of what academics have done to our words to verify their words. We want to be given the time, money, luxury, and security of academic credibility to define our own constructs from within our own languages and our own worlds and in our own time.

We struggle as contemporary Indian, Metis, and Inuit peoples to unlock the classificatory chains choking our dynamic languages and growing, changing lives. How can we learn how our language is structured, how our world of languages was created, if we still must parse, analyze, and chop them up to fit the grammar of other languages? How can we define who we are, what we see, and what we think when the public, politicians, and policy makers have accepted the prepackaged images of who we are, as created by anthropologists?

I am an Odawa. I speak Odawa, but anthropologists have preferred to say I speak Ojibwe. My language is an Algonquin language, I am told, and it is structured by describing things as animate or inanimate, so I am told. English definitions of the terms "animate" and "inanimate" lead people to think of things being alive or not alive. Is this how our language is structured? I think not. In Odawa all so-called inanimate things could not be said to be dead. Does animate then mean having or possessing a soul? Is this a sufficient explanation? I think not. Is the animate-inanimate dichotomy helpful in describing the structure of my language? I think that it is limiting, if not wrong outright. For in Odawa anything at some time can be animate. The state of inanimateness is not the denial or negation of animateness as death is the negation of the state of aliveness. Nor can something have a soul and then not have a soul and then acquire a soul again. In Odawa the concept of animateness is limitless. It can be altered by the mood of the moment, the mood of the speaker, the context, the use, the circumstances, the very cosmos of our totality. English terms imprison our understanding of our own linguistic concepts.

Having to define ourselves from the start with inappropriate English terms is not sufficient for our understanding. It is confining, and it is wrong. It seems that we must first defend ourselves against scholarly categories. We must find a way to break out of these cages. That takes a lot of unnecessary, unproductive time and energy and money.

In the last twenty years, Indian, Metis, and Inuit peoples have moved from reservations and isolated communities into places of greater visibility, but they are seen through the images built out of anthropological studies of them. We have been defined as "poor folks," members of a "minority" or "less sophisticated cultures"; we have been called "tribal," "underdeveloped," "nomadic," "less fully evolved." Therefore, real Indians are poor. You have provided us with the cop-outs: "Indian time" if we are late, "It's not the Indian way" if we don't want to do something. Employers have acquired cop-outs for not hiring Indians: Indians don't like competition, Indians don't like to work inside, Indians like seasonal employment. Teachers excuse the lack of Indian graduates. Indians themselves find excuses for their lack of employment, education, or dignity.

Now, we as Indian, Metis, and Inuit people want self-determination. We want self-government. When will anthropologists become instrumental to our ambitions, our categories of importance? How helpful is it to be called tribal or primitive when we are trying to negotiate with national and provincial governments as equal nations? Anthropological terms make us and our people invisible. The real people and the real problems disappear under the new rhetoric. Indian, Metis, and Inuit problems defined incorrectly lead to inappropriate solutions, irrelevant programs, and the reinforcement of the status quo. The real problems remain unresolved, and the Indian, Metis, and Inuit are again redefined.

The cumulative effects of all this are now evident. We have been redefined so many times we no longer quite know who we are. Our original words are obscured by the layers upon layers of others' definitions laid on top of them. We want to come back to our own words, our own meanings, our own definitions of ourselves, and our own world. Now scholars debate among themselves the ethics to be used in working in our communities and homes. It is as if they are organizing the feeding schedule at the zoo. We want to escape from the zoo. We want to be consulted and respected as not only human beings, at the very least, but as independent nations with the right to determine what transpires within our boundaries. We want to say who comes to our world, what they should see, hear, and take away. Most important, we want to appraise, critique, and censure what they feel they have a right to say about us.

We acknowledge, with gratitude, the attempts by the National Endowment for the Humanities and the American Anthropological Association to regulate researchers by guidelines or codes of ethics. However, for most of us, these efforts are part of the problem. For we must ask: Whose ethics? In this era of aboriginal self-government, it is not for the outsider to set the rules of conduct on our lands and in our communities. It is our right and responsibility as aboriginal nations to do that. It is the right and responsibility of researchers to respect and comply with our standards. The dictates of Western science and the standards of behavior enshrined by associations of researchers dedicated to the advancement of social science may or may not be compatible with the code of ethics of our aboriginal communities.

Creative approaches must be discussed and debated by aboriginal communities, academic institutions, and individual researchers to reach a working relationship that neither constricts the advancement of knowledge nor denigrates the aboriginal communities' legitimate authority over the integrity of their own intellectual traditions.

Let me close with a story. I had a dream that all the peoples of the world were together in one place. The place was cold. Everyone was shivering. I looked for a fire to warm myself. None was to be found. Then someone said that in the middle of the gathering of Indians, what was left of the fire had been found. It was a very, very small flame. All the Indians were alerted that the slightest rush of air or the smallest movement could put the fire out, and the fire would be lost to humankind. All the Indians banded together to protect the flame. They were working to quicken the fragile, feeble flame. The Indians were adding minuscule shavings from small pieces of wood to feed it.

Suddenly, throughout the other peoples, the whisper was heard: The Indians have a fire. There was a crush of bodies stampeding to the place where the flame was held. I pushed to the edge of the Indian circle to stop those coming to the flame so that it would not be smothered. The other people became abusive, saying that they were cold too and it was our responsibility to share the flame with them. I replied, "It is our responsibility to preserve the flame for humanity, and at the moment it is too weak to be shared, but if we all are still and respect the flame it will grow and thrive in the caring hands of those who hold it. In time we can all warm ourselves at the fire. But now we have to nurture the flame or we will all lose the gift."

Those are my words. *Meegwetch.*

7

Beyond Ethics
Science, Friendship, and Privacy

MARILYN BENTZ

During the emerging years of anthropology, the major ethical dilemmas concerned accuracy of data and validity of interpretation. Traditional Native American tribal values of extending generosity, hospitality, and sometimes friendship to strangers who were allowed into the community helped legitimize the tendency of anthropologists to consider their investigative inquiries as a high calling about which Native Americans should be, if not grateful, at least receptive. Although circumstances have changed, the ethics reflective of this early history continue to influence contemporary anthropological study.

Today, most Native Americans are literate. The results of anthropological research are likely to be disseminated and read by the communities studied. The potential for damaging interpersonal relationships or for making public information that could be harmful is real. In addition, Native Americans are no longer obligated by tribal social norms to be as gracious to inquiring strangers as in the past. If anthropologists are to continue their studies of Native Americans, they must become more conscious of their own motives and ethnocentric biases, and more sensitive to the interests of Native American populations.

Given the code of ethics of the American Anthropological Association, and the federal government's human subjects review requirements, contemporary anthropologists should at least be aware of recognized ethical boundaries. While some abuses are inevitable, anthropologists now avoid many of the excesses of the past, when the interests and welfare of informants were often ignored. My concern is not to belabor the sins of history or the deliberate violation of current ethical standards. Rather, it is to make a case for a more sophisticated and sensitive adherence to the spirit as well as the letter of current ethical standards and, in some cases, to argue for higher standards. In fact, it may be that certain types of research, those most vulnerable to abuse, need to be eliminated or at least modified. In particular, I am referring to studies that report life histories, provide accounts of personal interactions with informants,[1] and map kinship relationships. While the use of such data is currently well accepted and is not considered a violation of ethics, my experience with other anthropologists, my own work, and my reading of scholarly publications have caused me to question the legitimacy of such methods, many of which violate the friendship and the spirit of the human relationship that binds the anthropologist and his or her subject. I believe a more sensitive concern for the rights of informants also makes for better anthropology. Anthropologists should be more thoroughly trained in self-awareness and responsive to the well-being of the people they study before going to the field.

Life Histories

In my view it is not ethical to use life histories, or to report specific incidents from individual lives, if such information has the potential to prove embarrassing if the identities of these people were revealed. In most cases it is almost impossible to protect the anonymity of individuals in small communities where a researcher's activities and contacts are common knowledge. Moreover, concealing the geographic location of studies and using pseudonyms do not ensure protection for the individual within the community itself, where such knowledge can cause the most harm.

In conducting my own doctoral research, the importance of this concern became very clear. My dissertation was a comparison of the worldview of Indian students and that of non-Indian students, all attending the same off-reservation high school. Using an open-ended questionnaire, I categorized all phrases that, standing alone, could answer a given question. I listed the phrases within the appropriate category and then compared the categories of Indian and non-Indian responses. I naively believed that there was no possibility of anyone relating particular responses to specific individuals. In the years following the completion of my work, I became aware that many of the Indian students I had interviewed had read the study. In a conversation with one of the students who seemed to have read it with some care, I asked what had interested her the most. She replied that she and her friends enjoyed trying to figure out who had said what. I was dismayed to learn that they were so curious about the sources of individual responses. Moreover, I was chagrined when I found that they could actually identify individuals from the information I provided. I reread my study, and much to my consternation, realized that I had accounted for "deviant" comments by referring to students' backgrounds. For example, Indian students frequently made favorable comments about the reservation all-Indian school they attended prior to high school, whereas they rarely made positive comments about the integrated high school they were attending at the time. The only exceptions to this pattern were responses from two students, both of whom had lived off-reservation for long periods of time. In my textual analysis of the tables, I provided this information. Thus, immersed in trying to make sense of my data, I inadvertently gave information that the Indian students who knew each other well could use to identify these individuals.

In fact, pseudonyms do not protect research subjects even in urban areas. Although Native Americans are a small minority in most cities, many, especially first-generation migrants, often belong to a tight social network. While I was in graduate school, another student gave me the rough draft of his dissertation to read for comment.[2] I objected to the inclusion of life histories of several Indian women, some of whom had been helpful to him in making contacts for the study. The student refused to eliminate these life histories, arguing that it would be *unethical* since his committee had already approved the dissertation inclusive of the life histories. Furthermore, the student maintained, these women had signed human subjects permission slips and would not have given information they did not want revealed. From a literal standpoint, the student was correct, but I believe he was in violation of the spirit of the human subjects review requirement that the people studied be protected. Surely these women did not want embarrassing information about them revealed to the broader community. Once informed that I could easily identify these women, the student should have felt obligated to omit their life histories, particularly since they had nothing to do with the central issues in his thesis but were provided only as supplementary data in the appendix.

Anthropologists should always be aware that informants, especially when they have formed a personal relationship with the researcher, may provide information they would not want published. Informants may appreciate the opportunity to discuss a private matter with a sympathetic person in the expectation that the confidant will not disclose it. The need to share information about difficult life situations is often great among people who have experienced severe economic and social problems. In one of my research projects, most of the reservation people I interviewed divulged private information that was not relevant to my topic. The specific information I needed could have been gathered in one half-hour session with each informant, yet most of the interviews lasted from two to three hours. It is clear that the interview served a therapeutic purpose. My informants used these periods to relieve stress by speaking about painful matters to an outsider who, as a professional, could be expected to use discretion and keep this information confidential. They too signed a permission slip that gave me the right to publish any information they provided, but I would have been violating their rights if I used private information in that way.

Using the life history format is a legitimate and important method for gathering information. But reporting individual life histories of people without their approval is not. In the aforementioned example, the researcher could have made general statements about the stages in the lives of these women had the events of their lives formed a pattern helpful in the data analysis. If their life experiences did not present material directly relevant to the focus of the study, and merely reflected idiosyncratic life events, their personal histories might have been legitimate material for the popular press, but not for an anthropological interpretation.

Strategies for reporting life histories without violating the rights of the individuals studied are available. One strategy is to provide personal information only about individuals who have also given the researcher permission to divulge their names and the location of their residences.[3] This practice both ensures that researchers report only information that the subject knows could be made public and enables other researchers to check the accuracy of such information by talking to the informant. In addition, from the Native American perspective, it gives recognition to the individual who provides the information.[4] The most important guarantee of ethical reporting is allowing the subjects to read the study, then eliminating any information they do not want revealed.

Accounts of Personal Interactions with Informants

I also find objectionable revealing personal experiences with an informant without the informant's approval. Research goals can be attained in tribal communities only if these communities welcome anthropologists and cooperate in the collection of data. In remote areas such cooperation often includes providing housing and food. Moreover, unless the community has requested a certain study, anthropologists are generally accepted on personal grounds rather than solely on the merits of their research projects. In other words, anthropologists gain entry into the community by forging a human contract known as *friendship* with the hosts. In my view, reporting and analyzing the behavior of such "friends" with a cold, clinical eye in the guise of "science" is as much a betrayal as it would be to do that to friends in one's own community. The underlying assumption of such friendships, a signed permission slip notwithstanding, is that the researcher will not reveal any information that would be harmful if it were made public.[5] Such revelations are particularly objectionable because these are often considered reports of the anthropologist's "own" experiences; thus, it may be argued, permission slips signed by the informants are not required.

In a book of case studies entitled *Ethical Dilemmas in Anthropological Inquiry: A Case Book*, Jean Briggs reports on her deliberations about writing a personal account of her life in a small Eskimo camp during the two years she lived there. "My aim was to describe the ways in which the Eskimo people handle people who 'misbehave.' Thus, a good deal of 'bad' behavior—from the Eskimo point of view—is described in the book. Worse, since the book is written in a narrative, anecdotal style, the *dramatis personae* can be identified" (Briggs. 1978:202).

Briggs recognized that she might be violating the trust the community placed in her. She posed the ethical dilemma this way:

> The problem is, of course, to reconcile two mutually conflicting obligations. On the one hand, I feel a responsibility to contribute to scientific knowledge and to report honestly to the scholarly community the results of my research. On the other hand, I feel that I am equally responsible to the Eskimo, who

have welcomed and nurtured me during my visits and that, in return for their hospitality, I ought to avoid making statements that they might find embarrassing or that would create tension in their interpersonal relationships. (Briggs 1978:202)

Her decision to go ahead with the personal account that resulted in the book *Never in Anger* (Briggs 1970) was made in consultation with an Eskimo couple, missionaries living in another village, who served the group she studied and assisted her in gaining entry into the subject village. This couple assured her that such a book would contribute to dispelling the stereotype of the Eskimos as "Stone Age men" and "happy children." Moreover, even though some members of the community might not like it at first, as their culture changed they would be happy to have an account of their traditional ways.

I find this reasoning tenuous at best. If one really wanted to know and abide by the sentiments of the people studied, one would consult the people themselves, not missionaries, even if they were Eskimos. The people she studied, unlike the missionaries, had never been outside their territory and were probably unaware and unconcerned about any misconceptions others might have about their life. The important point Briggs misses here is that the interactions she made public were of a private nature, and in any cultural context that disclosure requires the consent of the individuals involved.

Some might argue that since these experiences were Briggs's, she had a right to reveal them. The ghost of truth in that argument ignores the fact that social research does not take place in a vacuum: Had it not been for the hospitality and cooperation of her hosts, Briggs would not have had access to the community or the experiences in the first place. The interactions she reported were as much the villagers' as they were hers. Ethical sensitivity demands that both villagers and Briggs agree to their being reported.

It is a credit to Briggs that she recognized her obligation to the Eskimo community. But her acceptance of a rationale that justified publication of this material because it would "ultimately benefit the Eskimos," even though they might not approve, is merely a specific manifestation of a generic and long-standing Eurocentric conviction that Western (white) civilization knows better than the savages what is good for them.

The most troubling part of this reasoning is that Briggs could assign equal weight to her obligation to "science" and to her debt to the people who had be-friended her — when other options existed that did not pose such an ethical dilemma. The analysis of Eskimo behavior could have been accomplished by generalizing about the behavior that Eskimos seem to find "good" and "bad," without jeopardizing the anonymity of her informants.

The real advantage of the personal account is that it is often more vivid, memorable, and readable, not that it is necessarily better science. Reporting specific detail is necessary in the physical sciences so observation and experi-mentation can be replicated. In anthropological fieldwork, however, replica-tion of human interactions is neither possible nor desirable. An ethnographic study has a totally different mission. Capturing the meaning or utility of human behavior in an ethnographic context relies on a global, holistic comprehension and interpretation drawn from one's knowledge of the culture. Providing and explaining examples of interactions are necessary, but they need not be tied to specifics by which the participants can be easily identified. An analysis that Briggs could have used just as effectively in describing the nature of Eskimo personal interactions can be found in Keith Basso's study of the use of silence among the Western Apaches (Basso 1970). He described situations in which si-lence is a mechanism employed to avoid potential conflict or misunderstand-ing. Basso discussed, for example, people meeting one another after a long sep-aration, couples getting to know each other during the first stages of courtship, and people associating with those who are mourning. Basso demonstrated how a researcher can provide a context in which behavior takes place without re-vealing specifics of the personal interactions. Thus, he met the needs of science without compromising the privacy of his informants.

Similarly, if the behavior revealed in Briggs's interactions with her hosts truly reflected what was considered "good" or "bad" behavior in that culture, it could have been substantiated by additional observations that confirmed her percep-tion of their cultural norms. There was no need to report personal behavior in a manner that risked identification of the participants by others in the community.

Kinship Studies

I also think kinship studies today should be avoided because they carry too much potential for embarrassing native people. I am referring primarily to those studies that diagram kinship relationships in which the identity of parents may be revealed, particularly when parents were not married or were of another tribe or race. I have been appalled to hear anthropologists, who would carefully avoid gossiping about their colleagues or neighbors, give me unsolicited information about the illegitimate parentage of Indian people in populations they have studied. Unless kinship relationships are important in the study of specific aspects of Native American culture, such as an understanding of ceremonial life, or how positions of status and authority are acquired, it is unnecessary to diagram them for contemporary communities. Knowing the precise nature of the kinship network is not as important to an understanding of social and political life as it was in the past. In most contemporary Native American communities it is enough to know that certain people are related; it is usually not necessary to discuss the precise nature of their relationships.

When the potential for abuses of the principles protecting research subjects is great, as is the case with life histories, accounts of personal experiences, and kinship studies, such studies of contemporary Native Americans should be discouraged. Although these strategies may have been ethical for studies of, for example, pre–World War II, nonliterate tribal peoples, today they transgress the ethical concern for the anonymity of the individuals studied.

The Need for Self-Awareness Training in Fieldwork

It seems that the anthropologists mentioned in the foregoing examples have accepted — subconsciously perhaps — attitudes that justify frivolous treatment of the human associations they make in the field. These attitudes lead them to weigh lightly their informants' interests. Through years of association with my colleagues, I am convinced that most anthropologists cannot escape the biases of their own culture. At a primary level they feel superior to the peoples they study, and it is this pervasive influence that allows them to betray friendships and to jeopardize research subjects under cover of the rationale that their "science" is paramount. I do not say this in reproach, because the tendency is probably only human. I think one could even argue that an individual who is not basically ethnocentric is unsure of his or her own identity. But anthropologists are supposed to be scientists engaged in seeking truth. If anthropologists are to be true to "science," they must recognize their attitudes on a conscious level, where they can at least try to prevent their biases from influencing their work.

Before I became an anthropologist I was a social worker. I received my degree in an era when social work training, still heavily influenced by Freudian theory, focused on intensely supervised fieldwork. We were required to write "process" interviews, in which we recapitulated everything we and our clients said. A supervisor reviewed and discussed these reports with us. Our objective was to ferret out and consider those of our behaviors that were responses to our own needs rather than those of our clients. Contemporary anthropologists would, I believe, benefit from similar training in self-awareness before they are allowed to go into the field.[6]

The following examples of contacts I have had with anthropologists indicate the need for such training. One colleague told me that he thought it would have been possible for him to have become a dancer in an Indian secret society and "learn all of their secrets." Another colleague, observing a winter dance, grew excited when it became apparent that the most sacred object associated with this ceremony was going to be used. He told me that although he had seen many of these dances, he had never observed this ritual before. He said that his hands were actually sweating in anticipation. I am not claiming that these anthropologists' interests in studying Native Americans were primarily voyeuristic, but I do believe that they were alarmingly unaware of those aspects of their studies that were motivated more by their own personal psychology than by their expressed scientific goals. At the very least, it was clear that they did not have the slightest understanding of what kind of impression they made on me.

According to one of the sacred tenets of anthropology, the outsider can be more objective than the insider in studying culture. It has been implied, to me and to other Indian anthropologists I know, that somehow our studies are not as valuable, or that we have not completed the full training track because we study only people from our own ethnic group. It is true that it might be difficult for Native Americans who study their own communities to be objective, but they would certainly be no more hampered than are the anthropologists previously mentioned. At least the curiosity Native Americans bring to such studies is not as likely to be mired in their own psychological symbolism — the search for the primitive Other. Indian anthropologists are also more apt to be sensitive to what Indian people really think about them and their work, and thus to be less brash in their pursuit of information.

Up to this point, I have provided examples of anthropologists whom I respect, and who I think have contributed a great deal to the field, in spite of an apparent lack of awareness of their own motivations and ethnocentrism. However, to illustrate how ethnocentrism leads to poor anthropology, I offer the following, admittedly worst-case, example from a study in which the researchers' insensitivity is beyond redemption. The following is from "Psychological States and Acculturation" (Boyer et al. 1989:461):

> Although they had anticipated their observation period positively, and have enjoyed working with Athapaskan Indians for some thirty years, both of the Boyers were struck with a feeling of uneasiness, a sense of something malevolent in the village. This began when the fieldworkers who were expected by the Upper Tanana, were stranded for hours without being transported across the river. They were in full view by the community. Travel by boat was the only means of access to the village. Although this occurrence was initially noted as "interesting," nothing more was made of the inconvenience. However, throughout their stay there was an undercurrent of hostility, not openly directed at the fieldworkers but, rather, an "aura," which pervaded the entire atmosphere: drunken male against drunken male; male versus female; mother antagonistic against teenage daughter. In the presence even of latency-age girls, Ruth Boyer, who never felt fear when working among Apaches of New Mexico, who are world-renowned for their cruelty to Anglos and Mexicans, experienced a constant but vaguely focused apprehension, an expectation of evil, perhaps only of thievery, perhaps of minor torment. She was happy to terminate observations. L. Bryce Boyer was even acutely fearful in the presence of some sober men in their 20s and 30s.[7]

Did these anthropologists really think they could do objective, unbiased research on personality in a place where they were obviously not wanted? If you informed people that you were to be visiting and they left you standing on their doorstep for several hours before they opened the door, it seems to me that you would take the hint and leave. If you persisted and gained entry, how could you separate the level of your hosts' latent anger from their reaction to the stress of having to deal with such an obtuse intruder, one, moreover, who persisted in involving them in activities which for them were unlikely to have meaning or utility? The fact that the Upper Tanana eventually capitulated and ferried the researchers across the river to their village, and even tolerated a somewhat invasive study, speaks for a high level of politeness, a strong feeling of social obligation, unusual patience, and a generosity of spirit. If the Upper Tanana really had the potentially explosive nature the Boyers' assessment implies, it is surprising that the Boyers are still with us. Few Indians today would suffer this kind of hit-and-run anthropology.

It is also most instructive that the scholarly journal *Ethos* published this article in 1989. This ethnographic study of acculturation uses Rorschach testing of the type that flourished in the 1950s and 1960s. If editors give publication preference to a study such as this, which breaks no new ground either methodologically or theoretically, while brimming with offensive, unscientific, generalized, intuitive characterizations of the Indians that were studied, perhaps anthropology has not moved as far as I thought it had in genuinely recognizing the integrity and rights of the people studied.

The Native American Community and Research Today
Abundant research possibilities still exist for anthropologists, but many Indians do not want to be bothered with studies that have no potential for benefiting their community in some substantial way. I was allowed to do education studies on a reservation because of the potential such research has for use in planning for the future. My hosts would have been far less receptive had I focused on more sensitive areas such as religion or personal aspects of life that concern drug and alcohol abuse or family interaction, even though a great deal of information on these topics was forthcoming from individual members of the community. The Indians in this community made it clear they want to control both the type and the amount of research that is done on their reservation. Increasingly, Native Americans everywhere will require that anthropological research in their communities serve humanity, as it should have all along, and will no longer allow humanity to serve science, as it often has in the past.

Acknowledgments
I am grateful to Tsianina Lomawaima and Gary Witherspoon for their thoughtful comments on this paper. I am indebted to David Spain for his detailed critique, which was immensely helpful in the development of my ideas.

Notes

1. While the designation "informant" does not adequately reflect the nature and extent of the contribution of native people in ethnographic studies, and also may bring to mind the idea of surreptitiously divulged information, I use it in this chapter in the absence of a more appropriate descriptive term. I considered both "interviewee" and "consultant," terms without the potential for negative association, but the former lacks any connotation of interpretive contribution and the latter implies too much. Within the confines of anthropology, the term "informant" historically has been used to indicate an individual who gives information, a depiction that seems more on the mark for the purposes of this chapter than the other two terms.

2. I am aware of the irony that in this paper I criticize anthropologists for reporting personal interactions with their research subjects, while using such examples from my own experience with anthropologists to develop my points. However, there is a difference. I did not gain the information through the hospitality of the anthropologists cited: they neither nourished nor housed me. My examples are taken from professional contexts or published accounts and did not result from interactions that they or I viewed as primarily social. Anthropologists should be held accountable for their comments and actions in their professional capacity. I have referred to all of the anthropologists mentioned in the example as "he," regardless of gender, in order to protect individuals from being identified.

3. Gary Witherspoon recommends this strategy. He never provides information about sources without giving names and where they can be located.

4. For a discussion of the native view on the tendency of anthropologists to let informants go unnamed, see Lomawaima 1989.

5. A good case could be made for maintaining that Indian cultures do not prepare individuals for understanding the concept of "objectivity," particularly in interpersonal contexts. Indians are likely to apply the friendship model, with all of its expectations, to anyone with whom they interact socially.

6. For a discussion of issues that would be appropriate in such training, see Paul 1953.

7. The use of the third person here by the Boyers is interesting in that it has the effect of making their highly speculative interpretations appear to be objective.

References

Basso, Keith. 1970. *The Cibecue Apache*. New York: Holt, Rinehart, and Winston.

Boyer, L. Bryce, C. W. Dithrich, H. Harned, A. E. Hippler, J. S. Stone, and A. Walt. 1989. "The Relation between Psychological States and Acculturation among the Tanaina and Upper Tanana Indians of Alaska: An Ethnographic and Rorschach Study." *Ethos* 17(4):450–79.

Briggs, Jean. 1970. *Never in Anger*. Cambridge, Mass.: Harvard University Press.

———. 1978. "A Problem of Publishing on Identifiable Communities and Personalities." In G. N. Appell, ed., *Ethical Dilemmas in Anthropological Inquiry: A Case Book*, pp. 202–4. Waltham, Mass.: Crossroads Press.

Lomawaima, Hartman N. 1989. "Commentary." In Lowell John Bean, ed., *Seasons of the Kachina*, pp. 165–71. Hayward, Calif.: Ballena Press.

Paul, Benjamin D. 1953. "Interview Techniques and Field Relationships." In A. L. Kroeber, ed., *Anthropology Today*, pp. 430–51. Chicago: University of Chicago Press.

8

The Anthropological Construction of "Indians"
Haviland Scudder Mekeel and
the Search for the Primitive in Lakota Country

THOMAS BIOLSI

> Can we divide human reality, as indeed human reality seems to be divided, into
> clearly different cultures, histories, traditions, societies, even races, and survive
> the consequences humanly?
> Said, *Orientalism*

Anthropologist Haviland Scudder Mekeel died suddenly of a heart attack in
1947 at the age of forty-five. His name is known in American Indian Studies for
his Yale dissertation on the Oglala Lakota of the Pine Ridge Reservation and a
handful of published articles on the history and contemporary (1930s) organization of Lakota people. In addition to his "pure" scholarship, Mekeel was eu-
logized by his colleagues at the time of his death for his "intellectual and emotional concern for the underprivileged" (Macgregor 1948:97). His obituary in
the *American Anthropologist* described his death as having "taken from this
country a man devoted to the causes of understanding the social and psychological problems of minority groups and of furthering their rights to participate
fully in a democratic nation" (Macgregor 1948:95). Mekeel had served as director of the Applied Anthropology Unit of the Office of Indian Affairs (OIA)
under Commissioner John Collier during the period 1935 to 1937. From that
position he sought to use the insights of anthropology to help implement the
new, reform federal Indian policy known as the Indian New Deal.[1] In 1945,
while a faculty member at the University of Wisconsin—Madison, Mekeel
published an article in the *Wisconsin State Journal*, a Madison newspaper, en-

titled "What to Do about Race Prejudice," in which he described racism as "an outlet to anxiety and hostility" and called for a world where "there would be no room for prejudice" (Mekeel 1945).

Given Mekeel's humane concerns for "the underprivileged," "minority groups," and ending racism, there is a surprising contrast in a passage from his ethnographic field notes. In the summer of 1930 he and his wife traveled by car from Yale University to the White Clay District on the Pine Ridge Reservation in South Dakota so Mekeel could begin collecting data for his dissertation. Shortly after establishing camp in Oglala, South Dakota, Mekeel made this entry:

> *Appear to be three main classes of Indians:*
>   1. Christian and trying to be acculturated.
>   2. Pagan and living as near as possible in old way, and perhaps succeeding *spiritually* to some extent.
>   3. *The in-betweens* — loafers, criminals, delinquents.
> The first two classes are fine individuals — the third (by far the majority) are all bums. (Mekeel 1930:9)

It is not a simple matter for a reader to reconcile a career dedicated to the welfare of the disempowered and the struggle against racism on the one hand, with the characterization of most Oglala people as loafers, criminals, delinquents, and bums, on the other. One could attribute the apparent racism and ill will in the field notes to the private and idiosyncratic thoughts of a complex individual: his field notes could be read as a diary in the strict sense of the term, certainly not the only time *that* kind of complexity has existed in an anthropologist. One can imagine that Mekeel might have felt comfortable entering into his field notebook personal thoughts that he would not incorporate into publications and that might indeed contradict his public, stage-managed, professional image. In other words, the contrast may be interpreted as an indication of the contradiction and ambivalence inherent in this individual's self.

One might also interpret the contrast as a function of intellectual growth. Mekeel labeled the passage quoted above "thoughts," as if to signal to himself and potential readers[2] that this classification of the Oglala was a preliminary and impressionistic mapping of the cultural landscape, one he was prepared to revise later as he learned more. One could easily interpret the 1930 characterization of Oglala people as a naive preliminary sketch by a young (twenty-eight-year-old) fieldworker from a privileged background, fresh from graduate course work at Yale, encountering Indian people for the first time in the midst of the Great Depression and drought on the Great Plains — experiencing what is colloquially called "culture shock." No anthropologist would be surprised that Mekeel's "thoughts" would change radically as he persisted in the field and as he became a more mature scholar. Few anthropologists would be puzzled that an anthropologist who apparently disliked most Indian people he met initially could later come to dedicate his career to correcting injustices visited upon Indian people and other disempowered peoples.

A third interpretation is also possible — the one I will be pursuing in this chapter. This interpretation seeks the significance of the contrast not in terms of Mekeel's individual personality or intellectual biography, but in terms of the contradictions inherent in the intellectual apparatus with which he went into the field. Mekeel was in all likelihood not unlike many others of his generation who studied Native Americans, and what should interest us, six decades later, is not how narrow-minded, Janus-faced, or complex he might have been as an individual, but how his intellectual vision was systematically *disciplined* by anthropology and by the wider intellectual climate of the period. Mekeel's negative characterization of the majority of the Oglala people was neither the private and idiosyncratic thought of an otherwise humane scholar, nor the naive impression of a novice fieldworker who eventually matured, but rather the direct intellectual effect of his search for the primitive.

The primitive is a concept generated out of the social and cultural dynamics of state-level societies and modernity. Stateless peoples certainly are real enough, but primitivity would have been invented by intellectuals in state societies even if primitives did not exist. The self-identity or subjectivity of people in state societies — or, for the purposes of this chapter about the 1930s, modern subjectivity — requires a concept of the primitive both to bound and to give content to the concept of the civilized. Primitivity is, by definition, diametrically opposite to modernity: the primitive may represent for modernity, negatively, the depths from which we have advanced and back to which we are in danger of regressing without continued vigilance, or, positively, the world we have lost that represents human possibilities undamaged by the oppressive disciplines of modernity. Hence the negative (heathen) and romantic (noble savage) representations of Native Americans that are a fundamental part of American culture and, more broadly, Western civilization. (On the social construction of the primitive Other in America and in general, see Appadurai 1988; Berkhofer 1979; Diamond 1974; Dippie 1982; Dorris 1987; Fabian 1983; Geertz 1988:chap. 5; hooks 1992:chap. 12; Jennings 1976:chap. 5; Kehoe 1985, 1990; Nabakov 1987; Pearce 1988; Rogin 1987; Simard 1990; Spurr 1993; Takaki 1982; Thomas 1994; Trouillot 1991; Wald 1993).[3]

Anthropology as a discipline has not been able to escape this conceptualization of the primitive, which is deeply embedded in the way Western civilization in general, and American civilization in particular, constitutes itself. In fact, the Western, modernist concept of the primitive is what makes anthropology intellectually possible. Anthropology did not invent the primitive; it has merely organized the concept and specialized in the scientific study of its cases (Trouillot 1991). One way that the field has organized the study of the primitive is through the conceptual apparatus of cultural relativism. The particular variant of cultural relativism that informed Mekeel's fieldwork in Lakota country in the 1930s was the "integrationist" relativism (Fox 1991:106) of Margaret Mead, Ruth Benedict, and Edward Sapir. In this view, a culture is an integrated, coherent whole, which is greater than the various shreds and patches that make up its parts. Furthermore, the world is filled with an array of distinct cultures, with discrete boundaries, not unlike species.[4]

This conceptual apparatus had the properties of a paradigm (Kuhn 1961) or a discursive formation (Foucault 1972) in that it undergirded an ethnographic worldview and determined what anthropologists saw on Indian reservations — what came to the foreground, what fell to the back, what was anthropological data, and what was annoying (even embarrassing) nondata or noise for anthropology. The conceptual apparatus constituted — made — the "facts" that were "found" in the field (see Nugent 1982:524–26). The cultural relativist apparatus generated a severe classificatory problem for Mekeel in which most Oglala people and most of what they thought and did in the real world of the reservation could not appear as authentically Indian. They were — by anthropological definition — not "proper natives" (Appadurai 1988:37; Thomas 1994:chap. 6). This is not to say that cultural relativism was the only conceptual framework that could cause an ethnographer or other western traveler to be disappointed in not finding the authentic primitive. Certainly modern Westerners of all kinds have commonly found real natives disappointing. Paul Gauguin came to find the Tahitians degraded primitives (Newberry 1980:233–34), and the equally romantic Mircea Eliade disliked and condemned the Eurasians he met in India (Buruma 1994). But the relativist apparatus has had a particularly strong influence in this regard for both anthropologists and Native Americans in its strong premising of autonomous, discrete, and internally integrated primitive cultures.

The Most Full-blood and Backward Place in South Dakota

The effects of the particular relativist worldview with which Mekeel worked can be seen in his choice of a field site as described in the field notes. Mekeel began his notes as he drove west from Minneapolis. The first concentration of Indian people he encountered was at Pipestone Indian School in Minnesota. Apparently he found little of interest at Pipestone, but the OIA physician told him that more "blanket Indians [lived] to the West" (Mekeel 1930:1).[5] Mekeel also stopped at the OIA's Flandreau Agency in eastern South Dakota, but he pushed on west to the Yankton Reservation. At Yankton Mekeel noted: "Indians here quite civilized in appearance. Made no contacts this day as I want to approach them slowly. Much curiosity among them as to my intents and purposes. A young buck with much beadwork on him called with an old man. They were out for work as interpreter and informant." Apparently Mekeel was not interested because he told them that he and Mrs. Mekeel were "just visiting" (Mekeel 1930:4). Mekeel also met a mixed-blood Santee man at Yankton who was "proud of [his] white blood, and mentioned several of his relatives that looked white" (Mekeel 1930:5). An OIA field employee on the Yankton Reservation confirmed what the OIA physician had told him at Pipestone: Yankton, Rosebud, and Pine Ridge Reservations "gave in order a perfect picture of degrees of assimilation of culture," with Pine Ridge, the most western, being the least assimilated (Mekeel 1930:6).[6]

Shortly thereafter, Mekeel drove west on U.S. Highway 18 — as Vine Deloria, Jr., has noted, the perennial summer route of anthropologists on the trail of Indians in South Dakota (Deloria 1969:83). He passed through the Rosebud

Reservation and eventually through Wanblee, South Dakota, a town in 1930 of white settlers on the Pine Ridge Reservation with Indian camps on the out-skirts. Mekeel noted of the Indians in Wanblee: "These, for the most part, seemed to be riff-raff—about the same type one sees among whites hanging around street corners" (Mekeel 1930:7).

Mekeel eventually entered the White Clay District of the Pine Ridge Reservation, the western-most part of the reservation. He was "much struck by difference in Indians. Many more 'longhairs' and quantities of *horses*[7] and teams. A thick settlement along White Clay Creek. Learned that this is the biggest group of full bloods." He set up camp in the little community of Oglala and commenced fieldwork (Mekeel 1930:8). Eventually Mekeel conducted a household survey, engaged in participant observation at powwows, a sun dance, rodeos, and tourist fairs, and interviewed elderly informants on band organization, religion, and other subjects of ethnographic import.

Mekeel was convinced that the Oglala area of the White Clay District was the right place for an anthropologist to be in Lakota country. In his first publication, an article in the *American Anthropologist* in 1932, he described his subjects: "This group of about nine hundred and fifty people, most of them descendants of the hostiles under Red Cloud, occupies White Clay district of Pine Ridge reservation, a district which has earned for itself the epithets 'full blood' and 'backward'" (Mekeel 1932a:275; see also Mekeel 1932b). In a 1936 article he stated that the White Clay District was "considered to be the most backward and to have the least admixture of white blood on the reservation" (Mekeel 1936:5).

What was it that Mekeel believed he had discovered in the White Clay District? The answer is clear enough in a letter to his wife in 1931 recalling an elderly Oglala, Kills Close to Lodge, they had both met in 1930: "You remember the tall, beautiful-bodied, 'long-hair' whom age has not yet bent. In shaking his firm hand and looking into his friendly face, I felt him a man—yet one who is on the other side of a chasm from me—both in race and culture—and alien. However, I felt his dignity and value" (Mekeel 1931:1). To Mekeel Indian people in White Clay represented the alien primitive Other, separated from him by a chasm of race and culture. Other Lakotas might be "Christian and trying to be acculturated," or "loafers," "criminals," "delinquents," "bums," or "riff-raff" (anthropological nondata and not even *Indian*), but in White Clay, one could find real, anthropologically significant, authentic Indians like Kills Close to Lodge.

Incommensurable White Clay

It was the relativist premise that cultures are discrete, bounded, autonomous, and (normally) internally integrated wholes—billiard balls on a global pool table in Eric Wolf's (critical) imagery (Wolf 1982:6)—that made Mekeel drive all the way across South Dakota to find a field site. Edward Sapir—Mekeel's professor at Yale and earlier at the University of Chicago (where Mekeel received his master's degree in 1929)—clearly had this relativist premise in mind when he wrote "Culture, Genuine and Spurious" (Sapir 1924). Written as a romanticist critique of American culture, the article also helped define the relativist concept of culture—and the relativist concept of the primitive—of the 1920s and 1930s (Stocking 1989:215–17). A genuine culture (and not all cultures are genuine) in Sapir's view is "inherently harmonious, balanced, self-satisfactory" (Sapir 1924:410), and the particular harmony and balance inevitably differs from culture to culture.

Ruth Benedict later elaborated on this early formulation of the relativist culture concept. The year Mekeel defended his dissertation, Benedict published "Configurations of Culture in North America" (Benedict 1932). In this paper, which George Stocking described as having had "major theoretical impact" on the culture concept (Stocking 1976:16), Benedict cited approvingly the hermeneutician Wilhelm Dilthey and wrote of "fundamental and distinctive configurations in [different cultures] that so pattern existence and condition the emotional and cognitive reactions of its carriers that they become incommensurables, each specializing in certain selected types of behavior and each ruling out the behavior proper to its opposites" (Benedict 1932:4). In *Patterns of Culture* Benedict further sketched out "configurational anthropology" (Benedict 1934:233), insisting that the Zuni, Dobu, and Kwakiutl contrasted on the basis of different culture traits but "still more because they are oriented as wholes in different directions" (Benedict 1934:223; see Hatch 1973:76–90). As Clifford Geertz summarized Benedict's imagining of cultural communities, "the Plains Indians are ecstatic, the Zuni are ceremonious, and the Japanese are hierarchal" (Geertz 1988:111; see also Mintz 1985:49–50). *Patterns of Culture* "seemed to carry the doctrine of relativity to its logical conclusion in the ultimate incommensurability of each human mode of life" (Stocking 1976:33).

Mekeel went into the field with precisely this relativist assumption of the discrete separation of incongruous cultural wholes. As he drove west from New Haven in 1930, Mekeel was looking for an Indian culture *incommensurably* alien from his — or at least noteworthy survivals of such a culture. This explains why Mekeel was so intent on finding "blanket Indians," why he was uninterested in "civilized" Indians and the mixed-blood proud of his white ancestry at the Yankton Reservation and the "riff-raff" in Wanblee, and why he was so attracted to Kills Close to Lodge and other full-blood "long-hairs" who rode around White Clay on horses instead of in automobiles. In Mekeel's vision, Kills Close to Lodge and others like him were authentic Indians because this small minority represented the incommensurably alien, authentically primitive, Lakota culture.[8]

Confronting the "In-Betweens"

Of course, this radical relativist apparatus could not but meet with problems in the ethnographic encounter, and Mekeel shored up the apparatus against the flood of messy real-world phenomena inconsistent with it. During his 1931 season in the field, he attended a mixed Indian-white dance. Some Lakota women at the dance wore beaded hide dresses and leggings, but most of the dancing was "non-Indian," couples-style. The orchestra was composed of mixed-bloods, and Fox Movietone News made a record of the evening. The whole situation of social and cultural interpenetration apparently disoriented Mekeel, who wrote to his wife: "I danced with Indian girls all evening. . . . I struck one . . . who could dance anything — a really graceful dancer. I have never had such a funny sensation in my life, holding in my arms a girl of a distinctly alien race and culture, dressed in buckskin and beads — yet dancing modern steps to modern music" (Mekeel 1931:26–27).

One might think that an experience like this would have caused Mekeel to reconsider his paradigm of two worlds separated by a chasm of race and culture.[9] Surely many situations existed on the reservation in which Lakota and white "cultures" — to the extent that they were distinguishable cultures — were

interwoven, perhaps even to the extent of its being less than logical to talk about
Lakota and white "cultures" as truly autonomous "configurations." Mekeel,
however, was able to preserve his "two-system model" (Moore 1986:281). He
managed to protect this paradigm by explaining away his worldly dancing part-
ner dressed in beaded buckskin (and, incidentally, wearing pumps despite
beaded leggings) as *not* a White Clay full-blood:

> She is mixed-blood, of course. . . . She comes from around Martin [on the
> eastern side of the reservation]. That is another thing I noticed — the Pine
> Ridge [a town east of the White Clay District] and Martin girls danced the
> best — been with white people more. The Oglala girls [from the White Clay
> District] I asked said they didn't dance white man's way. . . .
>
> One thing I was quite impressed with was the difference between dis-
> tricts. Dancing showed it up among the girls — drunkenness among the
> boys. I never saw as many drunks [in White Clay], and most of them were
> from other districts — especially Martin and Pine Ridge. Our Oglala district
> is less sophisticated and unspoiled — less troublesome — *has less whites* than
> any other district. (Mekeel 1931:26–27)

In short, Indian people who did not act "Indian" enough to fit Mekeel's relativist image of "Indians" could always be rejected as mixed-bloods or as people
from reservation districts tainted by white contact — less authentic Indians.

This intellectual mechanism not only had the effect of preserving the two-
system, billiard-ball view of cultures inherent in the relativist vision, it also had
the effect of consigning most Lakota people to a stigmatized liminal status in
Mekeel's thinking. The "in-betweens" were not just in between the two cultures, or just uninteresting scientifically. They were the "loafers, criminals,
delinquents," "bums," "riff-raff," and "drunks." For Mekeel, "Indians" by definition were *incarcerated* (Appadurai 1988) within an incommensurable, integrated, bounded culture. Any Lakota individual who acted outside that culture
was, axiomatically, inauthentic. Mekeel was hardly unique in definitionally
writing off native people who did not act "Indian" as less than Indian. Sapir
wrote in "Culture, Genuine and Spurious" (1924:414):

> When the political integrity of his tribe is destroyed by contact with the
> whites and the old cultural values cease to have the atmosphere needed for

their continued vitality, the Indian finds himself in a state of bewildered vacuity. Even if he succeeds in making a fairly satisfactory compromise with his new environment, in making what his well-wishers consider great progress toward enlightenment, he is apt to retain an uneasy sense of the loss of some vague and great good, some state of mind that he would be hard put to it to define, but which gave him a courage and joy that latter-day prosperity never quite seems to have regained for him. What has happened is that he has slipped out of the warm embrace of a culture into the cold air of fragmentary existence. What is sad about the passing of the Indian is not the depletion of his life on the reservation, it is the fading away of genuine cultures, built though they were out of the materials of a low order of sophistication.[10]

Clark Wissler, another of Mekeel's professors at Yale, wrote in 1929: "[O]n every hand, culture contact between a primitive group and a white presents a maze of conflict that cross-sections the life of the former" (Wissler 1960 [1929]:598). This is because of the inconsistency in the "close knit series of response patterns" (p. 597) between the two cultures. "Not only does the group break down in its functioning, but individuals fail" (p. 599). Benedict pointed out in *Patterns of Culture* that one could expect a culture on the border of culture areas—between two cultures—to be a "hodge-podge," "unco-ordinated" (Benedict 1934:224) or "disoriented" (p. 226). Margaret Mead, in *The Changing Culture of an Indian Tribe*, described the Omahas as plagued by "cultural breakdown" (Mead 1969 [1932]:219) resulting from contact, and she focused on sexual delinquency, particularly the increase in the number of "loose women" (p. 202).[11]

Of course, it would have been just as empirically correct to have characterized the "in-betweens"—recall that they were the majority of Lakota people Mekeel met—in admiring terms, as "bicultural" (Polgar 1960), as "150%" people (McFee 1968), as (actual or potential) creative syncretizers (Hoxie 1992; Wallace 1969), as *crossblood* cultural negotiators (Pasquaretta 1994; Vizenor 1990) in short, not as people "diminished," but as people whose "mazeways [had] become more complicated" (Clifton 1989:29) as they lived in and struggled against colonialism. Alternatively, Mekeel might have interpreted the "hodge-podge" of culture he was observing not as some kind of anomic interstice between genuine cultures, but rather as a local point in a larger "social field" (Lesser 1961) that *encompasses* reservation culture, or as we might now say, a "manifold" (Wolf 1982; see also Gupta and Ferguson 1992 and Mintz 1985) or an "ethnoscape" (Appadurai 1991). It is not enough to say that Mekeel worked before such ideas existed, because fragments of such ideas — even if not developed in their modern forms — were in circulation in the 1930s. In *The Pawnee Ghost Dance Hand Game*, for example, Alexander Lesser focused on the study of what he called assimilation, the process of "transforming aspects of a conquered or engulfed culture into a status of relative adjustment to the forms of the ruling culture." In Lesser's vision, and those of some other anthropologists of the 1930s, Native Americans and the colonizers were both integrated into the *same system*, a view that emphasized the inescapable connection of the local to a larger — even global — social and cultural order (Lesser 1933:ix; see Vincent 1988, 1990:chap. 3 on the availability of such — admittedly marginalized — ideas in the 1930s). Rather than following from a lack of alternative concepts, Mekeel's conceptualization of "in-betweens" was a positive effect — in the sense of a paradigm or discursive formation positively *producing* appearances and silences — of the relativist apparatus. The relativist concept of cultures as integrated, discretely bounded wholes made it inevitable that (what appeared as) "mixed" cultures and bearers of mixed cultures would be deemed inauthentic.

Ultimately, of course, anthropology did not solve its classificatory problem with "in-betweens" (who became more and more common in the places anthropologists worked) by using a field concept of global political or cultural economy. Rather, the concept of acculturation entered the field. The term was in use in the 1930s; Mekeel himself used it, but it did not yet have its subsequent sense of an empirically obvious process that has describable patterns and properties beyond nostalgic moral condemnation. For Mekeel and his colleagues in the early 1930s, acculturation was a tragic loss of cultural integrity by primitive tribes. What interested the relativist on contemporary reservations was *survivals*, not contemporary changes or transformed organization.

Robert Redfield set out some basic ideas for what was to become the study of acculturation in *Tepoztlan* (1930:10) and in a 1934 article in the *American Anthropologist*, but he still conceptualized acculturation as a process of "disorganization" (1930:13) even as late as *The Folk Culture of the Yucatan* (1941).[12]

It was not until 1936 that Redfield, Ralph Linton, and Melville Herskovits published their "Memorandum for the Study of Acculturation" (Redfield, Linton, and Herskovits 1936), which established a "new paradigm path" (Vincent 1990:203; but see Thurnwald 1932 for an earlier statement of the paradigm). This new paradigm allowed anthropology "to question the never-never land of isolated primitive peoples" (Vincent 1990:198) and focus on change as the subject of analysis rather than as an exogenous factor disturbing and disintegrating normally closed and internally integrated "configurations."

The first article in the *American Anthropologist* actually to examine culture change among American Indians in this spirit was Fred Eggan's "Historical Changes in the Choctaw Kinship System" (1937). Eggan argued that changes in the Choctaw kinship system could be arranged in a series that would constitute "a *general* type of change" (Eggan 1937:51). He did not suggest that disorganization takes place; in fact, this Chicago structural-functionalist and student of Alfred Reginald Radcliffe-Brown assumed that the kinship system *was a system* at each point along the series. His approach was a far cry from seeing cultural contact and change as resulting in "bewildered vacuity," a "hodgepodge," "breakdown," or "loose women." Herskovits further set out the paradigm in his *Acculturation: The Study of Culture Contact* (1958 [1938]), and Linton continued in this direction in his chapters in *Acculturation in Seven American Indian Tribes* (Linton 1963 [1940]).[13]

While they focused on change, the authors of these classic acculturation studies retained the premise of fundamentally distinct "cultures." They innovated by assuming that cultural transmission operated upon particulate materials (traits) that in culture "contact" got recombined with materials from other cultures, producing various grades of hybridization — "levels" or "degrees" of acculturation (see, for example, McFee 1968; Spindler 1955, 1962). They allowed the "in-betweens" to become not annoying noise but arguably the most interesting object of anthropological study of reservation cultures. Before this paradigm became anything like "normal science" in American anthropology, however, the relativist apparatus had reigned and had prevented Mekeel from seeing most people and most phenomena on the reservation as authentically Indian or worthy of anthropological scrutiny because most people and most phenomena had been heavily influenced by "contact." By positing unrealistically exclusive, essentialized, ahistorical, and rigid categories ("cultures," "configurations"), which only minimally applied to what was going on in the real world, the conceptual apparatus could not help actively constructing masses of interstitial people and phenomena. As with all faulty classificatory systems that are shored up by the classifiers rather than modified to better fit the referent, the liminal phenomena were avoided, outlawed, or labeled dangerous and polluting (Douglas 1966:52–53).[14]

Treaties Are Not Traditional

The relativist apparatus not only caused Mekeel to write off people "in between" cultures, it also caused him to distort seriously the nature of political and economic life on the Pine Ridge Reservation in his scholarly writing.

If anything is incommensurably and perennially Lakota in twentieth-century reservation political culture, it is the concern with treaties. It was there in 1900, when Clark Wissler and his associates — who incidentally also ignored the treaty issue — were collecting data, and treaties are still prominent in Lakota political discourse in the 1990s. Mekeel, however, like Wissler, could not see this concern as "culture" or an observable aspect of authentic Lakota political organization; it was, instead, anthropological nondata. The treaty discourse, in Mekeel's view, was a function of the Lakotas being spoiled by contact — and worse, contact with lawyers before the anthropologist could get there. In a paper published in 1936, he described the generation of Lakota people between the ages of thirty and the late sixties: "Their stomachs started on government rations and their minds were tuned to a parasitic life which was regarded as their inalienable right by treaty" (Mekeel 1936:6).

Mekeel considered the treaty discourse, at worst, a parasitic strategy on the part of people who did not want to work for a living and, at best, the rantings of old men. In 1931 he was visited by a chief named Turning Hawk, a member of the Oglala Council or Treaty Council on the Pine Ridge Reservation, a loose organization of older men who claimed that their authority to speak for the Lakotas was based on the Fort Laramie Treaty of 1868 (see Biolsi 1992). Mekeel wrote of the encounter: "[Turning Hawk w]anted to know what I was doing and whether my work would benefit the Indians in any way — whether I was doing good work. . . . He evidently had something to get off his chest. I thought the best plan would be to let him air his grievances — so I very seriously took notes. He rehearsed all the old treaties. Said they had fulfilled their part, the Government had not theirs — had never done anything for them, etc. — old stuff but with much truth to it, of course" (Mekeel 1931:24). Obviously, Mekeel was not interested enough to record the material seriously. At the time, the Oglala Treaty Council on Pine Ridge was embroiled in a conflict with the elected council officially recognized by the OIA on the reservation, the Council of Twenty-One. Treaty Council adherents cited their interpretation of the Fort Laramie Treaty of 1868 in this conflict, and Republican South Dakota Congressman William Williamson even took sides in the dispute because he believed it would help him win the Indian vote (Oglala Treaty Council 1931; Williamson 1931).

Mekeel was not interested in treaty rights, how the Lakotas interpreted their treaties, or how the issue related to reservation politics. Treaties, after all, were not Indian, and Indians who talked about them constantly were not really interesting as Indians in Mekeel's view. He was more interested in the aboriginal roles of *wakiconza* (chief) and *akicita* (soldier), which Wissler and his associates had described twenty years earlier (Price 1996:chap. 1; Walker 1982; Wissler 1912). Mekeel wanted to know if these roles, which were aboriginal and had nothing to do with the white man in his view, still survived. He found that they did, not in reservation communities, but during trips to tourist towns in the Black Hills. Groups of Lakotas, hired by Black Hills towns to attend fairs and rodeos for the benefit of tourists, organized their camps on the city fairgrounds under *wakiconza* and *akicita*. The towns, of course, wanted the Lakotas to perform as they had in the Wild West shows. Mekeel does not tell us how much the demands of the tourist trade influenced the organization of the camps, but he clearly believed that travel to these fairs and rodeos replaced the role of nomadic buffalo hunting for the Lakotas (Mekeel 1932a).[15]

In short, Indian politics *on the reservation* did not interest him because it involved treaties, a council based on treaties, an elected tribal government fostered by the OIA, and even the Republican and Democratic parties. How could all this be authentically Indian? True, reenacting chiefly and military society roles only at tourist spectacles in the Black Hills was not too authentically Indian either, but at least there was a palpable continuity with the buffalo days.

The Ancient Lakota Economy

In his search for survivals, Mekeel came to believe that Lakota values remaining from the "ancient economy" (Mekeel 1936:3) were still to be found in Lakota economic behavior. Among these values was generosity, something he theorized within his relativist paradigm to be essentially inconsistent with American culture:

> American society . . . utilizes the retention of wealth as one method of social ordination. . . . Teton Dakota society, on the other hand, has founded its cardinal values on the release of wealth. . . . Even at the present day this attitude toward wealth is one of the most outstanding characteristics of a Teton Dakota community and has proven to be one of the foremost stumbling-blocks to missionary and administrator alike. For there can be little compromise between such *diametrically opposed viewpoints* as the Teton and American on the symbolic use of wealth in the social scheme.
>
> . . . According to the existing pattern for hospitality a man, with his whole family, may visit his own or any of his wife's relatives for an indefinite period. When a man's food is low, or all gone, he may hitch up his team and take his family for a visit. Food is shared equally until none is left. The result of this actually is that no man, however industrious, can get very far ahead of those about him and still remain an active member of the community. He is literally eaten down to its level. Those with salaries, almost without exception, have, at the end of the month, grocery bills equalling, or in excess of their pay. Some give up their positions to relieve the drain, since they find themselves further behind than if they had no job. (Mekeel 1936:11; emphasis added)

Mekeel argued that the ancient Lakota values "virtually prescrib[ed] a state of socialism" (Mekeel 1936:11).

There are two problems with this image of the Lakota. First, it neglects the fact that the Lakotas Mekeel met were passionate about the protection of private property — that is, their individual land allotments on the reservation (see Biolsi 1992, 1995). They saw no conflict between the private ownership of land and the life of traditional, full-blood Lakota. In fact, some Oglala full-bloods went so far as to suggest that ownership of an allotment is what *made one*

Lakota: mixed-bloods who had been fee-patented, had their allotments taken out of trust status, "became white" according to some Oglalas (U.S. Senate 1940:21459). Clearly, something more complex than stone-age socialists resisting American capitalism was going on here, but it was lost on Mekeel.

Second, Mekeel falsely attributed Indian poverty at least partially to these supposedly primordial values. Mekeel was looking for survivals, as he was in the case of political behavior, and the implication in his analysis is clear: customs left over from the buffalo days, in particular the ideal of generosity, are at least partly responsible for Indian poverty in the present. This was long a belief of OIA officials, and probably still is.

We now realize, however, thanks to the work of Patricia Albers (1982) and Joseph Jorgensen (1971:78–79; 1972:116, 232; 1978:66–68) that such customs are not the cause of poverty but the product. Because he was wedded to the paradigm of archetypal ways of life confronting one another, however, Mekeel could classify Indian behavior and thought only as (1) survivals of authentic Lakota culture; (2) pathological behavior of "in-betweens"; or (3) acculturated behavior. Sharing certainly was not acculturated behavior; it was too inconsistent with American society in his image. It was not exactly pathological either, since Mekeel recognized that it allowed people to survive in a marginal situation. So, it must have been a survival. His paradigm did not allow for emergent behavior that was essentially neither "traditional" nor "acculturated," but that was related to a class situation: political-economic marginalization. It would be many years before anthropologists would be centrally interested in the question of how Indian people live with marginalization, and how this compares with other class positions in a global world-system.[16]

Knowledge/Power

Mekeel actively *constructed* Lakota people–and less-than-Lakota people — and their culture in his thinking, in his field notes, in his doctoral dissertation, and in his publications, all within the confines of the cultural relativist apparatus. It would be a mistake, however, to assume that Mekeel's deployment of the relativist apparatus involved the construction of Indians only in an ideological sense, in the sense of making an anthropological fiction that existed only in the minds of anthropologists. Thinking by colonizers about colonized peoples is, after all, seldom very far from power. "The Indian" was being invented and developed as a concept, for example, at the same time that Native Americans were being forcibly removed from the East to Indian Territory — a place more suitable for conceptual "Indians" (Maddox 1991; Pearce 1988; Wald 1993). Just as "ideas about the Orient drawn from Orientalism can be put to political use" (Said 1979:96), so the particular image of the Lakota shaped by the relativist paradigm was put to political use.

In 1935 Commissioner of Indian Affairs John Collier hired Mekeel to head the OIA's Applied Anthropology Unit. It is likely that Mekeel was hired at least partly because of a memo he had written to Collier in 1934 lauding the Wheeler-Howard bill (which, modified, became the Indian Reorganization Act) and emphasizing the importance of taking traditional social structure into account in organizing tribes for self-government. As part of his responsibilities, Mekeel provided technical assistance in drafting the tribal constitutions for the Pine Ridge and Rosebud Reservations under the provisions of the Indian Reorganization Act. Mekeel and the Rosebud superintendent collaborated in designing what became known as the "community plan" — the political districting of the reservations on the basis of supposedly aboriginal, supposedly stable, bands *(tiyospaye)* left over from the buffalo days. The community plan, however, met with such resistance from Lakota people — including the most traditional people, who demanded larger political districts — that it was deleted from the Pine Ridge constitution, although it was pushed through at Rosebud. For Mekeel and the superintendent, real Lakota political organization was based on the *tiyospaye*, notwithstanding what real Lakota people might say. Mekeel and the superintendent insisted that the *tiyospaye* was the only appropriate form of political organization for the Lakota, and that other units of organization — those being demanded by many Lakotas, for instance — represented inappropriate forms resulting from the effects of reservation life and the breakdown of aboriginal organization. Furthermore, the constitutions were completely devoid of any reference to the Treaty of 1868 and the Lakota interpretation of it, which was clearly an important element of Lakota political organization at the time. Bands were presumably "ancient" structures, even if they existed more in the minds of anthropologists and administrators than in the real political life of the reservations, while treaties in this Orientalist view were hardly traditionally Lakota, even if traditional Lakotas seemed to be profoundly concerned with them (Biolsi 1992).

Thus did a powerful anthropological vision of the primitive help construct, not just an idea about the Lakota, but one of the very real, very material, colonial structures through which the Lakota would be allowed to be Lakota in twentieth-century America — their official tribal governments. These Lakota governments, operating under constitutions Mekeel had some role in shaping, are in place today, and the absence of a role for treaty rights in the shaping of the tribal governments remains a problem for many Lakota people and a source of conflict between the Lakota grass roots and their tribal councils. Clearly the relativist apparatus of the 1930s, as far as the Lakotas are concerned, had "power effects"; it contributed to the colonial situation. The object of anthropological knowledge was not only thought and written about but actively *made* through the deployment in law and policy of a radically relativist image of the primitive.

Conclusion

What is the significance of Haviland Scudder Mekeel and his career for generalizing about the history of Native Americans and anthropologists in America? Certainly Mekeel was a complex individual, as are all individuals, both anthropologists and Native American consultants. He was capable both of racist views and narrow-mindedness on the one hand, and of dedicating his life's work to understanding and eradicating social injustice on the other hand. What we should read in Mekeel's career as significant for us, sixty years later, is not his individual orientations so much as how he lived out and worked in a larger intellectual framework, a framework that had, and has, direct, concrete ramifications in the lives of Indian people.

To return to the epigraph with which this chapter opened, it remains an open question as to whether or not we and the Lakotas have *humanly* survived the consequences of the anthropological division of Indians and whites into "clearly different cultures, histories, traditions, societies, even races." Whatever the consequences, anthropological cultural relativism and its intellectual construction of the primitive and of authentic and inauthentic Indians had a great deal to do with that division. Anthropology needs to come to terms with the consequences.

Acknowledgments

I would like to thank Constantine Hriskos, David Nugent, and Joel Robbins for critical readings of earlier versions of this chapter. These three friends have been long-standing influences on my thinking. Permission to quote from Mekeel's field notes was granted by the Department of Anthropology Archives, American Museum of Natural History.

Notes

1. On the Applied Anthropology Unit, see Kelly 1980, 1985; Kennard and Macgregor 1953; McNickle 1979; Taylor 1975.

2. It is not possible to know whether Mekeel considered that his field notes might eventually be read by colleagues, let alone analyzed as they are here.

3. Of course, there is a danger of overstating the unitary and historically persistent character of representations of the primitive Other and "the Indian" (Thomas 1994). I am not arguing that the representation of Indians in America is unchanged through five hundred years of history, uncontested or identical to representations of *other* primitive Others. My point here is simply that an embedded — if hardly unproblematic — Western discursive terrain preceded both Mekeel and anthropology, and that we must take notice of this terrain if we are to ask how anthropology constructs "Indians." Closely linked to the social construction of the primitive Other is the construction of the country as the opposite of the city (Williams 1975; see also Marx 1964) and the American West as the opposite of the East (Smith 1950).

4. This is not to suggest that anthropology in general or cultural relativism in particular made no difference in the way the primitive was conceptualized, that anthropology was merely old Orientalist (or primitivist) wine in a new bottle. On the contrary, the specifically anthropological discourse made it difficult to see the primitive as merely the *inversion* of the civilized, since anthropology emphasized the range of cultural difference in the world (see Berkhofer 1979; Thomas 1994). For present purposes, however, Mekeel was concerned with how the Lakotas were essentially different from non-Indians in ways that set up a *binary* relation — and this *is* an old story in the representation of "the Indian."

5. Internal evidence in the notes suggests that Mekeel may have already decided by this point to look for a field site on the Rosebud Reservation or perhaps on the Pine Ridge Reservation, west of the Missouri River (Mekeel 1930:4).

6. The linkage of presumed evolutionary relationships (between the civilized and the primitive) with *spatial* relationships (between the metropole and the hinterland) recurs in the social construction of the primitive. Not only is it obvious in Robert Redfield (1930:220–22; 1934; 1941:339–40), but in Peruvian intellectual discourse (Orlove 1993), and even in Thomas Jefferson (Takaki 1982:57).

7. Gerald Sider has noted the fascination of anthropologists with Plains Indians' horses as opposed to mules, which were critical in Plains societies, because mules "make Native Americans seem more like us" (Sider 1993:184). Interestingly, a conference on Plains Indian cultures held in 1994 was entitled "Power and Beauty: Horses on the Plains Indians."

8. At least one Lakota informant eloquently paraphrased the relativist paradigm. A

man Mekeel interviewed on the Cheyenne River Reservation told him: "The Indian is given a different generation from the white," which is to say that the Indians were created separately from the whites. The man drew two circles in the dirt and said: "Now here is one circle and here is another with the ocean between. Now in this circle the Calf Pipe was brought and the Indians lived in tipis and hunted the buffalo, and this is the difference between the Indian and the white. Now over here across the ocean God sent his son here and appointed the white man to live in a square house. Now this is the white man's way; now these two ways which should have been separate are now all mixed up" (Mekeel 1931:45). As Edward Bruner reminds us, both anthropologists and American Indians are "caught in the same web, influenced by the same historical forces, and shaped by the dominant narrative structures of our times" (Bruner 1986:149–50) (even if there remain critical differences in culture and power), so we should not be surprised that Lakota informants and American anthropologists jointly reproduce the same imagery.

9. I first encountered this kind of situation — made unexpected for me by the conflict between the anthropological premise of bounded, local "cultures," and the concrete fact of globalization of culture — when I "entered" my "field site" on the Rosebud Reservation for my dissertation research in 1985. Across the street from my house Lakota teenagers practiced break dancing. They were not only skilled at it but obviously familiar with it from satellite television (cable and VCRs are now very common in households on Rosebud). My "funny sensation" was that these teenagers — and their parents — knew more about pop music and culture, and professional sports, than I did, since I never paid much attention to these things. In the same vein, the only Tupperware party I have ever attended was in the Rosebud Tribal Office, and the only dances (rock) I have been to as an adult were on Rosebud.

10. For Sapir the problem was not so much that contemporary Indian people were betwixt and between two cultures, but that they had succumbed to the spurious culture of industrialized America. Contemporary Indians suffered from "bewildered vacuity" because they had at one time known a genuine culture, whereas whites had not and therefore had no knowledge of what they were deprived of.

11. Some of Mekeel's senior colleagues were less sanguine then he was about the possibility of finding a distinct and authentic Indian culture on Indian reservations. In *Tepoztlan* Redfield wrote that rural blacks had the only folk culture in the United States, while mountain people, lumbermen, and cowboys were quasi folk. American Indians did not even merit the label of quasi folk (Redfield 1930:4). Benedict in *Patterns of Culture* remarked that the culture of the Plains Indians "has not been functioning for some time" (Benedict 1934:238). Despite these kinds of doubts about the primitive authenticity of contemporary Indian communities in the United States, Native Americans have been preserved as an appropriate non-Western object for anthropological careers. For example, a 1994 advertisement in the *Anthropology Newsletter* for a job at a prestigious northeastern university involving participation in the university's Non-Western Studies Program pointed out: "Note that Latin America & native N America count as non-western in this prog; eastern Europe does not."

12. For Redfield, as for Sapir, the disorganization was a function less of mixing nor-

mally autonomous configurations than of non-Western cultures becoming more *like* those of the West. Both Sapir and Redfield were romanticists who saw primitives as possessing desirable cultures lost by the industrialized West (see Lewis 1951:435; Stocking 1976, 1989; Vincent 1990).

13. This new paradigm of acculturation did not prevent some relativistically inclined anthropologists from continuing to see change as essentially disintegrative. In 1955 Clyde Kluckhohn wrote that most Indians had lost their native cultures but had not yet acquired the culture of Americans: "Hence, in effect, they have for a time no culture at all" (Kluckhohn 1962 [1955]:339). "Personal and social disorganization is presently rampant among the Navajo," he asserted. "Navajo culture is becoming an ugly patchwork of meaningless and unrelated pieces, whereas it was once a finely patterned mosaic. This is due primarily and chiefly to the disintegrative power of alien ideas and values" (p. 340).

14. The specter of cultural disorder that seems to have haunted some of the cultural relativists when they observed border phenomena exhibits a remarkable congruity with racialist thinking concerning inferior vigor of "hybrids" produced by the "miscegenation" of pure "races" (see Stocking 1968:48–53). This congruity suggests that there may have been a fetishizing of *types* in both evolutionary and cultural studies. While hybridity of all kinds — biological and cultural — was increasingly a *fact*, some of the dominant intellectual frameworks of the first half of the twentieth century insisted upon the authenticity of clearly delineated taxa, whether "races" or "cultures." In the present, if we now recognize "that there are no races" (Appiah 1985:21), it is more difficult for anthropology to move beyond a "taxonomical" approach to cultural difference (Appadurai 1991:205) and to consider the possibility that there are no *cultures* in the sense of "programs" (Geertz 1973:44) characterized by "coherence, timelessness, and discreetness" (Abu-Lughod 1991:147). For a clear example of this kind of taxonomic thinking about Native Americans, and a critique of it, see Martin 1987 (especially chapters by Calvin Martin) and Biolsi (1989).

15. "Cultural tourism" remains a potential resource for Lakota people. The Rosebud Sioux tribe, for example, has a Tourism Task Force.

16. In fact, Mekeel did leave open the possibility that the value of generosity survives among the Lakotas because it is adaptive, but the thrust of his paper is that generosity is an ancient vestige.

References

Abu-Lughod, Lila. 1991. "Writing against Culture." In Richard G. Fox, ed., *Recapturing Anthropology: Working in the Present*, pp. 137–62. Santa Fe, N.Mex.: School of American Research Press.

Albers, Patricia C. 1982. "Sioux Kinship in a Colonial Setting." *Dialectical Anthropology* 6(3):253–69.

Appadurai, Arjun. 1988. "Putting Hierarchy in Its Place." *Cultural Anthropology* 3(1):36–49.

———. 1991. "Global Ethnoscapes: Notes and Queries for a Transnational Anthropology." In Richard G. Fox, ed., *Recapturing Anthropology: Working in the Present*, pp. 191–210. Santa Fe, N.Mex.: School of American Research Press.

Appiah, Anthony. 1985. "The Uncompleted Argument: Du Bois and the Illusion of Race." *Critical Inquiry* 12(1):21–37.

Benedict, Ruth. 1932. "Configurations of Culture in North America." *American Anthropologist* 34(1):1–27.

———. 1934. *Patterns of Culture*. Boston: Houghton Mifflin.

Berkhofer, Robert F., Jr. 1979. *The White Man's Indian: Images of the American Indian from Columbus to the Present*. New York: Vintage.

Biolsi, Thomas. 1989. "The American Indian and the Problem of Culture" (review article). *American Indian Quarterly* 13:261–69.

———. 1992. *Organizing the Lakota: The Political Economy of the New Deal on Pine Ridge and Rosebud Reservations*. Tucson: University of Arizona Press.

———. 1995. "The Birth of the Reservation: Making the Modern Individual among the Lakota." *American Ethnologist* 22(1):28–53.

Bruner, Edward M. 1986. "Ethnography as Narrative." In Victor W. Turner and Edward M. Bruner, eds., *The Anthropology of Experience*, pp. 139–55. Urbana: University of Illinois Press.

Buruma, Ian. 1994. "Indian Love Call." *New York Review of Books*, September 15–22, pp. 27–29.

Clifton, James A. 1989. "Alternate Identities and Cultural Frontiers." In James A. Clifton, ed., *Being and Becoming Indian: Biographical Studies of North American Frontiers*, pp. 1–37. Chicago: Dorsey Press.

Deloria, Vine, Jr. 1969. *Custer Died for Your Sins: An Indian Manifesto*. New York: Macmillan.

Diamond, Stanley. 1974. *In Search of the Primitive: A Critique of Civilization*. New Brunswick, N.J.: Transaction Books.

Dippie, Brian W. 1982. *The Vanishing American: White Attitudes and U.S. Indian Policy*. Middletown, Conn.: Wesleyan University Press.

Dorris, Michael. 1987. "Indians on the Shelf." In Calvin Martin, ed., *The American Indian and the Problem of History*, pp. 98–105. New York: Oxford University Press.

Douglas, Mary. 1966. *Purity and Danger: An Analysis of Concepts of Pollution and Taboo*. Baltimore: Penguin.

Eggan, Fred. 1937. "Historical Changes in the Choctaw Kinship System." *American Anthropologist* 39:34–52.

Fabian, Johannes. 1983. *Time and the Other: How Anthropology Makes Its Object*. New York: Columbia University Press.

Foucault, Michel. 1972. *The Archaeology of Knowledge*, trans. A. M. Sheridan Smith. New York: Pantheon.

Fox, Richard G. 1991. "For a Nearly New Culture History." In Richard G. Fox, ed., *Recapturing Anthropology: Working in the Present*, pp. 93–113. Santa Fe, N.Mex.: School of American Research Press.

Geertz, Clifford. 1973. *The Interpretation of Cultures*. New York: Basic Books.

————. 1988. *Works and Lives: The Anthropologist as Author.* Stanford, Calif.: Stanford University Press.

Gupta, Akhil, and James Ferguson. 1992. "Beyond 'Culture': Space, Identity, and the Politics of Difference." *Cultural Anthropology* 7(1):6–23.

Hatch, Elvin. 1973. *Theories of Man and Culture.* New York: Columbia University Press.

Herskovits, Melville J. 1958 [1938]. *Acculturation: The Study of Culture Contact.* Gloucester, Mass.: Peter Smith.

hooks, bell. 1992. *Black Looks: Race and Representation.* Boston: South End Press.

Hoxie, Frederick E. 1992. "Exploring a Cultural Borderland: Native American Journeys of Discovery in the Early Twentieth Century." *Journal of American History*, December, pp. 969–95.

Jennings, Francis. 1976. *The Invasion of America: Indians, Colonialism, and the Cant of Conquest.* New York: W. W. Norton.

Jorgensen, Joseph G. 1971. "Indians and the Metropolis." In Jack O. Waddell and O. Michael Watson, eds., *The American Indian in Urban Society*, pp. 67–113. Boston: Little, Brown.

————. 1972. *The Sundance Religion: Power for the Powerless.* Chicago: University of Chicago Press.

————. 1978. "A Century of Political Economic Effects on American Indian Society." *Journal of Ethnic Studies* 6(3):1–82.

Kehoe, Alice B. 1985. "The Ideological Paradigm in Traditional American Ethnology." In June Helm, ed., *Social Contexts of American Ethnology, 1840–1984* (Proceedings of the American Ethnological Society, 1984), pp. 41–49. Washington, D.C.: American Anthropological Association.

————. 1990. "Primal Gaia: Primitivists and Plastic Medicine Men." In James A. Clifton, ed., *The Invented Indian: Cultural Fictions and Government Policies*, pp. 193–209. New Brunswick, N.J.: Transaction Publishers.

Kelly, Lawrence. 1980. "Anthropology and Anthropologists in the Indian New Deal." *Journal of the History of the Behavioral Sciences* 16:6–24.

————. 1985. "Why Applied Anthropology Developed When It Did: A Commentary on People, Money, and Changing Times, 1930–1945." In June Helm, ed., *Social Contexts of American Ethnology, 1840–1984* (Proceedings of the American Ethnological Society, 1984), pp.122–38. Washington, D.C.: American Anthropological Association.

Kennard, Edward A., and Gordon Macgregor. 1953. "Applied Anthropology in Government: United States." In Alfred L. Kroeber, ed., *Anthropology Today: An Encyclopedic Inventory*, pp. 832–40. Chicago: University of Chicago Press.

Kluckhohn, Clyde. 1962 [1955]. "Indian Americans in a White Man's World." In Clyde Kluckhohn, ed., *Culture and Behavior: Collected Essays of Clyde Kluckhohn*, pp. 336–42. New York: Free Press.

Kuhn, Thomas. 1961. *The Structure of Scientific Revolutions.* Chicago: University of Chicago Press.

Lesser, Alexander. 1933. *The Pawnee Ghost Dance Hand Game.* New York: Columbia University Press.

———. 1961. "Social Fields and the Evolution of Society." *Southwestern Journal of Anthropology* 17:40–48.

Lewis, Oscar. 1951. *Life in a Mexican Village: Tepoztlan Restudied.* Urbana: University of Illinois Press.

Linton, Ralph. 1963 [1940]. *Acculturation in Seven American Indian Tribes.* Gloucester, Mass.: Peter Smith.

Macgregor, Gordon. 1948. "H. Scudder Mekeel, 1892–1947." *American Anthropologist* 50:95–100.

Maddox, Lucy. 1991. *Removals: Nineteenth-Century American Literature and the Politics of Indian Affairs.* New York: Oxford University Press.

Martin, Calvin, ed. 1987. *The American Indian and the Problem of History.* New York: Oxford University Press.

Marx, Leo. 1964. *The Machine in the Garden: Technology and the Pastoral Ideal in America.* New York: Oxford University Press.

McFee, Malcolm. 1968. "The 150% Man, a Product of Blackfeet Acculturation." *American Anthropologist* 70:1096–1107.

McNickle, D'Arcy. 1979. "Anthropology and the Indian Reorganization Act." In Walter Goldschmidt, ed., *The Uses of Anthropology,* pp. 51–78. Washington, D.C.: American Anthropological Association.

Mead, Margaret. 1969 [1932]. *The Changing Culture of an Indian Tribe.* New York: AMS Press.

Mekeel, Haviland Scudder. 1930. "Field Notes, summer of 1930, White Clay District, Pine Ridge Reservation, South Dakota." Department of Anthropology Archives, American Museum of Natural History, New York.

———. 1931. "Field Notes, summer of 1931, White Clay District, Pine Ridge Reservation, South Dakota." Department of Anthropology Archives, American Museum of Natural History, New York.

———. 1932a. "A Discussion of Culture Change as Illustrated by Material from a Teton-Dakota Community." *American Anthropologist* 34:274–85.

———. 1932b. "A Modern American Community in the Light of Its Past." Ph.D. diss., Yale University, New Haven, Conn.

———. 1936. "The Economy of a Modern Teton Dakota Community." *Yale University Publications in Anthropology* 6:3–14.

———. 1945. "What to Do about Race Prejudice." *Wisconsin State Journal,* February 18.

Mintz, Sidney, ed. 1985. *History, Evolution, and the Concept of Culture: Selected Papers by Alexander Lesser.* New York: Cambridge University Press.

Moore, Sally Falk. 1986. *Social Facts and Fabrications: "Customary" Law on Kilimanjaro, 1880–1980.* New York: Cambridge University Press.

Nabakov, Peter. 1987. "Present Memories, Past History." In Calvin Martin, ed., *The*

American Indian and the Problem of History, pp. 144–55. New York: Oxford University Press.

Newberry, Colin. 1980. *Tahiti Nui: Change and Survival in French Polynesia, 1776–1945*. Honolulu: University of Hawaii Press.

Nugent, David. 1982. "Closed Systems and Contradiction: The Kachin in and out of History." *Man* 17:508–27.

Oglala Treaty Council. 1931. Minutes, February 19, File 1131–1924–054, Pt. 1, Pine Ridge, Central Classified Files, Record Group 75, National Archives and Records Administration, Washington, D.C.

Orlove, Benjamin. 1993. "Putting Race in Its Place: Order in Colonial and Postcolonial Peruvian Geography." *Social Research* 60(2):301–36.

Pasquaretta, Paul. 1994. "On the 'Indianness' of Bingo: Gambling and the Native American Community." *Critical Inquiry* 20:694–714.

Pearce, Roy Harvey. 1988. *Savagism and Civilization: A Study of the Indian and the American Mind*. Berkeley: University of California Press.

Polgar, Steven. 1960. "Biculturation of Mesquakie Teenage Boys." *American Anthropologist* 62:217–35.

Price, Catherine. 1996. *The Oglala People, 1841–1879: A Political History*. Lincoln: University of Nebraska Press.

Redfield, Robert. 1930. *Tepoztlan, A Mexican Village: A Study of Folk Life*. Chicago: University of Chicago Press.

———. 1934. "Culture Changes in Yucatan." *American Anthropologist* 36(1):57–69.

———. 1941. *The Folk Culture of the Yucatan*. Chicago: University of Chicago Press.

Redfield, Robert, Ralph Linton, and Melville J. Herskovits. 1936. "Memorandum for the Study of Acculturation." *American Anthropologist* 38:149–52.

Rogin, Michael Paul. 1987. *Ronald Reagan, the Movie: And Other Episodes of Political Demonology*. Berkeley: University of California Press.

Said, Edward. 1979. *Orientalism*. New York: Random House.

Sapir, Edward. 1924. "Culture, Genuine and Spurious." *American Journal of Sociology* 29:401–29.

Sider, Gerald M. 1993. *Lumbee Indian Histories: Race, Ethnicity, and Indian Identity in the Southern United States*. New York: Cambridge University Press.

Simard, Jean-Jacques. 1990. "White Ghosts, Red Shadows: The Reduction of North-American Natives." In James A. Clifton, ed., *The Invented Indian: Cultural Fictions and Government Policies*, pp. 333–70. New Brunswick, N.J.: Transaction Publishers.

Smith, Henry Nash. 1950. *Virgin Land: The American West as Symbol and Myth*. New York: Vintage Books.

Spindler, George. 1955. *Sociocultural and Psychological Processes in Menomini Acculturation*. University of California Publications in Culture and Society, vol. 5. Berkeley: University of California Press.

Spindler, Louise. 1962. *Menomini Women and Culture Change*. American Anthropological Association, memoir 91. Menasha, Wisc.: Banta and Sons.

Spurr, David. 1993. *The Rhetoric of Empire: Colonial Discourse in Journalism, Travel Writing, and Imperial Administration.* Durham, N.C.: Duke University Press.

Stocking, George W., Jr. 1968. *Race, Culture, and Evolution: Essays in the History of Anthropology.* New York: Free Press.

———. 1976. "Ideas and Institutions in American Anthropology: Toward a History of the Interwar Years." In George Stocking, Jr., ed., *Selected Papers from the American Anthropologist, 1921–1945,* pp. 1–53. Washington, D.C.: American Anthropological Association.

———. 1989. "The Ethnographic Sensibility of the 1920s and the Dualism of the Anthropological Tradition." In *History of Anthropology,* vol. 6, *Romantic Motives,* ed. George W. Stocking, pp. 209–76. Madison: University of Wisconsin Press.

Takaki, Ronald. 1982. *Iron Cages: Race and Culture in Nineteenth-Century America.* New York: Knopf.

Taylor, Graham D. 1975. "Anthropologists, Reformers, and the Indian New Deal." *Prologue* 7:151–62.

Thomas, Nicholas. 1984. *Colonialism's Culture: Anthropology, Travel, and Government.* Princeton, N.J.: Princeton University Press.

Thurnwald, Richard. 1932. "The Psychology of Acculturation." *American Anthropologist* 34(4):57–69.

Trouillot, Michel-Rolph. 1991. "Anthropology and the Savage Slot: The Poetics and Politics of Otherness." In Richard G. Fox, ed., *Recapturing Anthropology: Working in the Present,* pp. 93–113. Santa Fe, N.Mex.: School of American Research Press.

U.S. Senate. 1940. *Survey of the Conditions of the Indians of the United States.* Hearings before a Subcommittee of the Committee on Indian Affairs, 76th Congress, Pt. 37. Washington, D.C.: Government Printing Office.

Vincent, Joan. 1988. "Ahead of His Time? Production and Reception in the Work of Alexander Lesser." *American Ethnologist* 15(4):743–51.

———. 1990. *Anthropology and Politics: Visions, Traditions, and Trends.* Tucson: University of Arizona Press.

Vizenor, Gerald. 1990. *Crossbloods: Bone Courts, Bingo, and Other Reports.* Minneapolis: University of Minnesota Press.

Wald, Priscilla. 1993. "Terms of Assimilation: Legislating Subjectivity in the Emerging Nation." In Amy Kaplan and Donald E. Pease, eds., *Cultures of United States Imperialism,* pp. 5–84. Durham, N.C.: Duke University Press.

Walker, James R. 1982. *Lakota Society,* ed. Raymond J. DeMallie. Lincoln: University of Nebraska Press.

Wallace, Anthony F. C. 1969. *The Death and Rebirth of the Seneca.* New York: Random House.

Williams, Raymond. 1975. *The Country and the City.* Frogmore, Eng.: Paladin.

Williamson, William. 1931. Letter to Commissioner of Indian Affairs, March 10, Pine Ridge Reservation File, Box 4, Williamson Papers, Richardson Archives, University of South Dakota, Vermillion.

Wissler, Clark. 1912. "Societies and Ceremonial Associations in the Oglala Division of the Teton-Dakota." *American Museum of Natural History Anthropological Papers* 11, pt. 1, pp. 1–99.

———. 1960 [1929]. "The Conflict and Survival of Cultures." In Margaret Mead and Ruth Bunzel, eds., *The Golden Age of American Anthropology*, pp. 592–601. New York: George Braziller.

Wolf, Eric R. 1982. *Europe and the People without History.* Berkeley: University of California Press.

9

Informant as Critic
Conducting Research on a Dispute between Iroquoianist Scholars and Traditional Iroquois

GAIL LANDSMAN

I originally prepared the first version of this chapter for a session at the American Anthropological Association meeting entitled "When the People We Write about Read What We Write."[1] Although I welcomed the opportunity to participate in the session, I found the paper surprisingly difficult to write. I procrastinated; I tried to forget I promised to write it; I hoped it would just go away. The task was difficult because its source was a very painful professional experience. Although the chapter in part discusses having one's work about Indians read by those Indians, a not uncommon experience for contemporary anthropologists, the more revealing aspect of the experience I describe deals with the consequences of using an avenue of research less often traversed in the discipline: using scholars as informants.

I was a young, idealistic university freshman when Vine Deloria's *Custer Died for Your Sins* appeared twenty-some years ago. At the time, I was not well enough schooled in what would become my discipline to catch the biting humor of Deloria's analysis of anthropology and its practitioners, but the impact of the critique the book offered was nevertheless profound and affected the framing of my future work.

A child of the sixties, I was drawn to anthropology as an undergraduate because it seemed to speak directly to the burning issues of the time: warfare, racism, ethnic conflict, and poverty. I believed anthropology offered conceptual tools that could be used to explain how these had come to be the conditions of our world; even more exhilarating to me, anthropology presented potential alternatives to these conditions. The contemporary works of cultural anthropologists detailing diverse worldviews and ethos suggested to this fledgling scholar that the terms of life were not, after all, cast in stone. In the midst of all the confusion of those times, anthropology provided a vision of hope.

Deloria's message came along at the same time. I was also receptive to it in that it condemned my elders. "Indians have been cursed above all other people in history," Deloria proclaimed, for "Indians have anthropologists" (Deloria 1988 [1969]:78). These anthropologists had so buried Indian communities "beneath the mass of irrelevant information that the total impact of the scholarly community on Indian people has become one of simple authority" (Deloria 1988 [1969]:81). As my generation's motto was to "question authority," Deloria's words resonated with my own goals. Furthermore, Deloria directly addressed the great concern with what we called relevance. Indians, he argued, should reject knowledge for knowledge's sake, and "should not be objects of observation for those who do nothing to help us" (Deloria 1988 [1969]:94). I knew then (and still believe) that individuals have an obligation to act in this world. The ivory tower was a myth; we were all responsible for the consequences of our knowledge and the means by which we obtained knowledge.

Yet Deloria's message did not stop there. He challenged my own romantic use of Indian peoples as a means for developing a critique of my society. He targeted not just those anthros who had used Indian peoples in the past but also me in the present. Naively seeking in Indian cultures a guide for organizing a more just world, I too could be accused of being just another "ideological vulture" (Deloria 1988 [1969]:95), of attempting to re-Indianize Indians according to the white man's idea of what Indians were in the past or should be in the future (Deloria 1988 [1969]:91). No anthropologist found a safe haven in this critique.

It was then, and still is, commonplace for anthropologists to point out the impact of dominant white culture on native life. What was new in what we were hearing from Indian people themselves was the other side of the relationship — that no more than we could understand Indians without addressing white culture, could we understand our *own* lives as scholars without addressing our connections (and thus our responsibilities) to Indians. Contributions from feminist anthropology and the recent reflexive mood in the discipline have encouraged anthropologists to recognize that as scholars we possess "situated knowledges" (Haraway 1988:583) and write from particular positions. But our Indian critics pointed that out long ago. Our particular (privileged) positions, they suggested, are made possible and structured by the lives of Indian peoples. The message I heard as an undergraduate was thus both simple and frustratingly complex: We are all to be held accountable.

This message preceded my earliest education in the discipline. Therefore, many years later, when I chose to conduct research on American Indian political activism, I was well aware that I was committing myself to work in an environment in which informants "talk back" to anthropologists. Working with contemporary Indians, I would not be allowed any illusions of "being adopted" or "loved" by the people I studied; no "Margaret Mead fantasies" (Davis 1990) existed for those of us conducting research in native North America. I assumed (and worried) that those about whom I wrote — Indian activists — were simultaneously informants and potential critics.

Would the same apply to anthropologists themselves when they serve as informants? What can the attempt to write about scholars tell us about the distancing and power relations between anthropologist and informant still inherent in anthropologists' endeavors? These questions emerged for me for the first time when then graduate student Sara Ciborski and I engaged in research on a developing dispute between traditionalist Iroquois Indians and some non-Indian Iroquoianist scholars, both anthropologists and historians.

The Conflict

In response to criticism by some Iroquois Indians of a new social science syllabus being field-tested for the seventh and eighth grades, the New York State Education Department decided in 1987 to produce a curriculum resource guide written by Iroquois people.[2] This guide was to be used not as a replacement for the social science syllabus but as an optional supplement. The head of the Native American Education Unit of the State Education Department was at the time a "traditionalist" or "Longhouse" Iroquois. Largely because of her efforts, Iroquois traditionalists were asked to serve as the researchers and writers of the guide.

In preparing the resource guide, Indian traditionalists took upon themselves the task of representing their history to the public with the somewhat unusual explicit support of state government. The Indians made choices to accept or reject particular historical and cultural representations from the existing and extensive literature on the Iroquois; they in turn contributed to that literature. The audience for the Iroquois curriculum resource guide was purposefully and explicitly *external* as well as internal — it was to be used to educate both the Indian and non-Indian school-age population of New York State about the Iroquois.

A first draft of the guide, over three hundred pages in length, was written and given the title "Haudenosaunee — Past, Present, and Future: A Social Studies Resource Guide Draft." Its stated aim was to supplement the current syllabus by presenting an "indigenous peoples' perspective." By using the term "Haudenosaunee" (generally referring either to the League of the Confederacy or to traditionalist Iroquois people in general), the guide excluded from its discussion both Christian Indians and the elective system of government that was then in competition with traditionalist governments in various Iroquois communities. The draft included a version of the Iroquois creation myth and provided lessons on the formation of the League of the Iroquois, government treaties, recent federal and New York State policy toward Indians, native diet, and arts and crafts; it pointed to the foresight of various Iroquois leaders of the past, emphasized the superiority of the Iroquois lifestyle, provided a long section on contributions of the Iroquois to American life — including the concepts of representational government and individual freedom — and encouraged teachers to make explicit comparisons between aspects of American and Iroquois cultures.

Five non-Indian Iroquoianist scholars were among the more than thirty people asked by the state in 1988 to evaluate the draft prepared by traditionalist Iroquois writers. These scholars were extremely negative in their reviews, and some demanded that the project director be fired. They criticized the Indian writers for failing to cite standard, accepted historical sources, characterizing the guide as "worthless," a "disaster," "harmful to the children of this state," biased, and marred by errors ranging from avoidable inaccuracies to "grievous, and even irresponsible distortions of fact." Among the distortions cited was the Iroquois writers' claim that the Iroquois had influenced the founding fathers in their conception of the U.S. Constitution. In presenting the "influence argument," Indian writers of the curriculum resource guide draft brought into a new arena what was then, and still remains, a bitter conflict between some "mainstream" Iroquoianist scholars and traditionalist Indian activists and scholars of the "influence school" over the construction of Iroquois history (see Johansen 1990; Newman 1988; Tooker 1988, 1990). The conflict over how history should be presented in the state's resource guide was exacerbated when copies of the negative reviews came into the hands of the traditionalist Iroquois writers. Indian responses to these reviews varied, with some calling for an end to Iroquois cooperation in research projects in which the scholars were involved.

When Sara Ciborski and I chose to examine this controversy over the curriculum resource guide, we sought not to determine the truth value of the guide's content but rather to explore the process whereby history is constructed, represented, and contested by both natives and scholars. Our research involved using Indian participants and state education officials as informants; in addition, it redefined the academic historians and anthropologists (those who had reviewed the guide for the State Education Department) as informants as well. Over the course of the research process, it became evident that using scholars as informants for this research not only brought about a conflation of the normally opposed subject and object, scholar and native, but also rendered ambiguous normal power relations.

One outcome of our research on the curriculum resource guide controversy was a draft paper entitled "Representation and Politics: Contesting Histories of the Iroquois." In this work we attempted to explain how the controversy had come about and to offer an interpretation of how it had contributed to a rift in the relations between scholars and natives. We explicitly positioned ourselves as neither advocates for either of the two sides nor as neutral observers; our goal was to provide a nonoppositional, third reading of the event.

Anthropologists, historians, and Indian writers in the conflict had all publicly presented their arguments over the guide using the discourse of objectivist history (see Novick 1988); in our paper we presented evidence suggesting that two distinct conceptual matrices underlay the convergence in the discourse of objectivist academic history. Scholars used a matrix of objectivist history, we argued, while Indians used a conceptual matrix of radical ethnicity or nationalism. We also implied that the influence argument mattered because the U.S. Constitution is valued in the dominant society; that it would be a significant part of "authentic" Iroquois history otherwise was not at all clear. We suggested that it was the hegemony of the dominant discourse that led Indians to attempt to portray — in the legitimizing academic style — the Iroquois Great Law as a major influence on the Constitution. We proposed that, if the conflict were to be understood not in the terms of the truth of history but in terms of the incommensurability of the different conceptual matrices brought to the debate over publicly *representing* history, options other than the current state of mistrust and anger might appear. In our conclusion we took the position that anthropology and history are themselves cultural discourses which cannot occupy "some fixed perspective outside the play of signification of other discourse" (Hanson 1989:899), and raised the prospect of negotiated representations of Iroquois history.

When we wrote the paper, I had not yet come across the work of the historian Elsa Barkley Brown. I have recently come to see the relevance of her discussion of strategies for teaching African American women's history to our argument. Brown suggests that we think in terms of the aesthetics of jazz, in which "each musician has to listen to what the other is doing and know how to respond while each is, at the same time, intent upon her/his own improvisation" (Brown 1989:925). If one were to apply this metaphor to the state's social studies curriculum, the existence of two or more interpretations (improvisations?) of history might then appear as related contributions to a "polyrhythmic" whole, rather than as either/or options in competition for one truth. Note that this position is *not* one of relativism, in which one "truth" is considered as good as any other, but rather a recognition that each version is partial and situated. Without the advantage and eloquence of the jazz metaphor, we had tried to make a similar point. A draft of our paper was sent to each person we had interviewed — non-Indian and Indian scholars, traditionalist Iroquois writers, and State Education Department representatives — for their comments.

Clifford (1986), Myers (1986), and others have pointed out how informants now look over our shoulders and may demand commitments in exchange for their cooperation. Having rejected the concept of culture as a reified and bounded unit, and having adopted a "process approach" with its "analytic emphasis on continuous production and construction without differentiating in that respect between repetition and innovation" (Moore 1987:729), my coauthor and I chose not to examine a specific culture or community. We took instead as our unit of analysis a conflict, or social drama, with conflicting participants as our informants.[3] As a consequence, the informants looking over our shoulders did so from varied positions and were overtly in competition with each other. Each was quite conscious of the other and had constructed his or her narrative in relation to the narrative of others. Layer upon layer of observations of the other had stacked up to create the present event.

The very demand to write the guide, initiated by a Mohawk artist and public school teacher and supported by other traditionalist Iroquois, was itself a response to Indians having read earlier works by anthropologists, historians, and educators about the Iroquois. As is common in nationalist discourse, Indians attempted to correct what they saw as mistakes in earlier works. Mainstream Iroquoianist scholars read the traditionalists' counternarrative and wrote negative reviews. Indians in turn read these negative reviews and publicly countered those scholars' claims. Meanwhile, two anthropologists observed and analyzed these conflicts between natives and scholars and distributed a written interpretation to participants in the conflict. Participants then responded to the anthropologists' interpretation. These responses were observed and became the basis for yet another interpretation, now given written form in this chapter. Although often in conflict, throughout the controversy scholar and native never truly stood separate and apart from each other.

William Fenton as Symbol

The Iroquois are among the most extensively studied of North American Indian groups (Wallace 1984:2). One man in particular, the anthropologist William Fenton, stands out among Iroquoianist scholars. All of Fenton's research has been on the Iroquois. His publications span a period of over fifty years; he initiated the annual Conference on Iroquois Research in the 1940s and is now widely acknowledged as the dean of Iroquois Studies. Anthony Wallace has pointed out the implications of the title "dean" that need to be made explicit to convey the nature of Fenton's contribution. "The term implies that there exists a community of scholars, among whom the 'dean' holds his place as a productive member and at the same time serves as the leader, organizing the education of the newcomers and facilitating the research of his mature colleagues. In this sense, Fenton fully deserves the title" (Wallace 1984:2).

Although much recent scholarship on the Iroquois has departed from Fenton's program for the field, much research in Iroquoian studies also continues in the culture-historicist framework Fenton originally established. The editors of a recent interdisciplinary collection assert that "it is clear to those who know Fenton's work that a recounting of his career amounts to a recounting of the development of Iroquoian studies as a whole" (Foster, Campisi, and Mithun 1984:xv), and Fenton is credited with having guided or encouraged the best-known ethnographers, linguists, archaeologists, and ethnohistorians of the Iroquois (Wallace 1984:8–9). Fenton continues to hold a special place in Iroquoian studies for Iroquoianist scholars. Of greater significance for my research, however, is that, regardless of his influence (or lack thereof) on contemporary scholars, Fenton is unquestionably seen as the dominating force in the field of Iroquoian studies by traditionalist Iroquois Indians.[4]

Fenton's centrality in the resource guide controversy is clear, despite the fact that Fenton himself neither contributed to nor reviewed the guide. For the traditionalist Iroquois writers and their supporters, Fenton symbolizes the opposition of academia to native control over the representation of their own culture, history, and identity (Landsman and Ciborski 1992:428). This view in part stems from Fenton's role in a bitter controversy over repatriation of wampum belts held in the New York State Museum in Albany.

Fenton argued against the return of the belts, and as Jose Barreiro states, "It is hard to present even a short history of the Haudenosaunee wampum belts repatriation issue without perceiving the presence of Fenton both as a major scholar and as controversial personality" (1990:15).[5] I have never heard Indians refer to the scholars researching their culture and history as "Iroquoianists," the term used in the literature and conversation of Iroquois Studies; taking it for granted, I often used the term in conversation with some of the Indians with whom I spoke. But the traditionalist Iroquois we interviewed referred to those who expressed their negative reaction to the resource guide by either or both of two terms: "Fentonites" and "Trolls."[6]

Traditionalist Iroquois see Fenton as having control over all scholars working in the field, and an Indian scholar criticized our paper for not including a
section on the politics of academia regarding Indians in general and William
Fenton's role in particular. The interchange between this Iroquois critic and
myself provides a useful example of the place Fenton holds for traditionalist Iroquois in their current efforts to write their history and define their identity. This
critic faulted not only the draft of the paper that Sara Ciborksi and I had written but the work of all non-Indian scholars of the Iroquois (placing us in that
category). He stated that we, like our colleagues, on some level needed Fenton's validation. He then directed me to observe scholars at the annual conference on Iroquois research in Rensselaerville seeking their "yearly anointment"
from Fenton.

This traditionalist Iroquois scholar also referred to an earlier conversation
during which he had asked me why I didn't disregard Fenton (or, as he put it,
"tell Bill Fenton to go to hell"). The conversation took place at a conference of
Iroquoianist scholars where the informant also teased me about how I constantly looked over my shoulder as we spoke. At the time I offered a quick and
embarrassed verbal response; later I provided a somewhat more "elaborate" response in the form of a letter. In the letter I stated that Fenton had made significant and worthwhile contributions and that, while I had indeed publicly
disagreed with Fenton on points relating to theory, I preferred to deal with those
differences in terms that would not create personal animosity, particularly as
the issues involved were not personal ones. I explained that I did not cower before Fenton but simply requested that, in light of theoretical differences, he not
be a reviewer of my work; I added that while there may be some truth to the notion that Fenton acted as gatekeeper for Iroquoian studies, I directed my research findings to those outside Iroquoian studies and thus did not need to use
him for validation of my work. To this my Iroquois critic responded with appreciation for my comments regarding myself but also with a reaffirmation that
the Fenton issue "needs to be explored." He argued that in spite of my own personal arrangements, the larger significance of Fenton remained: as an individual scholar, my dealings with Fenton were different from those of the Iroquois
as a people.

Other Iroquois with whom I worked on this research echoed this view of

Fenton. For instance, another traditionalist Iroquois scholar whom we consulted asserted that it was time for Fenton and his followers "to make room for other scholars — native or non-native." Native scholars like this one had entered the arena, though the mainstream Iroquoianists had "thought we'd never get there."

Informants as Critics

In some ways Fenton as symbol set the standard against which Indian writers judged our interpretation of the controversy. To the extent that our work could be viewed as in the same mold as Fenton's, we were judged as having failed. But to the extent that our tone was seen to differ from what is considered Fenton's exclusionary and authoritative voice, we were appreciated. That is, inasmuch as contrary to Fenton and some of his students, we interpreted *all* representations of history (including those by non-native scholars as well as by Indians) as politically informed, and considered traditionalist Indian voices, although not portraying accurate facts, as nevertheless worthy of a hearing, our work was perceived by Indians as fair. Upon viewing a draft of our paper, one Indian writer referred to my earlier warning that he should not expect to find in me or my research an ally. He concluded that indeed he did after all sense in me an ally, inasmuch as I did not call him a liar or a racist and did not suggest that he had a political agenda. "An ally is someone who will listen, and . . . will believe that I'm telling the truth as I see it."

Upon reading our analysis, some Iroquois also disavowed any tie to academic discourse we had imputed to them; two took the occasion to further discredit Fenton by claiming he had been tricked by his informants many years ago into presenting falsehoods as facts. Somewhat contrary to the reaction for which we had braced ourselves, however, Iroquois informants posed no objections to our framing the conflict in terms of the politics of representation rather than the "truth" of history. While maintaining that the history portrayed in the guide was true, they also accepted that we might not ourselves take their representation as historically accurate. What seemed to matter more was that we affirmed their equal right to their representation.

However, the issue raised by one Indian informant — whether the Iroquois in question had indeed gotten into the scholarly arena — was crucial for the non-native critics of the guide. It figured in their criticism not only of the guide but also of the paper we wrote about the controversy over the guide. One criticism made by Iroquoianist scholars of our analysis was that we had not taken it upon ourselves to discredit the credentials of the native writers. "Is everyone a historian?" asked one scholar, going through a list of names. "Do we have standards or don't we?" Another scholar, in an anonymous review of a version of the paper submitted to a journal, claimed that the title of our article was misleading, because the different accounts were not actually "contesting histories"; this reviewer considered the Iroquoianist account history and the Native American version "propaganda mythology." Both sides conceptualized the issue in terms of who should rightfully control the representation of Iroquois history; each publicly justified their claim to control in terms of unique access to, and willingness to put forth, the "truth" of Iroquois history.

In retrospect, my coauthor and I appear to have been extraordinarily naive. We were intellectually fascinated by the conflict, to be sure, and also sought the advantages that accrue to those who write and publish papers, but our real motivation and passion for the research stemmed from an innocent hope that by shifting analysis from the content of history to the politics of representation we might offer an alternative perspective to the apparent stalemate and thereby might repair and head off further hostilities between traditionalist Iroquois and scholars. I have much less optimism today. Judging from the responses of Iroquoian scholars who served as both our informants and critics, we were notably unsuccessful in convincing them of the value of interpreting the conflict in terms other than the content of history. Interestingly, this was the case not only for scholars who had been negative in their comments about the guide but also for those scholars of the influence school to whom Indian writers had apparently sent copies of our paper for comment.

Throughout our research we rejected taking either of the two sides as presented in the conflict, but in the end some Iroquoian scholars chose sides for us. Mainstream Iroquoian scholars criticized us for failing to assess the standing in the academic community of the sources cited by Indians (accusing us, for instance, of assuming that one academic degree is as good as another, regardless of discipline, level, or institution), and of thereby being apologists for the Indians. These scholars faulted us for not examining in greater detail the individual political agendas of specific, named Iroquois people; yet they reserved for themselves detached and unlocatable positions through their claims to a totalizing objectivity. Donna Haraway likens the latter position to the "god-trick," a way of seeing that promises "vision from everywhere and nowhere equally and fully" and that, like relativism, denies "the stakes in location, embodiment, and partial perspective" (Haraway 1988). Above all — and true to their commitment to objectivist history — these scholars continually responded that it was necessary for us as scholars to disprove specific historical mispresentations in the guide, including that of Iroquois influence on the Constitution. To fail to do so was to betray the canons of the discipline.

Anthropology from the Inside

The accusation of betrayal of scholarship and of scholars suggests a variation on the insider anthropologist dilemma. Anthropologists have recently focused on the ability to conduct research in a community of which one is a member (see especially Cerroni-Long 1995; Jackson 1987; and Messerschmidt 1981). In such settings questions often arise about sympathies — usually of ethnicity, political ideology, or class — that might impede objectivity or place constraints on publication. But to be an anthropologist studying scholars sets up yet another dynamic, and perhaps an untenable situation, for a somewhat different set of reasons.

As a route to understanding this dynamic, I offer the following painful example. A version of our paper "Representation and Politics" had been sent to a journal for review. Among the criticisms offered by one reviewer was the very serious suggestion that I had violated standards of research integrity in my handling of certain quotes. The quotes in question were statements made by scholars in public in the context of scheduled academic conference sessions. Although in one instance a similar statement had been made to me in conversation, it was also made in the above-described context, and for this reason I had judged it acceptable to publish. All quotes in the paper were unattributed and none were taken from private conversations with me at conferences or from conversations overheard at such conferences. In the anonymous review, however, the reader compared my methods to those of journalists, and apparently drawing an analogy mistakenly stated that I had attended conferences and quoted off-the-record conversations without verifying the accuracy or intent of the remarks. This reader also offered an ominous warning: scholars who collect data in such ways endanger their scholarly reputations and their future access to meetings of this kind.

The reader's response left me troubled and confused for reasons that went beyond fear of ostracism by specialists in Iroquois Studies. I was forced to recognize the problematic nature of this aspect of our research strategy not only in this case but in the discipline as a whole. On the one hand, the much touted advantage of participant observation is precisely that it allows one to gain access to less formal, self-conscious, and "produced-for-the-anthropologist" data. I had simply chosen to conduct my participant observation in a community of scholars of which I was nominally, at least, a member. On the other hand, I concede that my coauthor and I may have been "wrong" in using academic meetings as field sites. After all, we had used data collected in one context for purposes for which it had not originally been generated. In doing so we had also objectified those about whom we wrote.

The irony, of course, is that these are sins I and others regularly commit in the course of being anthropologists. They are a source of complaints that Indians have long made against us, and that we in turn have long defended in the name of objective scholarship. Regardless of what I had actually done or not done, being called on this point by scholars at the particular moment I was taking *scholars* as my object brought to the fore the question of whose interests are served by keeping the academic process secret and our informal conversations out of the public domain. It went far toward revealing anew the privileged position we hold for ourselves *vis-à-vis* those we study, as well as the institutional response awaiting those who "refuse to guard the order" (Fine 1991:6).

Using as an example research in an Essex village, Marilyn Strathern correctly notes that just being a member of the larger, overarching culture in question does not mean the anthropologist will render an account that is recognizable to the local group studied. "Indigenous reflection is incorporated as part of the data to be explained, and cannot itself be taken as the framing of it, so that there is always a discontinuity between indigenous understandings and the analytical concepts which frame the ethnography itself" (Strathern 1987:18; see also Greenhouse 1985). In the case of our analysis of the Iroquoianist scholars, however, the "indigenous reflection" was itself in the form of academic discourse. Our ethnographic account of the conflict, while at variance with scholars' indigenous reflection, was nevertheless perceived by scholars as falling within the very same domain as that reflection. This circularity perhaps accounts for those scholars' unwillingness to set aside the issue of the truth or falsity of Iroquois claims in their response to our work. They had assumed a commonality of academic culture between us and them, a commonality that, if indeed it had ever existed, was violated by the imposition of the anthropologist-informant relation.

Framing scholars' "reflections" as ethnographic data rather than as historical analysis propelled our analysis into the rugged terrain of academic politics. When members of groups more often studied by anthropologists disapprove of what is written, the recourse available to those studied generally remains outside the domain of academia. The criticisms leveled may be devastatingly painful to the anthropologist in an emotional or personal sense, all the more so when the perceived insult to the group was unintended, but ultimately careers are rarely threatened. Our usual informants may have access to the popular media, or to their own media through which they vent their criticisms and embarrass a scholar. In the worst-case scenario (for the anthropologist), they may cut off the anthropologist's access to future informants. But such critiques rarely discredit the anthropologist in the circle of the academy. They are taken to be polemical, political, nonobjective, and essentially irrelevant for the validity of research findings. I by no means suggest that we ignore such criticisms or fail to address the concerns of those about whom we write. I am simply acknowledging that, although the situation may be changing, in raw terms most of our informants simply do not yet have the means to punish scholars where it hurts.

In attempting to treat scholars as informants, we potentially equalize the asymmetrical power relationship that usually exists between the scholar and the Other, and thus like other insider anthropologists, even with the best of intentions, we can inadvertently set the scene for accusations of betrayal. But in reaction to what we perceive as betrayal, we as scholars do have the power to hurt those who write about us. We publicly review one another's publications, we referee grant proposals and articles for prestige-conferring journals, we evaluate one another for promotion and tenure. Unlike the case for most of our other informants, scholar-informant disagreements can be vented within the anthropologists' own domain. Within that domain we can portray politics as commitment to objectivity, to defense of good scholarship. To separate politically based criticism from something we might call pure academic criticism is impossible. The attempt merely leaves an author open to charges of whining. Paul Rabinow's comment that an anthropology of anthropology would include attention to the less glamorous but immediately constraining conditions of academic politics (1986:253) is here quite pertinent.

A full accounting of this experience, then, would require further analysis of the "micropractices of the academy" (Rabinow 1986:253), as well as of the relation of scholar to informant. As I strive to give coherence and meaning to this particular experience of having those about whom I write read what I write, I find that it has raised a most unsettling question. If, indeed, we ourselves resist the role of informant, should we expect any less of the others about whom we write?

Acknowledgments

I am grateful to Caroline Brettell, organizer of the AAA session "When the People We Write about Read What We Write." I thank as well the other panel members for stimulating discussion of the topic. I would also like to express appreciation to James Collins and Phyllis Pease Chock for their useful comments and encouragement.

Notes

1. The full title of the session was "When the People We Write about Read What We Write: Doing Ethnography in Complex Societies," annual meeting of the American Anthropological Association, New Orleans, La., November 1989.

2. For a fuller discussion of the conflict, see Landsman and Ciborski 1992.

3. Victor Turner elaborated the notion of conflict as social drama (Turner 1974). For more recent discussions and examples of using moments of social discord as the unit of analysis for studies of social process, see Ginsburg 1989, Landsman 1988, Landsman and Krasniewicz 1990, Moore 1987, and the various essays in Ginsburg and Tsing 1990. Moore argues that such moments of discord can serve as "diagnostic events" revealing a "multiplicity of social contestations and the voicing of competing cultural claims" (1987:729), and should be privileged as a source of ethnographic data.

4. Fenton's place in traditionalist Iroquois politics was attested to by Iroquoianist scholars themselves. One scholar, in an anonymous review of a version of our paper submitted to a journal, chose to recount his or her own experience in being "assailed" by Native American scholars. This reviewer held that being associated with Fenton (whom

the Indian scholars treated as their enemy and called "vile names," in the reviewer's words) was enough to incur hostile criticism.

5. See Fenton 1971 for Fenton's own arguments against repatriation; see Barreiro 1990 for a native activist's discussion of the history of the belts, efforts to have them returned to Iroquois hands, and Fenton's role in the controversy. Barreiro criticizes the argument made by "prominent anthropologists that the old Iroquois Confederacy died two hundred years ago"; such anthropologists, he claims, have failed "to take into account the cultural traditions through the families and clans" and have incorrectly focused on "the ceremonial moment and on the icons of culture" (Barreiro 1990:20).

6. The latter term is used because the Iroquois writers conceptualized their role in preparing the guide as building bridges between people; their critics, in particular the "Fentonites," are defined as the trolls lurking beneath those bridges. In this paragraph I draw on the first section of Landsman and Ciborski 1992: 427–28.

References
Barreiro, Jose. 1990. "The Return of the Wampum." *Northeast Indian Quarterly* 7(1):8–20.
Brown, Elsa Barkley. 1989. "African-American Women's Quilting." *Signs* 14:921–99.
Cerroni-Long, E. L. 1995. "Insider Anthropology." *NAPA Bulletin*, 16 (National Association for the Practice of Anthropology, Arlington, Va.).
Clifford, James. 1986. "Introduction: Partial Truths." In James Clifford and George Marcus, eds., *Writing Culture: The Poetics and Politics of Ethnography*, pp. 1–26. Berkeley: University of California Press.
Davis, Dona. 1990. "Unintended Consequences: The Myth of 'the Return' in Anthropological Fieldwork." Unpublished paper presented at the annual meeting of the American Anthropological Association, November.
Deloria, Vine, Jr. 1988 [1969]. *Custer Died for Your Sins: An Indian Manifesto.* Norman: University of Oklahoma Press.
Fenton, William N. 1971. "The New York State Wampum Collection: The Case for the Integrity of Cultural Treasures." *Proceedings of the American Philosophical Society* 115(6).
Fine, Michelle. 1991. "Passions, Politics, and Power: Feminist Research Possibilities." Unpublished manuscript.
Foster, Michael, Jack Campisi, and Marianne Mithun. 1984. Preface. In Michael Foster, Jack Campisi, and Marianne Mithun, eds., *Extending the Rafters: Interdisciplinary Approaches to Iroquoian Studies*, pp. xiii–xvi. Albany: State University of New York Press.
Ginsburg, Faye. 1989. *Contested Lives: The Abortion Debate in an American Community.* Berkeley: University of California Press.
Ginsburg, Faye, and Anna Lowenhaupt Tsing, eds. 1990. *Uncertain Terms Negotiating Gender in American Culture.* Boston: Beacon Press.

Greenhouse, Carol. 1985. "Anthropology at Home: Whose Home?" *Human Organization* 44(3):261–64.

Hanson, Allan. 1989. "The Making of the Maori: Culture Invention and Its Logic." *American Anthropologist* 91(4):890–902.

Haraway, Donna. 1988. "Situated Knowledges: The Science Question in Feminism and the Privilege of Partial Perspective." *Feminist Studies* 14(3):575–99.

Jackson, Anthony, ed. 1987. *Anthropology at Home.* London: Tavistock Publications.

Johansen, Bruce. 1990. "Native American Societies and the Evolution of Democracy in America, 1600–1800." *Ethnohistory* 37(3):279–90.

Landsman, Gail. 1988. *Sovereignty and Symbol: Indian/White Conflict at Ganienkeh.* Albuquerque: University of New Mexico Press.

Landsman, Gail, and Sara Ciborksi. 1992. "Representation and Politics: Contesting Histories of the Iroquois." *Cultural Anthropology* 7(4):425–47.

Landsman, Gail, and Louise Krasniewicz. 1990. "'A Native Man Is Still a Man': A Case Study of Intercultural Participation in Social Movements." *Anthropology and Humanism Quarterly* 15(1):11–19.

Messerschmidt, Donald A., ed. 1981. *Anthropologists at Home in North America.* Cambridge: Cambridge University Press.

Moore, Sally Falk. 1987. "Explaining the Present: Theoretical Dilemmas in Processual Ethnography." *American Ethnologist* 14(4):727–36.

Myers, Fred. 1986. "The Politics of Representation: Anthropological Discourse and Australian Aborigines." *American Ethnologist* 13(1):138–53.

Newman, Michael. 1988. "Founding Feathers." *New Republic,* November 7, pp. 17–18.

Novick, Peter. 1988. *That Noble Dream: The "Objectivity Question" and the American Historical Profession.* Cambridge: Cambridge University Press.

Rabinow, Paul. 1986. "Representations Are Social Facts: Modernity and Postmodernity in Anthropology." In James Clifford and George Marcus. eds., *Writing Culture: The Poetics and Politics of Ethnography,* pp. 234–61. Berkeley: University of California Press.

Strathern, Marilyn. 1987. "The Limits of Auto-anthropology." In Anthony Jackson, ed., *Anthropology at Home,* pp. 16–37. Cambridge: Cambridge University Press.

Tooker, Elisabeth. 1988. "The United States Constitution and the Iroquois League." *Ethnohistory* 35(4):305–36.

———. 1990. "Rejoinder to Johansen." *Ethnohistory* 37(3):291–97.

Turner, Victor. 1974. *Dramas, Fields, and Metaphors: Symbolic Action in Human Society.* Ithaca, N.Y.: Cornell University Press.

Wallace, Anthony, F. C. 1984. "The Career of William N. Fenton and the Development of Iroquoian Studies." In Michael Foster, Jack Campisi, and Marianne Mithun, eds., *Extending the Rafters,* pp. 1–12. Albany: State University of New York Press.

10

The End of Anthropology (at Hopi)?

PETER WHITELEY

> The pure products of America go crazy.
> William Carlos Williams (via James Clifford)

Scene I: The Ritual

It is August in the dusty pueblo plaza. Two lines of ritually attired men emerge from underground kivas and make their way to an arbor. The first group, the Antelopes, white-kilted and with white zigzags painted over a gray ground down their torsos, marches past the arbor, stamping on a plank-drum, and then lines up in front of it. The Snakes, brown-painted and kilted, march behind the Antelopes, stamping on the plank, and line up to face them. A short song and dance follows. Then each Snake man goes to the arbor and procures a live snake. He places the back of its neck between his teeth and dances the snake around the plaza. At the conclusion, the Snake men set all the snakes down into a cornmeal circle, where they are sprinkled with cornmeal by Snake women; the men then pick up the snakes again and race them out of the plaza.

You thought I was talking about the Hopi Snake Ceremony, right? *Pay qa pam 'i'*, "That's not it," as a Hopi clown says when he introduces his *tawi*, or pun-story, whose words depend on newly coined meaning, sometimes obscene or perverse, for existing verbal representations. No, I'm talking about the *Smoki*

This chapter was previously published as "The End of Anthropology (at Hopi)?" in the *Journal of the Southwest* 35 (summer 1993):125–57 and is reprinted by permission.

Snake Dance, an ersatz performance, which coins new meaning, probably obscene, certainly perverse, for Hopi ritual representations. In the Smoki Snake Dance, the performers are white, the "pueblo" is plywood, the snakes are all bull (whereas rattlers are the key snakes for Hopis) — in short, the ritual is a racist parody.

Founded in 1921 by Prescott businessmen to burlesque Indian ceremonies, the Smokis soon became more earnest, initiating into a fraternal order, founding a museum with Indian artifacts and ethnographic books, and claiming to preserve Native American culture: the (racist) joke turned serious. The group has typically included men of influence in white Arizona (Barry Goldwater was a member and performed three times; Brinkley-Rogers 1990:2).[1]

The dance itself is a mishmash. Elements are close to the Hopi original — the kilts, for example, were probably purchased from Hopis in the past, the body paint and arbor setup are roughly accurate, some of the dance movements mimic the real thing — and my description might indeed be of the Hopi ceremony. But I was selective. I neglected to mention that the painted backdrop was illuminated by floodlights (it was night; the Hopi ritual occurs in daylight); that participants — divided into "warriors," "braves," and "squaws" under the leadership of "Chief Hairlip" (*sic*) — wore red bandannas over black long-hair wigs; that drummers (there are none at the Hopi ceremony) dressed like Hollywood Navajos pounded out a Western-movie Indian track, a four-four bar heavy on the first beat; that the rattles were painted coffee cans; and that the "songs" (Oh! ah! oh! ah! oh! ah!) and dance movements seemed choreographed by the same characters who do "tribal" dances in Tarzan movies.

To begin, the public-address system intoned a script while an elderly Smoki mimed to costumed children, and the story was enacted by other Smokis stage-left. The story, purporting to be the snake myth, was obviously taken from Hopi ethnography, though with a heavy dose of savagist ambience: "The old Snake priest gathers his grandchildren and the children of the tribe and the story begins. Many moons ago, the chief's son, Tiyo, wondered about the universe. His father told him to go to the underworld to seek out Spiderwoman. . . ." After this, the paying audience applauded from their bleachers (payment, applause, and bleachers are absent from the original) amidst the drone of the highway (likewise) from outside the roadside arena. Then, on to the ceremony itself:

"Ladies and gentlemen, the world-famous Smoki Snake Dance!" the voice boomed in Western twang.[2]

Scene II: The Land

Twelve miles south of Holbrook, Arizona, rises a volcanic cinder cone known as Woodruff Butte, after a Mormon who founded a nearby settlement in the 1870s. In Hopi it is *Tsimontukwi*, Jimson-Weed Butte, a rather important place, which has carried this name since time immemorial. It houses one of nine major shrines *(tuutuskyam)* that mark the boundaries of *Hopitutskwa*, Hopi land (Page and Page 1982; Whiteley 1989). The butte also contains clan shrines, for the Bearstrap and Water clans — both formerly lived in the vicinity — and shrines for the *Porswiwimkyam* curing society. Some plant medicines are collected there. The two named clans also have property rights in eagles in the vicinity, which Hopis continue to gather every May. The area is particularly sacred to the Water clan because of an establishing myth in which a boy and a girl were sacrificed there to appease *Paalölöqangw*, the Water Snake spirit of *Paayu*, the Little Colorado River.[3]

Tsimontukwi is not on a reservation; it has been "privately owned" by a local white family since 1935. The Bearstrap clan shrines, which used to be on top of the butte, were destroyed in the 1960s when a radio tower was erected. In September 1990, the owners leased the butte to a gravel mining company. The Hopis protested, sending religious leaders and tribal officials. The lead owner, Norman Turley, knew of the place's significance but apparently cared little ("Woodruff Journal" 1991), challenging the Hopis to buy him out for a million dollars. The tribe sought a legal appraisal, which came in at $45,000, and made a counteroffer.

Meanwhile mining went ahead. The priests, terribly concerned, continued to visit the butte. While Eldridge Koinva, chief of the Antelope society (and a leader of the Bearstrap clan) from Shongopavi, looked on helplessly, the boundary shrine itself was felled by a bulldozer.

The controversy has grown, and mining operations ceased temporarily. But the owner is not amused. Angered by the Hopi offer, Turley at one point threatened to blow up the whole butte rather than return it to the Hopis (telephone conversation with the Hopi Office of Cultural Preservation, July 1991). The mining area has been fenced off, a large "No Trespassing" sign was put up, and to make sure the Indians got the message, a dead coyote was pinned to it.[4]

Scene III: The Sacra, or, *Ahöla's* Nose Is out of Joint

Sotheby's auction house in New York City is in a posh setting on the Upper East Side. A sale of May 1991 featured "Fine American Indian Art" (Sotheby's 1991), including three Southwest "masks,"[5] one possibly Navajo, the other two Hopi, an *Ahöla* and a *Kooyemsi.* Despite Hopi protests (Wallach 1991a,b; Reif 1991a), Sotheby's insisted that the masks were "legitimately acquired" (Natalie Wolcott, personal communication May 18, 1991), although it refused to disclose the identity of the seller.

The auction room was buzzing—the press was on hand. The buyers were mostly wealthy "Indian art" patrons, all white as far as I could see, both "old money" and arrivistes, in Madison Avenue haute couture or Santa Fe chic. Bids that outstrip most Hopi families' annual incomes were casually mounted. Finally *Ahöla* was swung round on a revolving platform, surrounded by a gray cloth ground—transformed into "fine art." He went for $24,200. As he came into view, I saw the nose had been dislocated, cocked slightly to one side.[6] Of course, no one would care; the object's new found commodity status, not its Hopi meaning, was the sole criterion of value. Nonetheless, the disjointed nose seemed somehow appropriate—an index of incongruities—born of the clash of cultural meanings and standards.[7]

Scene IV: The Texts

[T]he Hopi are a fascination in the public mind. More than any other group in North, Central, or South America, the Hopi have retained their aboriginal culture, with its religious expression in its purest form. And they embody a philosophy of life totally in balance with their physical and spiritual environment. . . . Within Hopi rituals and sacred ceremonies, the ancient knowledge of early humanity is deposited. It is brought to us without interruption or corruption. Most of us will go to Hopi driven by the force of the primeval need to be in communion with the source. (Boissiere 1986:20–22)

North American Indians, because of their culture, hold a special place among aboriginal peoples of our world. The Hopi, in turn, are esteemed among Native North Americans. Mythology is the central feature of Hopi culture. The Hopi prophecy plays a central role within Hopi mythology. At the center of that prophecy we find Pahana, the Elder White Brother, for whose return the Hopi wait. There is thus a connection between our hopes concerning the wisdom of tribal people and the Hopi expectation for the return of Elder White Brother. (Kaiser 1991:85–86)

We have . . . a specific link between New-Age thinking and the worldview of indigenous peoples and of nature religions. We sense that our dualistic distinctions between spirit and matter, God and the world, humans and nature, subject and object, do not apply in their view of things. Instead there is an understanding of the holistic connectedness of all that exists. For a people holding such a holistic view of the world, everything would be sacred, imbued with the Spirit, part of a greater Whole, inseparably interwoven. (Kaiser 1991:116)

These excerpts from Robert Boissiere's *Meditations with the Hopi* (1986) and Rudolf Kaiser's *The Voice of the Great Spirit: Prophecies of the Hopi Indians* (1991) illustrate a wide-ranging interest by "New Age" groups from North America and Europe. The Hopi are held up as icons of spiritual wisdom, exemplars for a quest toward new meaning in the malaise of modern life (compare A. Geertz 1987, 1994).

Popular literature on the Hopi, especially since Frank Waters's *Book of the Hopi* (1963), produced an influx of seekers and yearners in the 1960s, and while these eventually departed, the legacy has remained. During Hotevilla's *Powamuy* rituals in 1981, for example, a mysterious, black-garbed German woman interrupted *Angwusnasomtaqa's* (Crow Mother's) distribution of bean sprouts, grabbing handfuls and offering them grandiosely to spectators, before being shooed away by a Hopi woman. Another mysterious character in a red robe camped for a while by Oraibi and went around at night claiming to be Maasaw, a prominent Hopi deity. And recently, Hopis visiting the *sipaapuni* emergence shrine in Little Colorado River Canyon have found, to their dismay, crystals and other pseudo-offerings. Radically decontextualized reinterpretation of Hopi traditional and prophetic representations by New Agers and their fellow travelers has thus begotten another clash of representations between the Hopi and the dominant society. The clash reached an apogee at the "Harmonic Convergence":[8] "[L]arge numbers of people gathered at many sacred sites all over the world . . . [i]ncluding Prophecy Rock on the Hopi reservation. A small group, between thirty and fifty people, made sacrificial offerings, drew astrological signs on the ground in front of Prophecy Rock and, at sunrise on 17 August, raised their hands toward the sky, turning east toward the rising sun, in the direction faced by Prophecy Rock for thousands of years" (Kaiser 1991:119). None of the celebrants, so far as I am aware, was Hopi; Hopi religious leaders specifically repudiated the connection, denying any recognition of this alien convergence or its association with the so-called Prophecy Rock. The Hopi meaning of this petroglyph-marked site is contested, but it has been greatly reworked by Thomas Banyacya, a Hopi guru to many New Agers and the subject of much controversy in Hopi discourse (see A. Geertz 1994:257–87).[9]

In each of these four cases, cultural conceptions that are critical to Hopi identity — religious rituals, a sacred landscape, deity masks, metaphysical beliefs — are fundamentally violated by various elements from the dominant society. Core Hopi representations and meanings are (1) directly parodied (the Smokis), (2) actively scorned and destroyed *(Tsimontukwi)*, (3) commodified and transmuted into an alien register of value *(Ahöla)*, and (4) self-servingly reimagined into the canons of a new universalizing religious cult (the New Agers).

Broadly, each case involves different interest groups, though all are predominantly white. The respective interests intersect along a number of axes, including capital gain (both material and symbolic), regional identity (particularly for the Smokis), class, and ethnic-supremacist ideology (conscious or not), among others. These cases and their attendant interests by no means exhaust the manipulation of Hopi representations by outsiders. I choose them to illustrate recent, particularly acute violations of Hopi cultural and religious sovereignty. Moreover, all occur outside the direct application of U.S. sociopolitical and ideological domination (although this serves as ultimate guarantor), such as by federal laws and BIA police, BIA schools, missionary religions, and the metropolitan economy. They involve a subtler process of cultural hegemony, a politics of representations wherein a dominant group appropriates and refigures a subaltern's cultural symbols to its own purposes (compare Çelik 1992; Lavie 1990; Vizenor 1987).

This distortion of symbols[10] has reflexive effects back home: it conditions interactions between Hopis and non-Indians, and partly undermines the symbols' established meanings and transformative power. Tourists arrive with arrogant assumptions about heathen rituals and their rights to sample them; illegal plunder of artifacts and sites proceeds apace; many items of traditional culture (notably including Kachina dolls)[11] have been commodified for the "ethnic-art" market; and interference with shrines and rituals is ongoing. A promiscuous traffic in Hopi representations thus occupies multiple nexuses of meaning. Hopi has for the last century been progressively inundated by a dominant society that has sought in myriad ways to impose its political, economic, religious, and sociocultural control. The Hopi are still technically wards of the U.S. government, "domestic dependent nations" (for example, Deloria and Lytle 1984), their land is held in trust, and they have very limited real political sovereignty. Perpetuation of traditions must battle imposed institutions like schools and missions, supermarkets, wage labor, television, and other forms of cultural imperialism. All of this has had profound effects: many Hopi children do not understand the language, prefer heavy metal over Hopi songs, Coke and Big Macs over *yoywwala* (rainwater) and *piiki* (wafer bread), and expect jobs off reservation rather than engagement in the subsistence economy.[12]

Collecting Hopi Culture

> The relations of power whereby one portion of humanity can select, value, and collect the pure products of others need to be criticized and transformed. (Clifford 1988:213)

At the same time as overt domination, the national society, or elements of it, has continuously fetishized aspects of Hopi culture — especially rituals and artifacts — into its own canons of value. Appropriation and sale of religious objects has occurred for over a century. At Hopi private collectors and formal museum expeditions, especially at the turn of the century (notably including the Smith-sonian Institution, Chicago Field Museum, Harvard Peabody Museum, Southwest Museum, and the Museum of the American Indian), have made off with great quantities of artifacts, some of irreplaceable sacred worth (for example, Wade 1985). Recently, the "primitive-art" market has caused a re-newed proliferation of pothunting and thefts. The Hopi Reservation is difficult to patrol: some pothunters (many, apparently, northern Arizona whites) fly in by helicopter at night, ransack sites, and are out again in no time: this is big business.

The anthropological world has been quick to condemn pothunting, but in their effects, the "professional" excavation of "sites" and removal of artifacts to university museums seem hard to distinguish from the pothunter's practice. In both cases, important materials are alienated from Hopi, or from the collective spiritual patrimony of Hopi ancestry. Generally speaking, Hopi belief man-dates that remnants of the past be left alone, to serve as sources of power and meaning in the landscape; eagle gatherers, for example, revisit ancient habita-tion sites, because eagles who dwell there reincarnate clan ancestors. The re-ality that formal archaeology may protect such sites from vandalism and theft does not alleviate this basic contradiction of Hopi sacred values.

For the collector, prehistoric items gain a special cachet of symbolic capital because of their antiquity and finitude. Items in current ritual use are also prized, partly from motives of aesthetic primitivism (Torgovnick 1990), but also as spoils of a vicarious raid into a resistant exotic Other's inner sanctum. Some Hopis, whose loyalties are subverted by the need for cash (compare Price 1989:69), have dealt with the culture vultures, but in most cases they have no authority over, have effectively stolen, sacra that they sell. Art dealer arguments about "legitimate acquisition" thus gain credence: "this was bought from a Hopi." Yet here again a politics of ethnic domination appears: vulgar stereo-types of communitarian "tribal societies" — which lack order, laws, or coherent decision-making processes — are subtextually invoked; a willful failure to rec-ognize legitimate Hopi authorities, or whether particular individuals are ad-hering to Hopi religious precepts, justifies expropriation.

Collection of Hopi representations follows a patterned division in the com-modification of "tribal art" and "artifacts" into, briefly, fine art, folk art/craft, and tourist art (Clifford 1988:223–26; see also Price 1989). Though the categories overlap, this division reflects a hierarchy of interest groups in many instances coincident with class divisions in the dominant society. The panoply of cultural and social registers of interest is especially noticeable among tourists, and national class is not the only configuration of difference: ethnicity — indigenous, national, and international — is also prominent. A typical Hopi ritual, for example, is viewed by a multiplicity of outsiders, including (1) *kyavakvit*, Hopis from other villages; (2) other Native Americans, especially Navajos and Pueblos — often from Zuni, Laguna, Cochiti, and Santo Domingo; (3) many non-native Americans — the great majority white, but also Hispanics, African Americans, and Asian Americans — of different classes, age groups, regions, and subethnicities; (4) Europeans, especially Germans, French, Italians, occasional British, Spanish, and others; (5) Japanese and other Asians, including sometimes Pakistanis, Tibetans, and Indian Sikhs;[13] (6) and perhaps the odd African, Latin American, Indonesian, and white Australian, or even a Jamaican reggae entourage (see note 12). In addition to their intrinsic attraction as performers of exotic rituals and producers of acquirable tribal art, Hopis are on a major American tourist circuit because of their proximity to the Grand Canyon and Monument Valley. In short, outside interests in and valuations of Hopi people and their representations are anything but monolithic.

The invention of tribal art in the dominant society as a marketable commodity (which objectifies and reflects the identity and often prestige of its owners) confounds the artifacts' indigenous meanings. Whatever it is that collectors see in Hopi artifacts, it is not their Hopi saliences. Rather, an alien code of value supervenes: that of symbolic capital and its acquisitive worth in the construction of Western selves (Clifford 1988:220). Inasmuch as Hopi objects evoke some notion of Hopiness for their collectors and observers, the cultural recognition is typically no more than "ethnocentric sentimentalism in the absence of a knowledge of what those arts are about or an understanding of the culture out of which they come" (C. Geertz 1983b:119).

As with museum objects, the artifacts of an exotic culture, or even photographs of its members, allow the metropolitan aesthetic gaze to empathize on its own terms. In earlier times, cultural exhibitions often included individual "natives," too, shipped in for display (Çelik 1992; Rydell 1984). Contemporary American Indian arts-and-crafts fairs perpetuate this practice in modified form. Some Hopi friends regularly demonstrate plaque weaving and pottery in St. Louis and Washington, D.C., where they have occasionally been asked to wear buckskins and sit in front of tepees.

Modern transportation and a developed tourist industry (whether in Papua New Guinea, the Amazon, Borneo, or the U.S. Southwest) recapitulate the self-absorbed fetishizing gaze, but in situ. At home, Hopis often don stereotypical personae for tourists, both to ensure real privacy and because it eases cash transactions for crafts (compare Lavie 1990 on constructions of Bedouin identity).

So, graven images (in museums, private collections, or coffee-table texts),[14] briefly visited ritual performances, and staged cultural identities and practices enable outsiders, in the seclusion of their imaginations, to envisage Hopi (among Others') experience insulated from its material realities. Psychological realization of an aesthetic impulse (involving a sort of primitivist cathexis) — through voyeuristic attributions of "beauty," "dignity," or "ingenious handiwork" — effectively discharges human obligation and diverts any real social concern. In general, aestheticization defuses social responsibility: "An aestheticizing reference to painting, sculpture or literature . . . resorts to the neutralization and distancing which bourgeois discourse about the social world requires and performs" (Bourdieu 1984 [1979]:45).[15]

In some instances, fetishizers of Hopi culture have been centrally involved in overt political domination (Snake Dance visitors at the turn of the century — a period of coercively "directed culture change" — often included political dignitaries; see note 1).[16] The New Agers, by contrast, ideologically (and, as in the Marxist sense, with false consciousness) deny or oppose establishment values present in governmental domination: for them, fetishized Hopis become metonymic emblems of a millenarian struggle against old meanings. And hautbourgeois art patrons, if they care, deny complicity in domination by setting their fetishism in a sublime category apart (neutralizing and distancing in Bourdieu's terms) from the grime of a material politics, that is, "Art" or "Aesthetics" — entrenched categories of bourgeois taste and self-identification (for example, Price 1989; Williams 1977:150).

Writing Hopi Culture

Contemporary Hopi life is indetachably positioned within the political-economic and aesthetic-cultural interests of a national polity and its local forms under the control of Anglo-Americans. Hopi perspectives on the dominant society and its interests in them are inextricably tied to contexts of interaction instanced in the above abuses of their representations. Anthropology is deeply implicated here, both as a principal source of outside knowledge about Hopi and as another mode of collecting, analyzing, and reordering Hopi practices to its own registers of significance. Ethnographic knowledge about the Hopi has been accumulating for more than a century (see Laird 1977). The first real monograph, J. G. Bourke's *The Snake Dance of the Moquis of Arizona*, appeared in 1884. Since then, ethnographic research and writing have proliferated: every conceivable area of Hopi life — from sexuality to astronomy, herpetology to child psychology — has come under scrutiny at one point or another. Moreover, anthropologists are often indistinguishable for Hopis from other "ethnographic" inquirers, academic and otherwise: "No ethnic group of comparable size has had as much attention trained on it as the Hopi Indians of Arizona. Ethnologists and religious specialists, linguists, art historians and collectors, hippies and 'Indian-freaks,' ecologists, spiritualists and pursuers of esoterica — interest in this people oscillates among extremes" (Kunze 1988:jacket, my translation).

Many Hopis are deeply suspicious of *any* graphic representations of their culture, particularly ritual knowledge and practice. For years now, all villages have featured signs prohibiting photography, note taking, painting, and sketching (in Hopi, the same term, *peena*, to represent graphically, covers all these inscriptional modes). The signs may as well say "No Ethnography." While much anger is focused on Frank Waters's *Book of the Hopi*, a great deal is directed at more serious ethnographic publications, both the older studies of esoteric ritual detail, like those of H. R. Voth, A. M. Stephen and J. W. Fewkes, and also recent works treating religious ritual and belief.

Traditionally, academic scholars have privileged their practice and mystified its politics.[17] They do this via institutionally supported prestige techniques and discourses, including the blanket invocation of old shibboleths — "academic freedom" (to inquire) and "freedom of speech" (to publish). Further, they distance their work from all "amateur" interests not sanctioned by the academy.

So, (we) self-righteous anthropologists can be appalled by Smokis, art collectors, or New Agers, while conveniently blinding ourselves to a family resemblance with our own representations of Hopi culture. In claiming an exalted ground of "pure research," scholars disavow the political situation underpinning their work: the state of dominance and subordination between their society of origin and those of their subjects (compare Asad 1973).

It is little wonder that subject societies are often unconvinced of the virtues of academic research, especially if they know any published representations will be open to abuses affecting their cultural sovereignty.[18] Again, fine distinctions among serious and less serious inquiries are often irrelevant to Hopi interests. Both the scholar — whether blithely bent on "pure research"[19] or genuinely interested in a sensitive portrayal of Hopi perspectives — and the dabbler ask similar kinds of questions, and often produce written representations with analogously disruptive effects.

Moreover, fear or dislike of misrepresentation is not the only issue. Voth's and Stephen's work (for specific sources, see Laird 1977) and some recent publications on religious ritual, for example, are targeted specifically for their accuracy. One Hopi friend commented ironically after reading Voth's *The Oraibi Summer Snake Ceremony* (1903), "Thank you; now I am an initiate." And others have indicated a preference for spurious, plainly inaccurate accounts, because at least these keep the reality private by misleading their audience: truth, in this context, is held more dangerous than fiction (compare Scott 1985).

The desire for privacy and autonomy is a function of both the inundation of inquisitors and the internal sociology of Hopi knowledge. Knowledge conferred by initiation simultaneously endows instrumental power over actions and events in the world (Whiteley 1987). Much ritual power/knowledge is held secret within specific sectors of Hopi society: secrecy and the attendant social care and respect accorded to esoteric knowledge guarantee both authority conferred by initiation and instrumental efficacy when the power/knowledge is activated. Prescriptions for individual conduct in ritual — namely, a purity of thought, emotion, and intention — and proscriptions against the misuse of ritual knowledge, which specify supernatural retribution, are utterly central in Hopi discourse. Dissemination of ritual knowledge, either orally to unentitled parties or *ipso facto* in published accounts, violates ritual sanctity and effectiveness, and may damage the spiritual health of the community.[20]

In light of this and of the abuses adumbrated above, it is not surprising that the Snake Dance has recently been closed to non-Indians, or that in 1992, for the first time ever, most villages closed down Kachina dances, following an issue of Marvel Comics' *NFL Superpro* (in March 1992), which featured the steroid-inflated white superhero in a "gut-stomping" contest with named Hopi Kachinas, impersonated by a white mafioso gambling cartel.[21] Nor then should it be surprising that Hopis have actively sought to prevent publication of a work on religious pilgrimage that identifies shrine locations (Raymond 1990). Tribal officials are debating specific restrictions on research; not a few argue for a total moratorium, as Tribal Chairman Vernon Masayesva (1991) pointed out in a recent speech at Northern Arizona University: "As people we have been studied as 'social artifacts' or quaint vestiges of a primitive existence. Our legends, handicrafts, and even the bones of our ancestors have been collected and studied outside of the subjective view of our own ways of life." He went on to note two cases of research (by scholars from Arizona universities) that Hopis found offensive, one suggesting Hopis were cannibals until the 1700s (contrary to Hopi historical knowledge), the other on the salt-trail pilgrimage:

> I learned that [the] University could not take any action on my complaint since the research was protected by a sacred university tradition called "academic freedom." It is this type of research that is causing many Hopis to pressure the Hopi Tribal Council to enact an ordinance prohibiting all future research activities on the Hopi Reservation. . . .
>
> Although the [salt-trail] research wears the cloak of scholarly enterprise, its publication denotes to us a lack of sensitivity to our religious values and the way we organize and conceptualize our sacred traditions. Research needs to be based on the reality of our existence as we experience it, not just from the narrow and limited view American universities carried over from the German research tradition.

The End of Anthropology? Or Déjà Vu?

> To anthropologists I say, put your own house in order because what you may regard today as just a skirmish with Indians may tomorrow become a worldwide problem. (Ortiz 1970:91)

In 1987 Palestinian American critic Edward Said suggested, before the American Anthropological Association, that the anthropological project itself be abandoned, for its collusion with the colonial domination of its subjects. In some respects anthropology has been experiencing an ontological crisis recently, and critiques, both academic and popular, are mounting (for example, *Anthropology on Trial* 1984; Clifford 1988; Dwyer 1982; Malcolmson 1989; Marcus and Fischer 1986; McGrane 1989; Minh-ha 1989; Said 1989; Sass 1986; Torgovnick 1990). But, as with much social analysis of the 1980s and 1990s, there is a sense of déjà vu here.[22]

In 1969, Native American critic Vine Deloria, Jr., challenged anthropologists in similar ways to Said. For a while, a more genuine dialogue ensued between native scholars, at least, and academic anthropologists (for example, American Anthropological Association 1970), and this was associated with revisionary contemplations of the discipline's ethical foundations (for example, *Current Anthropology* 1968, 1971; Hymes 1972) . The 1960s, as we nostalgically rhapsodize, was a watershed for cultural and political critique. Deloria's challenge came at a time of serious questioning more widely within and beyond the discipline. Revisionary theoretical challenges (such as Leach 1961) coincided with critiques of anthropology's colonial associations,[23] producing a serious examination of both the intellectual and moral condition of the discipline, and its relations with its constituted subjects. Critique of theory was explicitly associated with critique of practical political effects on subject communities.

In the 1960s the critique of anthropology had clear theoretical and political targets in functionalism, on the one hand, and obvious colonial structures, on the other. At present, while the political (for example, Third Worldist) critique still involves resistance to old and neocolonial structures, it is hard to even identify a central body of theory. And perhaps indeed it is a question more of absence than presence. If we choose, say, postmodernism as a recent ethnographic episteme, this is less easily assailable than functionalism — as an intellectual collusion with formal power — because of its philosophical diffuseness, its emphasis on continuous deconstructing and decentering, and its own avowed critical stance on colonial structures. While the de Man affair may reawaken a more contextualized historicism (see Lehman 1991), much postmodern critique disenables a politics of action because of its emphasis on the radical contingency of events, meanings, and perspectives. Postmodern cultural analysis depends on the same bourgeois social distance and aestheticizing valorization—but here of academic-intellectual discourse itself—present in culture-collecting. If signification is only self-referential, social recommendations seem irrelevant and postmodernists may sit comfortably on their ivory fences.

If anthropology is really in crisis at present, rather than some anthropologists cultivating a fashionable, careerist neurosis, it might be hard to notice. Almost twenty-five years ago, Asad (1973:10) noted a similar paradox:

> [T]he Association of Social Anthropologists flourishes as never before; it holds academic conferences whose proceedings are regularly published in handsome hardcover and paperback editions. Monographs, articles and text-books by writers calling themselves anthropologists appear in increasing number. . . . The subject is now being taught in more university and college departments than ever. . . . Seen in terms of its public activity there is no crisis in social anthropology.

If we change the references to a North American context in the 1990s, all of these characterizations hold true, as the American Anthropological Association annual meetings continually attest.[24]

What has changed in the last twenty years or so is the role of Native Americanists and their subjects within anthropology. Both have become marginal in critical debates and prestiged discourses of the discipline (see Lurie 1988)—a factor reflected in both teaching and research. In graduate-level teaching of anthropological theory, contemporary texts on Native North Americans figure sparingly. Most teaching of Native American ethnography probably occurs at an undergraduate level. Moreover, undergraduate textbooks typically reproduce stereotypical vignettes of native cultures, selected for their topical imaginative appeal, as different from or models for a critique of the students' own cultures. Of the Hopi, for example, undergraduates are most likely to learn that they have no concepts of time and little gender inequality.[25] Images of Native Americans constructed through canonical ethnographic texts, textbooks, and other representational modes "invent" Native Americans for their audience (Deloria 1969; Vizenor 1987). Some presumptions I attributed above to New

Agers derive in part from classroom inventions of Native Americans: timeless, historyless spiritualists at harmony with one another and in tune with nature — and this is the story many students continue to want to hear.

Moreover, ethnographic monographs are proving insufficient teaching tools for the interpretation of cultures. Student criticism (some of which I share) of ethnographic texts — that they are dry, jargon-filled, and distant from the lived experience and interpretations of their subjects — causes me to assign a mix of (auto)biography, Native American literature, and criticism, along with formal ethnography. Meanwhile, few ethnographic texts by Native Americans are being produced, because there are very few native ethnographers (as academics, anyway). Native American academics for the most part have pursued other disciplines, indicating, *inter alia*, a signal failure of anthropology in its stated goal of serving as a vehicle for genuine, usable intercultural understanding. The most interesting "ethnography" by, and to some extent of, Native Americans today is literary (Louise Erdrich, Leslie Marmon Silko), or based in cultural critique (Gerald Vizenor), or visual (Victor Masayesva, Jr.),[26] rather than strictly anthropological.

With respect to research, graduate students are urged to work in Highland New Guinea, Amazonia, Indonesia, or some other suitably exotic, overseas elsewhere. Native Americans have "lost their culture," become "proletarianized," or at any rate been "overworked" (in the manic careerist bazaar of "original" research projects) — they have been "done" already. Central concerns in contemporary theory — like power, the self, gender, the body, discourse, agency, hierarchy, textual representation — are best worked out in those distant locales where these things are somehow more authentically constitutive of lived experience (compare Appadurai 1986). Reciprocally, Native Americanists no longer lead in key debates and, with a few exceptions (largely in archaeology and narrative translation), inhabit the intellectual peripheries of key arguments.

This alleged marginalization may come as a shock to Hopis (and other native peoples) who each summer — with the appropriate seasonality their "biological" worldviews are held to prescribe[27] — experience the perennial arrival of neophyte anthropologists, often from less prestigious graduate programs and, in the West especially, from local universities. Like beaching driftwood on the flood-tide of tourists, in "field schools," or just off their own bats, they appear on the reservation to investigate some "problem," usually devised without the benefit of any local input.[28] Native communities remain proving grounds — boot camps — for apprentice researchers. That this is possible bespeaks the same political domination that underwrites the abuses of Hopi representations I began with.

The research picture is further complicated by the "blurring of genres" (C. Geertz 1983a). Anthropologists are increasingly not the only academics interested in Hopi. Occasional linguists, psychologists, and philosophers have studied there since the 1930s at least, but recently a gaggle of linguists and narratologists, students of comparative religion and art history, have entered the fray, very often examining the same questions as anthropologists, but blithely unaware of the ethical standards and cultural understandings anthropology has genuinely accumulated (partly as a result of its history of interaction with Native Americans).[29] For Hopis, the many faces of research get ever muddier.

Possibilities

[I]t would be wise for anthropologists to get down from their thrones of authority and PURE research and begin helping Indian tribes instead of preying on them. (Deloria 1969:104)

[Anthropology] can be abused, but it can also be used humanely and ethically, as well as scientifically. (Ortiz 1970:87)

I had a call from a graduate student at a department quite close to Hopi that will remain nameless. He said he was writing a paper on Hopi "tipony" and wondered if I had any advice. After I determined that he meant not a small horse but *tiiponi*, an important ritual emblem, I suggested he go and talk to some Hopis. No, he said, he was not going to do that; he just wanted to read up on it and come to his own conclusion. He would then present his paper — on a religiously sensitive matter — to the world (actually to the AAA meetings). I had another call from a novelist in New Jersey. He said he had read my book (Whiteley 1988) that focuses on the deliberacy of Hopi political decision-making. He had also heard about the theft of the *Taalawtumsit*, important ritual figures used in manhood initiation, from Shongopavi. Their theft in the late 1970s has been deeply hurtful to Hopi sensibilities (perhaps as Catholics might feel if the Sistine Chapel were blown up by atheist terrorists), and both ritually and socially disruptive. The novelist had an idea; he wanted to write a Tony-Hillermanesque tale set at Hopi, whose plot would focus on how the Shongopavi priests deliberately got rid of these religious figures for some dark purpose. I advised him against this. The already damaged community would be gravely offended by this adding of insult to injury.

How naive can outsiders get about the social effects of their representations? The West's liberal conscience was shocked when Ayatollah Khomeini issued a death sentence on Salman Rushdie for *The Satanic Verses*. "Freedom of speech" again was the rallying cry. But as Talal Asad (1990) has pointed out, the protests ignored the social context of embattled subaltern Muslim communities, particularly in Britain; the book's implicit critique of Islam — as well as the Muslim world's reaction to it — has already been transmuted into another tool of cultural oppression by the dominant white, non-Muslim majority.

While the management of Hopi representations must be partly regulated internally, it is clear that the U.S. government would put down forcible Hopi resistances, like death sentences against ethnographers or novelists, as it has repeatedly shown with numerous subaltern activist groups, from AIM to the Black Panthers. So, for their part, anthropologists must take an initiative and decide whether they are willing to be complicit in processes of oppression or whether they will work in various ways — both in terms of their representations and their social action — for Hopi interests against this oppression. The moral situation is of course more complex than this framing of choice, but not thereby grounds for its avoidance (see Maclean, Montefiore, and Winch 1990). It may already be too late: the crisis of bad faith has been compounded in so many ways that Hopis may well elect to simply exclude ethnographers (as Masayesva's speech indicates).

In the atmosphere of cultural subversion that my four initial examples point to, the question remains whether anthropology, or various sister disciplines, have any practical or intellectual utility within Hopi society or can genuinely enhance intercultural respect, appreciation, and understanding, in a way that overrides potential abuses. Anthropologists (and others) can no longer sustain the illusion that their work occurs in a political or representational vacuum.

They *must* now address the likely effects disseminating ethnography in the dominant society will have on Hopis.

As for my own work, I want mostly to leave that to the judgment of others: emphasis on the self-scrutinizing author's voice in recent ethnographic writing often seems to me simple narcissism designed to obviate dialectical critique and mask unconsidered subtexts. I am concerned, however, that my representations were read by this novelist and put together into his dark little plot. And given what I have said, I think it unwise at present to publish on a topic of great personal interest and substantial research over the last decade, Hopi place names; I would have to subtitle it "A Site Guide for New Age Tourists and Pothunters." Though here again, the politics of representations are complex: if *Tsimontukwi* had been widely known about among those sympathetic to Hopi interests in the dominant society, it just might not have been desecrated.

Third World critic Trinh Minh-ha (1989:68) has characterized anthropology fundamentally as gossip. As anthropologists know, gossip can be a powerful technique for social control in any community. In the contemporary global community, if their representations are going to have any use to their subjects, anthropologists must make their gossip more controlling on behalf of their subjects and less for their subjects' oppressors. The "speaking for others" at the heart of the anthropological enterprise must come to terms with the moral responsibilities latent in all such practice (Alcoff 1991). This will involve, in part, not just an account of resistance, but a full-blown focus on the multiple processes whereby the West has exerted its hegemony on colonized societies, forcing them to reconfigure numerous social and cultural practices and concepts (Asad 1992). If anthropologists are to survive and pursue any of their stated goals to further intercultural understanding, they must move their cultural inquiries into a different register. With regard to Hopi, first, what is badly needed in ethnographic description are Hopi perspectives — social, cultural, critical, historical, ecological, and so on. It is the height of absurdity (in any event, but especially after more than a century of ethnography), for example, to read a recent account that cites me as the authority for an observation that Hopis know they need water to grow crops (Loftin 1991:10).

Second, the literature already has more than enough accounts of Hopi ritual detail: we do not need to encourage "tipony-ism." Regarding ritual, an-

thropologists should start explaining to their audience, in a socially constructive way, how Hopis situate, evaluate, and feel about their actions in contemporary circumstances, why privacy needs to be respected, why many accounts
of ritual are subversive, and that Hopis want members of the dominant society
to appreciate and learn from Hopi practice but without desecrating it. In short,
the intersocietal environment conditioning both Hopi and non-Hopi interpretations of ritual needs foregrounding as the critically salient site of present cultural explanation. In many instances Hopis are glad to share their perspectives
and what they perceive as the uniquely beneficial aspects and effects of their
culture's worldview. As one friend put it, accounts of Hopi for the outside world
are acceptable "so long as it positively enhances their lives, their understanding." Hopis see their culture not as some abstract expression, but as having instrumental effects: ritual dramas, for example, are performed for the material
benefit of the whole world. It is only with great reluctance and significant opposition, therefore, that even after decades of Smoki and other kinds of abuse
the priests felt they had no alternative but to close down the Snake Dance. In
other words, it runs counter to Hopi first principles to want to restrict all outside representations of them: they are simply tired of the abuses.

Third, anthropologists must attend and conform to the interests of local
communities in constructing research projects. The graduate school rationale
of constructing "problems" *in vacuo* to pursue in "the field" — and here, I think,
lies the epistemological key to anthropology's contemporary intellectual reproduction of colonial oppression — has simply got to go. If this means giving
up cherished theoretical procedures, and being skeptical of knee-jerk invoca-
tions of "academic freedom," then so be it: we stand to gain far more, for theory itself, in a discipline devoted to the study of culture, if we genuinely engage
different cultural perspectives.[30]

And fourth, a corollary of the preceding, constructing research projects dif-
ferently is the only way anthropology can become truly multicultural. I like to
tell my undergraduate students, in the current classroom debates about culture, that anthropology is the most sophisticated potential tool for understanding cultural realities, dialogically bridging difference, and therefore engaging a
truly multicultural perspective. But this remains potential. Why, after so much
research for so long on Native American cultures, are there still so few native

anthropologists? It is particularly ironic, given the discipline's stated interests, to see year after year the annual meetings of the American Anthropological Association utterly dominated numerically by whites. If anthropology is to become a genuine vehicle of intercultural understanding, rather than a bourgeois language-game about the oppressed, it must reform its thought and its institutional structures, both to be of interest to members of subaltern ethnicities and to provide them formal access to its practices and discourses: in the present global society, anthropology, more than any other subject, drastically needs "affirmative action" to include practitioners from all communities.[31] For this to happen, and it sounds utopian, anthropology must not only "rethink" and "reinvent," to allude to previous efforts at revision, but radically restructure both its thought and its institutional underpinnings. If it does not make such efforts and quickly, it will probably die a slow, lingering death from disinterest, increasingly irrelevant to cultural interpretation in the emergent cosmopolitan order.

In terms of social action, it is easy to pontificate and issue conscious-salving hard-line calls to the barricades. But earlier attempts to do this (such as Moore 1971) have largely failed. At the same time, it seems clear that "action-oriented," activist, or applied anthropology must become a component of *all* anthropological practice, rather than being ghettoized into a subdiscipline. I do not mean to trivialize the problematics of activism and advocacy (see Hastrup and Elsass 1990; Wright 1988), but at a basic level, if anthropologists are not interested in the fates of their subjects, then what use can their knowledge have, either to the community itself or to any genuine "science of man"? Hopis experience plenty of social and cultural problems that the particular skills of anthropologists could help with: land loss, language loss, cultural loss, intellectual property violations, alcoholism, diabetes, all deriving from decades of U.S. cultural hegemony. But anthropologists must have the political will to do so and must show this actively if they are to be perceived as beneficial to Hopis. Again, Deloria (1969:269) pointed the way over two decades ago: "If I were asked to make a list of the useful anthropologists, it would be very short. But this group of people could be critical in helping American society to understand the concepts involved in equality — real equality. I believe that they should offer themselves as volunteers to the various tribes and apply their skills in research to real problems." Some of this is taking place at present, and by no means all anthropologists studying at Hopi are exclusively self-interested. Still, researchers have a long way to go, in the atmosphere I have described, to overturn Hopi impressions of cultural exploitation as the sole motive for their presence. Let me close with some more of Vernon Masayesva's (1991) remarks, which resonate with several of these arguments:

> I hope you [the academic community] can help us find common ground. Together we need to examine the issue of research and the manner in which scholars will conduct research so that Indian views will be respected. I propose an inclusive agenda . . . involving Indian people in formulating research questions. In the process you can help us become effective researchers. The inclusive agenda would involve mutual study, not just one person or group objectively studying the other. The key to our survival as Indian people is not just preserving our cultural ways, but in devising ways to effectively interact with the dominant society and other cultures with which we coexist. I believe the university has a major responsibility in sharing its academic tools with us. . . . However, let me caution you again that any university-sponsored project, regardless of how noble its aim might be will surely fail if consultation with Indian tribes is not part of the planning process from the project's inception.

Epilogue: The Pure Products Go Crazy, Part 2

Lest I risk overemphasizing anthropologists' self-importance as cultural representers, it is worth recalling that they are not the only ones to practice or utilize ethnography as a medium of intercultural impression management (compare Basso 1979; Lavie 1990). Hopis, while oppressed materially and representationally by the dominant society, are not just passive receptors of the traffic in their representations. Though I have argued that anthropologists can be of assistance in some cultural spheres, and that we need more Hopi anthropologists in a cosmopolitan program of intercultural and intersocietal studies, Hopis are working out many of their own intercultural experiences in their own traditional ethnographic modes.

It is August in the dusty pueblo plaza. . . . Well, actually it's June, but you get the picture: I am talking about a Snake Dance. But this time it is a Hopi plaza

(Kykotsmovi, circa 1985) with a mixed Hopi and non-Hopi audience. The performers are Hopi clowns,[32] the snakes are of the store-bought bamboo-segment variety, the songs are histrionic Hollywood-tribal, and the dance steps are, as my friend put it, "you know, white-man-style" (which I took to mean, in the first place, rhythmically inept, overgestural, and uncoordinated). They are burlesquing the Smoki Snake Dance, ridiculing its racism and incongruities, reasserting sovereignty over Hopi representations, parodically turning the parody back on itself, emptying it, for the time being at least, of its oppressive meaning and power. The Hopi part of the audience — with a trace of nervousness, because, as with much clown ethnographic-allegory, this gets rather close to the bone — dissolves in laughter.

Acknowledgments

Versions of this chapter were presented at a session of the 1991 AAA meetings in Chicago entitled "Native Americans, Anthropology, and Ethics"; at the Royal Anthropological Institute's third International Festival of Ethnographic Film, held at Manchester University in September 1992; and to the doctoral program in anthropology at the City University of New York in October 1992. I am grateful for comments and encouragement in Chicago to Leigh Jenkins, Kurt Dongoske, Roger Echohawk, and Larry Zimmerman; in Manchester to Marilyn Strathern, Paul Henley, Stephen Hugh-Jones, and Barbara Babcock; in New York to Louise Lennihan, May Eibhara, Delmos Jones, and Gerald Sider. Many thanks for comments also to Tom Biolsi, Arnold Krupat, Nicole Polier, and Hans-Ulrich Sanner. I am grateful, as well, to Vernon Masayesva for permission to quote from his speech at Northern Arizona University.

Notes

1. The contexts of this interethnic play of identity and difference are multiple and complex, but one deserves emphasis. The Hopi Snake Dance had been since the 1880s a major feature of the Southwest tourist trade, annually drawing large parties of wealthy, socially connected tourists particularly from "back East" and Europe; Teddy Roosevelt visited in 1913; D. H. Lawrence (of course!) came in 1924 (Lawrence 1924). Frontier Anglos in Arizona were thus on one edge of an intercultural representational play: while the exoticism of local Indians was celebrated, with a quasi-erotic mixture of disgust and fascination — a look-at-the-savages-with-snakes-in-their-mouths sort of zoo-gaze — their own identity and difference with these Eastern sophisticates was equivocal. No doubt their provinciality, their Westernness as opposed to Easternness — a significant dimension of white-American class-status games — was slighted. In short, Arizona white identity was partly refracted through images of frontier otherness epitomized by the Hopi Snake Dance and its annual deluge of high-society pilgrims.

2. I should add that my ethnographer's representations are also counterfeit. I was not a "participant-observer" but watched all this on a VCR; a tape — punctuated by guffaws and wisecracks, as well as pregnant silences, from Hopi observers — was made by a Hopi videographer (Kaye 1991) as part of a large Hopi protest at the 1990 performance. My somewhat half-hearted plans to attend in 1991 were mercifully scotched by cancellation, owing to years of increasingly publicized Hopi protests (see, for example, Brinkley-Rogers 1990). For the time being, at least, the Smokis have ceased their major public performances, although it is reported that they continue to march in costume in Prescott parades.

3. The area is also sacred to Zunis (Zuni's land responsibilities go south of the butte, Hopi's north), Navajos, and White Mountain Apaches (Hardeen 1990).

4. After Woodruff Butte had been sold to another party, mining resumed in May 1996. A major area on top of the butte sacred to Hopis has now been completely destroyed. As of June 1996 Hopis were negotiating to preserve what is left. But again they have met with a wall of resistance and a new price to end mining of $2.3 million.

5. For Hopis, even the concept "mask" — implying representational falsity — in itself violates the items' sanctity. In English Hopis usually refer to them as Kachina "friends" (translating from the Hopi reference *ikwaatsi*, my friend), actively avoiding "mask."

6. At the preview the nose had been correctly aligned.

7. As a result of the prior publicity, the purchaser, Elizabeth Sackler, in fact bought it with the sole intention of returning it to the Hopi people (Wallach 1991b; Reif 1991b). While a noble enough act in itself, it scarcely solved the ironies and political-economic implications, the intercultural class and power inequities, or the clash of cultural values. Subsequently, the Hopi tribe has been approached by a number of collectors seeking to return Hopi sacra — as long, of course, as they can get a tax write-off for their generosity.

8. Kaiser (1991:118–19) explains Harmonic Convergence as follows: "On the basis of an intensive study of Aztec and Mayan stone calendars, he [Jose Arguelles, an astrologer] projected the transition to the Age of Aquarius to occur during the night of the 16th to the 17th day of August 1987."

9. Armin Geertz (1994:313) claims Thomas Banyacya in fact met and led New Age acolytes in the construction of an altar at Prophecy Rock. If this is so, Banyacya must have been working both sides of the issue, since his signature appeared on circulars (posted in prominent places around the reservation prior to August 16) condemning the celebration.

10. I am utilizing a (Clifford) Geertzian conception of cultural symbols here. Unlike many (e.g., Bloch 1989; Leach 1976), however, I disavow a separation between instrumental and expressive domains of culture. The *Ahöla* mask is, in Hopi conceptions, inseparable from the supernatural figure it represents; the mask is not just an expression but embodies the deity (cf. my remarks on the Snake Dance [1987:698]). My use of the term "symbols," then, should not be taken to imply a denial of their intrinsic instrumental power.

11. Here too there is a proliferation of counterfeits, including in the summer of 1991

a container-load of dolls from Hong Kong impounded by U.S. Customs in San Francisco (Leigh Jenkins, personal communication 1991).

12. More complexly, many young adults — often those without access to traditional ritual status and knowledge (because of their village, or clan, or family ideology) — favor an embryonic Third World/indigenist identity. This identity is socially underpinned by their experience of subalternity in the national society. It is culturally constructed especially through the politics and music of Caribbean reggae (Hopi is a major stop on Jamaican musicians' tours) along with a rather abstract acknowledgment of the wisdom of Hopi elders.

13. Sometimes white-bourgeois Sikhs from Española, New Mexico — known in local parlance, for their white turbans, as "diaper-heads" — are present too: at a Hopi dance, transgressive postmodern identities are refracted across multiple intersecting planes.

14. On Hopi coffee-table images, cf. Whiteley 1990.

15. In an incisive critique of the same process at work in Sebastião Salgado's photography — widely acclaimed in Western bourgeois circles for its supposed social consciousness — of dying children in the Sahel, Ingrid Sischy (1991:92) points out: "[T]his beautification of tragedy results in pictures that ultimately reinforce our passivity toward the experience they reveal. To aestheticize tragedy is the fastest way to anesthetize the feelings of those who are witnessing it. Beauty is a call to admiration, not to action."

16. Foucault's analyses of power (e.g., 1978) render implausible absolute distinctions between overt political oppression and aesthetic valuation. Gramsci's concept of hegemony (e.g., 1970) also keenly demonstrates the infiltration of power structures into cognitive, including aesthetic, processes. Eagleton (1990) takes up and extends these and other arguments on the social roles and effects of aesthetics.

17. This has been pointed out by a rising tide of critics (e.g., Asad 1973, 1992; Clifford 1983; Clifford and Marcus 1986; Deloria 1969; Dwyer 1982; Fabian 1983; Gough 1967; Hymes 1972; Maquet 1964; Marcus and Fischer 1986; Minh-ha 1989; Said 1989). As Said (1989:213) puts it: "[T]he by now massed discourses, codes, and practical traditions of anthropology, with its authorities, disciplinary rigors, genealogical maps, systems of patronage and accreditation have all been accumulated into various modes of *being anthropological*. . . . [T]he customary way of doing things both narcotizes and insulates the guild member. . . . To practice anthropology in the United States is therefore not just to be doing scholarly work investigating 'otherness' and 'difference' in a large country; it is to be discussing them in an enormously influential and powerful state whose global role is that of a superpower."

18. It is certain, for example, that the Smokis used ethnographic works on the Snake Dance by Voth and Fewkes, in particular.

19. Vine Deloria's witty polemic (1969:83–104) against "pure research" by anthropologists in Native American communities is still unequaled as an indictment of socially insouciant academic practice. For example: "The anthro is usually devoted to PURE RESEARCH. Pure research is a body of knowledge absolutely devoid of useful application and incapable of meaningful digestion. Pure research is an abstraction of schol-

arly suspicions concerning some obscure theory originally expounded in pre-Revolutionary days and systematically checked each summer since then. A 1969 thesis restating a proposition of 1773 complete with footnotes to all material published between 1773 and 1969 is pure research" (1969:85).

20. Secrecy, particularly regarding instrumentally powerful knowledge, is, of course, a universal social practice (see, e.g., Bok 1983). While in the United States, for example, academics and the press often trumpet an unproblematized version of "free speech," the same society has produced multiple secret praxes in military and other matters deemed to affect "national security." With regard to the ethnographic politics of ritual knowledge elsewhere, Australian aboriginal societies have (finally) had some particular success in persuading anthropologists to preserve secrecy (see Myers 1986).

21. One of the most acutely upsetting elements of this comic was that the Kachinas' masks were knocked off, revealing their human vehicles. The issue appeared on reservation newsstands right at the time of *Powamuy* initiation, when Hopi children are supposed to be learning some of the secrets of the Kachina society in a more orthodox way. The Tribal Council's protests to Marvel Comics produced a somewhat belated and ambiguous apology, and the withdrawal (well after their peak sales period) of the remaining copies.

22. After I had already titled my paper I discovered, tellingly, the identical title (minus the "[at Hopi]") in a 1966 paper by Peter Worsley. The recent debates on "endism" (e.g., Fukuyama 1989; Malcolmson 1989; McKibben 1989), from right and left, reproduce a precedent that is rather more full-bodied. Indeed compared to earlier critiques of anthropology, the later ones often seem lame — more a disengaged postmodern navel-contemplation than a call to social action.

23. For example, see Anderson 1968; Banaji 1970; *Current Anthropology* 1968; Goddard 1969; Gough 1967; Hooker 1963; Leclerc 1972; Lévi-Strauss 1966; Maquet 1964; and most especially Asad 1973, from which I take much of this history.

24. Indeed they hold less true in Britain, owing to the educational ravages of Thatcherism.

25. Whorf's depictions of the Hopi language as timeless remain popular despite Malotki's (1983) careful corrective. The theme of gender equality is especially associated with Schlegel's work (e.g., 1977).

26. In his film *Imagining Indians*, which appeared as the first version of the present chapter was going to press in 1992, Victor Masayesva, Jr., broaches some of the same issues (including some of the same examples) of appropriation, fetishization, and misrepresentation of Native American cultures — brilliantly, penetratingly — as are included here.

27. My jibe is intended particularly for Calvin Martin (1987).

28. Deloria's (1969:83) acid comments on this practice still hold true more than twenty-five years on.

29. See, for example, American Anthropological Association 1971, 1990; Fluehr-Lobban 1991.

30. Archaeologists, for example, in both their theory and praxis, have more often

than not systematically excluded the knowledges and interpretations of living Pueblo descendants — as they have with non-Western indigenous peoples worldwide (Bruguier and Zimmerman 1991; Ucko 1987). The intellectual grounds for exclusion, particularly in the now-old "new archaeology," exalt cold "scientific analysis" of mute material remains over indigenous oral histories: Natives need not apply. To me at least, this seems an appalling interpretive error (as well as a morally indefensible act in a genuinely plural society), cultural varieties of historicity notwithstanding. It is as if classical archaeologists were to simply throw out all Greek and Roman texts and deny a need to know the languages — an inconceivable circumstance. Yet I cannot think of a single southwestern archaeologist who has taken the trouble to learn a Pueblo language, for example.

31. The AAA's Committee on Anthropology in Predominantly Minority Institutions, founded in 1989, is a step in the right direction.

32. This account is taken from a Hopi friend who participated. I did not witness the performance, though I have seen many others over the years.

References

Alcoff, Linda. 1991. "The Problem of Speaking for Others." *Cultural Critique*, Winter, pp. 5–32.

American Anthropological Association. 1970. "Symposium on Anthropology and the American Indian." Published in 1973, San Francisco: Indian Historian Press.

———. 1971. *Statement on Ethics, Principles of Professional Responsibility.* Washington, D.C.: American Anthropological Association.

———. 1990. "Amendment to *Statement on Ethics, Principles of Professional Responsibility.*"

Anderson, Perry. 1968. "Components of the National Culture." *New Left Review* 50:3–57.

Anthropology on Trial. 1984. Nova Videograph (WGBH). New York: TimeLife Video.

Appadurai, Arjun. 1986. "Theory in Anthropology: Center and Periphery." *Comparative Studies in Society and History* 28(2):356–61.

Asad, Talal. 1990. "Ethnography, Literature, and Politics: Some Readings and Uses of Salman Rushdie's *The Satanic Verses*." *Cultural Anthropology* 5(3):239–69.

———. 1992. "Afterword: From the History of Colonial Anthropology to the Anthropology of Western Hegemony." In G. Stocking, ed., *Colonial Situation: Essays on the Contextualization of Ethnographic Knowledge*, pp. 314–24. Madison: University of Wisconsin Press.

Asad, Talal, ed. 1973. *Anthropology and the Colonial Encounter.* London: Ithaca Press.

Banaji, Jairus. 1970. "The Crisis of British Anthropology." *New Left Review* 64:71–85.

Basso, Keith. 1979. *Portraits of "the Whiteman": Linguistic Play and Cultural Symbols among the Western Apache.* New York: Cambridge University Press.

Bloch, Maurice. 1989. *Ritual, History, Power: Selected Papers in Anthropology.* London: Athlone.

Boissiere, Robert. 1986. *Meditations with the Hopi.* Santa Fe, N.Mex.: Bear and Company.

Bok, Sissela. 1983. *Secrets: On the Ethics of Concealment and Revelation.* New York: Pantheon.

Bourdieu, Pierre. 1984 [1979]. *Distinction: A Social Critique of the Judgment of Taste,* trans. Richard Nice. Cambridge, Mass.: Harvard University Press.

Bourke, John G. 1884. *The Snake Dance of the Moquis of Arizona.* New York: Charles Scribner's Sons.

Brinkley-Rogers, Paul. 1990. "Anglo 'Tribe' Dances Controversial Steps." *Arizona Republic,* August 5, pp. A1–A2.

Bruguier, Leonard R., and Larry J. Zimmerman. 1991. "Native Americans and the World Archaeological Congress Code of Ethics." Paper presented at the annual meeting of the American Anthropological Association (session on anthropologists, research ethics, and Native American rights).

Çelik, Zeynep. 1992. *Displaying the Orient: Architecture of Islam at Nineteenth-Century World's Fairs.* Berkeley: University of California Press.

Clifford, James. 1983. "On Ethnographic Authority." *Representations* 1:118–46.

———. 1988. *The Predicament of Culture: Twentieth-Century Ethnography, Literature, and Art.* Cambridge, Mass.: Harvard University Press.

Clifford, James, and George Marcus, eds. 1986. *Writing Culture: The Poetics and Politics of Ethnography.* Berkeley: University of California Press.

Current Anthropology. 1968. "Social Responsibilities Symposium." 9(5):391–435.

———. 1971. "Toward an Ethics for Anthropologists (symposium)." 12(3):321–56.

Deloria, Vine, Jr. 1969. *Custer Died for Your Sins: An Indian Manifesto.* New York: MacMillan.

Deloria, Vine, Jr., and C. M. Lytle. 1984. *The Nations Within: The Past and Future of American Indian Sovereignty.* New York: Pantheon.

Dwyer, Kevin. 1982. *Moroccan Dialogues: Anthropology in Question.* Baltimore: Johns Hopkins University Press.

Eagleton, Terry. 1990. *The Ideology of the Aesthetic.* Oxford: Blackwell.

Fabian, Johannes. 1983. *Time and the Other: How Anthropology Makes Its Object.* New York: Columbia University Press.

Fluehr-Lobban, Carolyn, ed.1991. *Ethics and the Profession of Anthropology: Dialogue for a New Era.* Philadelphia: University of Pennsylvania Press.

Foucault, Michel. 1978. *The History of Sexuality,* vol. 1, trans. Robert Hurley. New York: Pantheon.

Fukuyama, Francis. 1989. "The End of History?" *National Interest* 16:3–35.

Geertz, Armin. 1987. "Prophets and Fools: The Rhetoric of Hopi Indian Eschatology." *European Review of Native American Studies* 1(1:)33–45.

———. 1994. *The Invention of Prophecy: Continuity and Meaning in Hopi Indian Religion.* Berkeley: University of California Press.

Geertz, Clifford. 1983a. "Blurred Genres: The Refiguration of Social Thought." In Clifford Geertz, *Local Knowledge,* pp. 19–35. New York: Basic Books.

———. 1983b [1976]. "Art as a Cultural System." In Clifford Geertz, *Local Knowledge*, pp. 94–120. New York: Basic Books.

Goddard, David. 1969. "Limits of British Anthropology." *New Left Review* 58:79–89.

Gough, Kathleen. 1967. "Anthropology: Child of Imperialism." *Monthly Review* 19(11):12–27.

Gramsci, Antonio. 1970. *Selections from the Prison Notebooks*, ed. Q. Hoare and G. N. Smith. New York: International Publishers.

Green, Rayna. 1988. "The Indian in Popular American Culture." In *Handbook of North American Indians*, vol. 4, *Indian-White Relations*, ed. W. Washburn, pp. 587–606. Washington, D.C.: Government Printing Office.

Hardeen, George. 1990. "Apaches, Zunis Join Navajos, Hopis in Opposing Development of Sacred, Historical Landmark." *Navajo Times*, December 27.

Hastrup, Kirsten, and Peter Elsass. 1990. "Anthropological Advocacy: A Contradiction in Terms?" *Current Anthropology* 31(3):301–11.

Hooker, J. R. 1963. "The Anthropologist's Frontier: The Last Phase of African Exploitation." *Journal of Modern African Studies* 1:455–59.

Hymes, Dell, ed. 1972. *Reinventing Anthropology*. New York: Pantheon.

Kaiser, Rudolf. 1991. *The Voice of the Great Spirit: Prophecies of the Hopi Indians*. Boston: Shambhala Press.

Kaye, Merwin. 1991. *The 1990 Smoki Ceremonials* (videotape). Kykotsmove, Ariz.: Hopi Office of Cultural Preservation.

Kunze, Albert, ed. 1988. *Hopi und Kachina: Indianische Kultur im Wandel*. Munich: Trickster Verlag.

Laird, W. David. 1977. *Hopi Bibliography: Comprehensive and Annotated*. Tucson: University of Arizona Press.

Lavie, Smadar. 1990. *The Poetics of Military Occupation: Mzeina Allegories of Bedouin Identity under Israeli and Jordanian Rule*. Berkeley: University of California Press.

Lawrence, D. H. 1924. "The Hopi Snake Dance." *Theatre Arts Monthly* 8(12):836–60.

Leach, Edmund. 1961. *Rethinking Anthropology*. London: Athlone.

———. 1976. *Culture and Communication: The Logic by Which Symbols Are Connected*. New York: Cambridge University Press.

Leclerc, G. 1972. *Anthropologie et Colonialisme*. Paris: Fayard.

Lehman, David. 1991. *Signs of the Times: Deconstruction and the Fall of Paul de Man*. New York: Poseidon.

Lévi-Strauss, Claude. 1966. "Anthropology: Its Achievements and Future." *Current Anthropology* 7(2):124–27.

Loftin, John D. 1991. *Religion and Hopi Life in the Twentieth Century*. Bloomington: Indiana University Press.

Lurie, Nancy O. 1988. "Relations between Indians and Anthropologists." In *Handbook of North American Indians*, vol. 4, *Indian-White Relations*, ed. W. Washburn, pp. 548–56. Washington, D.C.: Government Printing Office.

MacLean, Ian, Alan Montefiore, and Peter Winch, eds. 1990. *The Political Responsibility of Intellectuals*. Cambridge: Cambridge University Press.

Malcolmson, Scott. 1989. "How the West Was Lost: Writing at the End of the World." *Village Voice* (literary supplement) 34(73):9–13.

Malotki, Ekkehart. 1983. *Hopi Time: A Linguistic Analysis of the Temporal Concepts in the Hopi Language.* New York: Mouton.

Maquet, J. J. 1964. "Objectivity in Anthropology." *Current Anthropology* 5(1):47–57.

Marcus, George, and Michael Fischer. 1986. *Anthropology as Cultural Critique: An Experimental Moment in the Human Sciences.* Chicago: University of Chicago Press.

Martin, Calvin, ed. 1987. *The American Indian and the Problem of History.* New York: Oxford University Press.

Masayesva, Vernon. 1991. "Native Peoples and the University Community (Research on Hopi: Concerns of the Tribe)." Speech delivered at Northern Arizona University Union, January 23.

McGrane, Bernard. 1989. *Beyond Anthropology: Society and the Other.* New York: Columbia University Press.

McKibben, William. 1989. *The End of Nature.* New York: Random House.

Minh-ha, Trinh T. 1989. *Woman, Native, Other: Writing Postcoloniality and Feminism.* Bloomington: Indiana University Press.

Moore, J. 1971. "Perspective for a Partisan Anthropology." *Liberation* 16:3443.

Myers, Fred. 1986. "The Politics of Representation: Anthropological Discourse and Australian Aborigines." *American Ethnologist* 13(1):138–53.

Ortiz, Alfonso. 1970. "An Indian Anthropologist's Perspective on Anthropology." In American Anthropological Association, "Symposium on Anthropology and the American Indian," pp. 85–92. Published in 1973, San Francisco: Indian Historian Press.

Page, Jake, and Susanne Page. 1982. "Inside the Sacred Hopi Homeland." *National Geographic* 162(5):606–29.

Price, Sally. 1989. *Primitive Art in Civilized Places.* Chicago: University of Chicago Press.

Raymond, Chris. 1990. "Dispute between Scholar, Tribe Leaders over Book on Hopi Ritual Raises Concerns about Censorship of Studies of American Indians." *Chronicle of Higher Education* 37(7):A6, 8–9.

Reif, Rita. 1991a. "Three Masks to Stay in Auction." *New York Times,* May 21, p. C18.

———. 1991b. "Buyer Vows to Return Three Masks to Indians." *New York Times,* May 22, p. C11.

Rydell, Robert. 1984. *All the World's a Fair: Visions of Empire at American International Expositions, 1876–1916.* Chicago: University of Chicago Press.

Said, Edward. 1989. "Representing the Colonized: Anthropology's Interlocutors." *Critical Inquiry* 15:205–25.

Sass, Louis. 1986. "Anthropology's Native Problems: Revisionism in the Field." *Harper's Magazine,* May, pp. 49–57.

Schlegel, Alice. 1977. *Sexual Stratification: A Cross-Cultural View.* New York: Columbia University Press.

Scott, James C. 1985. *Weapons of the Weak: Everyday Forms of Peasant Resistance.* New Haven, Conn.: Yale University Press.

Sischy, Ingrid. 1991. "Photography: Good Intentions." *New Yorker*, September 9, pp. 89–95.

Sotheby's. 1991. "Fine American Indian Art" (auction catalog), May 21, New York.

Torgovnick, Marianna. 1990. *Gone Primitive: Savage Intellects, Modern Lives*. Chicago: University of Chicago Press.

Ucko, Peter. 1987. *Academic Freedom and Apartheid: The Story of the World Archaeological Congress*. London: Duckworth.

Vizenor, Gerald. 1987. "Socioacupuncture: Mythic Reversals and the Striptease in Four Scenes." In Calvin Martin, ed., *The American Indian and the Problem of History*, pp. 180–91. New York: Oxford University Press.

Voth, H. R. 1903. *The Oraibi Summer Snake Ceremony*. Field Columbian Museum Publication 83. Chicago: Field Museum.

Wade, Edwin. 1985. "The Ethnic Art Market in the American Southwest, 1880–1980." In G. Stocking, ed., *Objects and Others: Essays on Museums and Material Culture*, pp. 167–91. Madison: University of Wisconsin Press.

Wallach, Amei. 1991a. "Indian Leaders Battle Auction of Sacred Items." *New York Newsday*, May 18, p. 2.

———. 1991b. "Top Bidder to Return Sacred Indian Masks." *New York Newsday*, May 22, p. 21.

Waters, Frank. 1963. *Book of the Hopi*. New York: Viking.

Whiteley, Peter. 1987. "The Interpretation of Politics: A Hopi Conundrum." *Man* 22(4):696–714.

———. 1988. *Deliberate Acts: Changing Hopi Culture through the Oraibi Split*. Tucson: University of Arizona Press.

———. 1989. "Hopitutskwa: An Historical and Cultural Interpretation of the Hopi Traditional Land Claim." Expert witness report presented to the District Court in Arizona for *Masayesva v. Zah v. James* ("The 1934 Reservation" case).

———. 1990. Review of *Dwellers at the Source: Southwestern Photographs of A. C. Vroman, 1825–1904*, and *The Hopi Photographs, Kate Cory: 1905–1912. American Indian Quarterly* 14(3):325–26.

Williams, Raymond. 1977. *Marxism and Literature*. New York: Oxford University Press.

"Woodruff Journal: After Mining, a Furor over a Shrine." 1991. *New York Times*, January 3, p. A12.

Worsley, Peter. 1966. "The End of Anthropology?" Paper prepared for the Sociology and Social Anthropology Working Group, sixth World Congress of Sociology.

Wright, Robin M. 1988. "Anthropological Presuppositions of Indigenous Advocacy." *Annual Review of Anthropology* 17:365–90.

Conclusion

Anthros, Indians, and Planetary Reality

VINE DELORIA, JR.

I appreciate the efforts of Tom Biolsi and Larry Zimmerman in organizing the panel at the 1989 annual meeting of the American Anthropological Association, at which we reviewed the two decades of development since the publication of the chapter on anthropologists in *Custer Died for Your Sins*. More so, I appreciate the calm and rational manner in which I was received at that meeting, since the 1972 AAA meeting in San Diego, where we had a heated discussion of anthropologists and Indians, had led me to believe that if no light had been shed on the relationship between Indians and anthros, a good deal of heat remained. Having read the papers in this volume, and been offered another opportunity to give my response, I hope I can take the discussion of issues to another plateau from which the next generation can move into new territory.

The twenty-eight years since the publication of *Custer* have been memorable in that predictable responses to my diatribe have been forthcoming from the anthropological community. At first it was quite humorous to find anthros speaking to me in confidence, like Nicodemus approaching Jesus secretly by night, telling me that they had been saying the same things all along but no one had listened. If such an internal critique had been operating before I leveled my broadside, it was certainly not evident from public speeches or printed articles in the literature. Each secluded conversation ended with the anthro confiding to me that he or she had always been an ethnohistorian anyway and did not much truck with anthros unless academic protocol demanded it. Younger anthros and graduate students then entering the field had two basic responses. They were determined to prove me wrong by being unusually sensitive to Indian needs, sometimes to the point of confessing to crimes they had not personally committed. And they would fiercely attach themselves to Indian groups in order to have some Indians speak on their behalf when anti-anthro activists attacked or criticized them. I found I had thus weakened one part of the scholarly attitude while forcing people to stress a different part of it. So reform was basically a draw.

During these twenty-plus years, however, a great deal has been done to transform the attitudes that American Indians have toward social scientists, and events in the world have conspired to present us with new challenges and a set of problems of which we could not have conceived in the early 1970s. Some immensely useful work has been done by anthropologists on behalf of American Indians. Dr. Barbara Lane, working with the tribes of western Washington, demonstrated skills bordering on pure genius in providing the ethnological background for the *U.S. v. Washington* fishing rights suit, which resulted in an important victory for the Indians of the Pacific Northwest. While I still believe that William Sturtevant possesses one of the great nineteenth-century minds, Bill has frequently gone out of his way to offer his considerable scholarly skills on behalf of Indian communities seeking federal recognition. Sturtevant is a gentleman of the first magnitude and possesses a heartfelt empathy for Indian people that is not surpassed by anyone working with Indians today.

A surprising number of anthropologists, most particularly Deward Walker and Larry Zimmerman, have taken a positive and sometimes aggressive stand on behalf of the Indian position on reburial of human remains. Jack Campisi has become a real force in assisting eastern Indians in clarifying their long-standing claims against the United States and in preparing petitions to submit for federal recognition of Indian communities. So the record is considerably better than what we saw from the anthropological community in the late 1960s. Scholars better understand their skills and the degree to which they can assist Indians, and Indians have come to rely on anthropologists once they are satisfied that the individual is competent and understands the nature of what they are trying to do. We have certainly not found paradise, but we have seen considerable light brought to bear on problems, and we can now make choices we could not make before.

There are some things, however, that cannot change because they are the foundations of the relationship. Anthropology carries with it some incredibly heavy baggage. It is, and continues to be, a deeply colonial academic discipline, founded in the days when it was doctrine that the colored races of the world would be enslaved by Europeans, and the tribal peoples would vanish from the planet. When we stop and think about it, we live in a society so rich and so structured that we have the luxury of paying six-figure salaries to individuals who know a little bit about the pottery patterns of a small group of ancient people, who know something of the language of an Indian tribe, or who specialize in ledger-book drawings or plant knowledge of remote groups of desert-dwelling tribal peoples. We still seem to find it more valuable to have an Anglo know these things and be certified to teach them to other Anglos in an almost infinite chain of generations of scholars than to change the configuration of the academic enterprise and move on to more significant endeavors.

American society is structured along a combination of racial and economic class lines that enable people with the proper connections to prosper and condemn the majority to a lifetime of meaningless or demeaning work. Since the publication of *Custer* there has been no concerted effort by the academic community, or by anthros themselves, to open the ranks of the discipline to American Indians. Anthropology departments still cling fiercely to the belief that it is more valid and scholarly to have an Anglo study an Indian tribe than to have a member of that tribe trained in anthropology. Beneath this view lie alarmingly distressing attitudes that have not been plumbed. The basic message is that Indians, even Indians who are trained in anthropology, cannot be trusted to be objective, to be analytical, or to understand what is happening in their own communities. The works of non-Indian scholars are still widely praised and reviewed. Research grants and fellowships still go to Anglos in disproportionate numbers. Professors in the classrooms still promulgate outmoded and erroneous characterizations of tribal practices and beliefs. We have made very little progress in building a bridge over which future generations can cross.

In America we have an entrenched state religion, and it is called science. When the debate about reburial and repatriation was at its most heated, a substantial number of anthropologists and archaeologists thought all they had to do was scream "Science" to win the debate. When asked to provide accurate information on just how valuable Indian skeletal remains were, in contrast to the possible use of Anglo remains, they registered a deafening silence. The University of California at Berkeley still considers the reburial issue simply a minor political squabble that has nothing to do with religious and cultural beliefs. And just as there were some closet Indian sympathizers when *Custer* first appeared, there are many scholars who are closet racists on the reburial issue today. It is simply impolitic for them to raise their voices at this time, but we will see them venting their spleen in the future.

The Indian world has changed dramatically in these years also. The elders who possessed accurate knowledge have left us. In their place we find several generations of educated Indians who obtain a good deal of their knowledge of tribal ways from books and reports. Reservations have been opened up to the outside world by the poverty programs in a manner completely unanticipated a generation ago, and there are few places on any reservation where people have the luxury of privacy. Connecting Indian reservations with electricity has meant an increase in modern conveniences for communities that had little contact with the modern world half a century ago. And this electric network has fundamentally changed Indian behavior. Instead of spending the winter evenings listening to stories of the elders, children now gather around the VCR and watch the same movies that their Anglo counterparts in Boston and Los Angeles are viewing.

Through a series of radical shifts in national politics, it has become possible for Indians to become gaming operators. Tribes now face the possibility of having their gambling "privileges" granted or revoked by state governments, which are themselves shifting to legalized gambling on many occasions. We have the potential for rapid unexpected wealth or instant poverty on the reservations, depending on the financial structure and political courage of local politicians. The economic world of many tribes has been turned upside down, and there is not a welcome prospect of any stability in the immediate future.

Indian activism of the 1970s brought a resurgence of interest in traditional religions. A strange kind of ecumenical theology has grown up around *Black Elk Speaks* and *The Book of the Hopi*, a theology that takes certain symbols, circles, directions, and the changing of the worlds and popularized tribal religions in the same manner and with the same effect as the "Jesus" movement of this period. Real and imagined "medicine men" have become hawkers of "spirituality," breaking the old circle of the people and introducing anyone who can pay the entrance fee. With a few exceptions anthropologists have not contributed to this bastardization of tribal religion and have maintained a respectful distance, hoping that Indians will come to their senses. But a self-righteous piety has swept Indian country, and it threatens to pollute the remaining pockets of traditionalism and produce a mawkish unreal sentimentalism that commissions everyone to be "spiritual" whether they understand it or not.

When we move to a planetary scale of activity we find the confusion of environmentalism, which lauds tribal peoples as the guardians of the planet but finds no way to prevent the industrial machine from grinding up both people and habitat in its insatiable need for raw materials. American Indian delegations have been active in world environmental movements but have brought only a romantic sentimentalism as their contribution. It is totally disheartening to see Indians interviewed in the seemingly endless documentaries about the environment and find them telling us that the earth is our mother. The interviewer nods wisely, the Indian looks solemn, and the destruction continues.

The New World Order looks startlingly similar to medieval feudalism in that the elite of each country has devised ways to keep political and economic power while the mass of humankind is unable to muster any sense of national or planetary will or sensitivity even to require political leaders to fulfill their constitutional duties. The last sense of national outrage in which we all shared in the United States was the impeachment of Richard Nixon, created by a relentless press that later allowed Ronald Reagan to sleep through eight years of poor leadership without challenging him at all. Saddam Hussein still has his job while millions of Americans have lost theirs, and we hear not a whimper from mainstream Americans. A Texas millionaire offers to purchase the presidency and he leaps to the lead in political polls.

We cannot discuss Indians and anthros apart from the context in which we now live. We live in an era of melt-down, breakdown, and disintegration. The machine that was Western civilization has ceased to function, and its peripheral activities, such as the social sciences of academia, have been revealed as the hobbies of the affluent class (which they always were). Species may be disappearing at a faster rate than we can catalog them. We have reason to believe that everything except what is technologically or economically feasible will disappear from higher education in another generation. Social sciences may well follow the humanities, which are today regarded as useless outmoded appendages to the true function of universities — the molding of personalities capable of accommodating corporate businesses. And we do not even have the luxury of time to adjust to our world.

Anthropology came to be in a world that had accepted Darwinism as an intellectual proposition, and although there are many complaints that evolutionary theory does not possess the facts to support it, academics are extremely reluctant to abandon it. Another writer in this collection boldly asserts that I unjustly accuse anthros of being slaves to cultural evolutionary theories, but if I press any anthros in a prolonged discussion on exactly why they study Indians and other tribal peoples and why they study anthropology at all, I am almost always informed that tribal people represent an earlier stage of human accomplishment and that we can learn about our past by studying the way existing tribal peoples live. I continue to argue that this attitude is at the base of anthropology and will always be cited as justification for doing what anthros do — in the last analysis as the discussion ends and we go our separate ways.

According to the dictates and doctrines of cultural evolution, things should always be getting better, we should be producing a smarter model of human being, we should be able to do more wonderful things at a faster pace. We should *not*, above all, see everything collapse on us. We are smarter than tribal peoples, and we are smarter than our own ancestors, and our grandchildren will supposedly be a much better brand of organism than we are.

In that case, one should argue that anthropology must study the ancestors of the Anglo Saxons since that group, for all practical purposes, has enjoyed virtual control of the planet for most of this century. It turned away German barbarianism twice in this period of time and built an atomic and then a hydrogen bomb, certainly evidence of the superiority of this expression of civilization. Unfortunately the focus of anthros during this century has not been directed toward the dominant society but has merely encouraged its practitioners to continue the task of anthropological pioneers, recording yet again the quaint behavior of smaller societies over which Western civilization had almost complete control. So it is very difficult now for anthropologists — or other social scientists — to offer any sane critique of modern civilization.

The conflict between Indians and anthropologists in the last two decades has been, at its core, a dead struggle over the control of definitions. Who is to define what an Indian *really* is? The generation of anthros now retiring and passing away has not been at all willing to surrender its entrenched position on this matter. In the last few years there has been a tremendous battle over the degree to which the Six Nations might have influenced the thinking of the Constitution's fathers. Here we have seen the anthros show their true colors. No sooner was the subject raised than a bevy of anthros, lacking even a rudimentary knowledge of the historical papers, charged into the fray spouting a confusing conglomerate of anthropological concepts that made no sense at all. Advocates of the Indian position have found themselves rejected for National Endowment for the Humanities grants, been denied positions at colleges and universities, and seen well-documented books rejected by university presses that feared the wrath of prominent figures in anthropology.

This fight over the Six Nations' influence has been a bitter one, and if it had been submitted to a jury for fair deliberation the anthropological profession would now be paying reparations to the Six Nations, for the evidence and the argument weigh heavily in favor of the Iroquois and their supporters. Beneath this quarrel over the right to define social — and Indian — reality lurks a more fundamental conflict that has not even been touched. Anthros have argued that the Iroquois could not have influenced the thought of the constitutional fathers since there is no traceable transfer of specific concepts; that is, there is no provision for women, say, to have a distinctive voice in political affairs in the U.S. Constitution. They make this argument under the assumption that non-Indian scholars know more about the Six Nations than do the Six Nations people.

The Six Nations people, however, contend that their ancestors in prolonged conversations with American political leaders promulgated certain kinds of political ideas that the Americans then adopted. It was not a case of the constitutional fathers wanting to become Indians but an instance of them listening to the manner of resolving problems used by the Six Nations and then creating their own version of the political principles involved. The argument has been reduced to the following statements. Anthros: the constitutional fathers did not adopt Six Nations culture; Six Nations: the constitutional fathers did discuss with our ancestors political principles of unification of states, and what they did reflects some of our way of doing things.

I will be the first to grant that the advocates for the position of the Six Nations have not used the best language and examples to present their case. And I will also grant that their response to anthropological efforts to maintain control of the definitions has not been phrased in the most polite manner. But let us clarify things even further. The Six Nations people understood that if they were recognized as the primary source of accurate information on themselves they would break the control in academia of a small group of scholars who had devoted their lives to becoming experts on the Iroquois. The fight has nothing to do with the Constitution and everything to do with who represents the source of reliable authority on the Iroquois — in short, who controls the definitions.

What should the Indian advocates have said to better present their case or to make clear exactly what they were suggesting? We are in the first generation of Indians who have been to college, in the sense that only since 1960 have we seen a massive entrance of Indians into colleges and universities. Social sciences on the whole have been hostile to Indians' becoming professors and expositors of the cultures they represent, and thus very few Indians are able to translate the Indian side of the discussion into concepts that will have immediate recognition among Anglo academics as an explanation worthy of consideration.

The real Indian argument, in my opinion, should be phrased as follows. The Six Nations contributed to the U.S. Constitution at least the idea that sovereignty could be split between the national government and the constituent states in a manner in which each entity would gain in political stature and power and not lose important aspects of its political existence. Between 1783 and 1789, when the Constitution was adopted, the United States governed itself by the Articles of Confederation, and under these provisions it was unclear where the national power actually rested. States could make treaties with Indian tribes, and presumably they could also regulate commerce and political relationships with other states and other countries if the need arose. Sovereignty of the states meant a weak national government and eventually the disintegration of the unity that the American Revolution had wrought.

The Six Nations had solved the question of a divided sovereignty by allocating seats on its national council to the respective five, and later six, nations, and then limiting the powers of the council. In different ways, each Indian nation was as powerful as the whole council of the league, but the pledge of peace and unity enabled the leaders of each nation to exercise national power responsibly. Because the Iroquois had a clan system, which served to provide national unity, the arrangement worked well until the Six Nations ruptured during the American Revolution because of its decision to allow individuals to take sides. The major problem in attempting to transfer some aspect of this arrangement to American political thinking was that no corresponding institution or provision to perform the function of the clan existed.

The American version of the distribution of sovereignty between states and the national government has been sporadically unsuccessful. The Civil War demonstrated that only by force could national sovereignty be maintained and that there would always be a conflict between states and the national government. The recent conservative movement to restore states' rights and control the powers of the federal government, particularly when the federal government threatens to create a superior national citizenship, is simply this century's effort to resolve the old problem of the allocation of sovereign powers. It is the supreme irony of history that the Republican Party, which led the fight to preserve the Union, now leads the struggle to negate it.

When we look at state-nation relations within the American constitutional framework we are looking at the Anglo adaptation of Iroquois thinking. Each time we are faced with the possibility of a third-party candidacy throwing the national presidential election into the House of Representatives, we worry about how the choice will be made and the equity of allowing a small state to have an equal vote with larger states. The strange arrangements that our Constitution provides are a direct result of consultations with the Six Nations. Where else were ideas of distributing national sovereignty articulated and practiced when the constitutional fathers were debating the organic documents of state? They certainly could not have looked to Europe for guidance, and there was no nation on earth at that time except the Six Nations that had grappled with this problem.

I have reviewed this issue because it helps me illustrate the deeper question that presently separates Indians from anthros and, by extension, from the rest of social science. Indians did, do, and will continue to express what they feel they are, and this feeling is a wholly subjective presentation. Anthros expect Indians to have the same perspective as they do — to have an objective culture that can and must be studied and that Indians themselves will study. The anthros' belief no doubt comes from the extreme materialism that has always been present in Western civilization and from their individual experiences in college and graduate school, when they had to study hard and long to master the rudiments of another culture. But knowing what others have observed about another culture does not mean that the scholar emotionally understands that culture, and this point many anthros miss completely.

Some of the chapters in this book suggest that the anthropologist has been greeted favorably by Indians. Indeed, one contributor writes that the Indians on reservations greeted her generously because they could not afford to purchase *Custer* and so did not know they were supposed to be hostile. I can only mourn and applaud such naïveté. What she experienced was simply the hospitality of Indians toward a stranger. You can bring almost anyone into an Indian community and Indians will greet him, feed him, invite him to ceremonies, spend time with him. As an activist, I am repeatedly dismayed when an obvious fraud or con artist is greeted effusively by Indians who seem not to exercise critical faculties at all.

What our fellow writer experienced was an acceptance of her as a person, not necessarily the endorsement of her as a scholar and researcher. Certainly anthros have Indian friends. If they did not they would know it in rapid order. But Indians discount the scholarly status of the individual and simply accept the person until he or she begins to disrupt the community. People in American society have virtually no personal identity in the sense that Indians experience it. When you inquire about an Indian, the first question is almost always, where do you come from? followed by, who are your relatives? In American society you are asked where you come from and what you *do*.

There is a universe of difference here. Employment or career achievement of academic or social status in American society does not have much standing in Indian society. It is family and community that count. I am constantly frustrated when I visit Indian groups and realize that for all my experience in politics and knowledge of law, what I suggest can be easily negated by anyone who has personal prestige and offers an alternative solution regardless of its sanity. Indians recognize expertise only when they accept you as a person. Some time ago a man appeared among the Sioux who said he could get the Internal Revenue Code changed so that whites within the 1851 treaty area would have to pay their taxes directly to the Sioux tribes. This proposition is preposterous and shows an appalling ignorance of basic principles of American government. Yet the man had and still has many supporters because he also has a good deal of personal charisma.

Anthros should not misinterpret the natural hospitality of Indians as an endorsement of anthropology or support for their work. Indians may like their work and admire their skills but only because they have first accepted the individual as a person; admiration for the work depends wholly on the integrity of the work. In this respect anthros are no different from good bronc riders, capable mechanics, or friendly teachers. If the sense of personal trust is broken, everything else falls apart also. It is indeed pitiful to listen to anthros recount their friendly reception from Indians and conclude that they have found some Indians who appreciate anthropology. Let the Indians detect a moral flaw in your personality and see how quickly the appreciation for your work changes.

When we have Indians in anthropology we find an even better example of how confusing the relationship between Indians and anthros is. Some prominent Indian anthros have announced at Indian meetings, "I'm an Indian, *but* I'm also an anthro." There is no question in this announcement that the individual has chosen the profession over the community. Once this happens, watch how quickly a cloud of suspicion envelops the Indian scholar. Such scholars may continue to travel in Indian circles, and they may think they have bridged the cultural gulf, but unless they prove to be momentarily useful they are never trusted again and people avoid them whenever possible.

Anthropology alleges to be the study of human behavior, values, and institutions. Let us suppose for the moment that Indians and tribal peoples really did have a sophisticated way of living in the world, wholly natural, and without pretensions to objective knowledge and superiority over other cultures and societies. Paul Radin once noted that these societies, although described as "primitive," were able to feed, clothe, and house all of their members and ensure that in hard times the burden of suffering fell relatively equally on everyone. We might further suppose, as do a significant number of people today, that the principles of organization and the values of these tribal or primitive societies might offer a new way of looking at the problems of industrial societies. Would not then the materials describing the behavior of tribal peoples and the tribal peoples themselves, whatever remnants now exist, be in a position to speak meaningfully to the modern world?

Could there, for example, be something in the kinship relations — a principle whereby civility could be restored to American society? Could the festivals by which people reestablished relationships with the natural world provide us with a vehicle for making our concern about the environment an actual change of behavior instead of a vague sense of warm sentiment about chipmunks? Could the allocation of roles and functions between genders practiced by tribal peoples enable us to resolve some of the gender problems of the modern world? Could principles of balancing emotional states and the natural environment become a new way of assuming responsibilities for our cities and neighborhoods?

During the period of its formal existence, anthropology has taken the values and institutions of Western civilization, acted as if they represented normality, rationality, and sanity, and leveled severe criticism of tribal societies, finding them lacking in the rudiments of civilized behavior. The policies of political institutions and the attitudes of American society toward tribal peoples have been shaped largely by the descriptions forged by the social sciences. Instead of possessing cultures that were different, but nevertheless a valid expression of how our species can live on this planet, tribal cultures have been understood as primitive efforts to become scientific and industrial, and failing efforts at that.

It is now time to reverse this perspective and use the values, behaviors, and institutions of tribal or primitive peoples to critique and investigate the industrial societies and their obvious shortcomings. As long as anthropology and anthropologists focus on Indians and other tribal peoples and report back to their own society about the quaint and sometimes romantic people they are studying, there is no respect for tribal peoples in spite of the pious disclaimers and pledges of emotional allegiance given by scholars. If, however, anthropologists and other social scientists begin to speak critically to the shortcomings of their own society using the knowledge which they claim to have derived from observation of the tribal peoples, that will be a signal that something of real value is contained within the tribal context.

The so-called New Agers are attempting to perform this task albeit in an overly romantic and inept fashion. They have demonstrated, however, a great willingness to listen to other ways of doing things. The fight over credentials, over who should or can speak with authority about Indians, should cease. Instead of the confrontation over whether or not the Six Nations had influence on constitutional thinking, the debate should shift to the question of whether or not an institution or a formal practice comparable to the clan system exists in industrial society, whether it is useful to that society, and what can be done to enable it to resolve problems that now plague modern peoples. As another example, agricultural surpluses today are the product of subsidizing the commodity markets; we should be considering how we can transform these surpluses to enable us to feed people.

I realize that asking anthropology to undertake a new task, particularly a task with such a high potential for disturbing the secure financial base from which scholars have always comfortably moved to examine the exotic tribal peoples of the world, is a rather hazardous request and one likely to be rejected out of hand. But it is a necessary request because it basically asks scholars to develop a personal identity as concerned human beings and move away from the comfortable image and identity of "scholar." If anthros did begin to offer intellectual and moral leadership in American society and became problem solvers, they would achieve the necessary objectivity they do not have at the present time.

It seems to me that after two decades of reasonably constructive reforms in the relationship between anthropologists and Indians, and with the passing of the elder generation of anthros who were victims of what Alfred North Whitehead described as "misplaced concreteness," we have an opportunity to leave the colonial mentality behind us and bring the accumulated knowledge and insights of anthropology to bear on the larger arena of human activities. And we have the responsibility to do so.

Index

Native American studies and, 191–
192; micropractices of the academy
and, 17, 173–174; NAGPRA and, 80,
81, 82, 105; postmodernism and,
190–191; power and, 150, 173–174;
privilege and, 191; publics and,
83–84; racial theory and, 95–96;
reflexive accounts and, 124–126;
representations of Indians and,
63–65, 72–74, 76, 95, 103, 117, 134,
136–139, 140–145, 145–146, 161,
191–192, 220; responses to Deloria's
critique and, 209–210; service to
Indian communities and, 210; views
on indigenous intellectuals of, 170;
violence of abstraction and, 115–
117. *See also* American Anthropological Association; American
Association of Physical Anthropologists; cultural relativism; ethics;
fieldwork; Society for American
Archaeology
art, American Indian, 180, 186
artifacts, collection of, 184
Asad, Talal, 4, 191, 194

Basso, Keith, 126
Benedict, Ruth, 136, 139, 142, 152n
Boyer, L. Bryce, 129–130
Boyer, Ruth, 129–130
Briggs, Jean, 124–126
Bureau of Indian Affairs (BIA), 149

Campisi, Jack, 210
class, 83, 87n, 185, 211
Collier, John, 149
colonialism: anthropology and, 12–14,
150, 187–188, 190, 211, 221; Hopi
situation and, 187–188
cultural relativism: holism, 136, 139–
140, 143, 151–152n; power and, 150;
stereotypes of Indians and, 117, 136–
137; view of the primitive and, 136

Custer Died for Your Sins: conference
panel on, 4; critique of anthropology
in, 3–4, 36–37, 161, 197–198,
201–202n

Deloria, Vine, Jr.: critique of anthropology, 3–4, 36–37, 45–47, 54–55, 57,
63, 77, 92–93, 161, 190, 197–198,
201–202n, 211, 214, 215, 218, 219,
220, 221; executive director of NCAI,
57–58; family background of, 28–29;
influence on anthropology, 36, 41,
44–46, 48, 59, 190; marginalization
of, 30; opinions of his impact, 27–28;
publications of, 30–33 passim; representations of Indians, 53–54
dialogism, 166
discourse, 136, 143, 148–149, 165

Eggan, Fred, 144
ethics: AAA code, 4, 6, 92, 118, 120;
anonymity of informants, 121–123,
126–127; archaeology and, 106–108;
contradictions and limitations of, 83,
118, 121, 122–123, 124; false dilemmas, 124–125; informed consent,
41–42, 43, 122, 123–124; institutional review boards, 37–38, 43; SAA
code, 79–80, 83, 108
ethnocentrism (of anthropologists),
127, 128–130
evolutionism, 94–95, 117, 127, 151n,
214

Fagan, Brian, 64–65
feminist perspectives, 85, 161
Fenton, William, 166–169, 174–175n
fieldwork: American Indian movement
and, 38–39, 63; ethnocentric bias
and, 129–130; genealogies and, 126–
127; life histories and, 121–124;
reflexive accounts and, 124–126;
training for, 128

TE DU